# The Psychotic Wavelength

*The Psychotic Wavelength* provides a psychoanalytical framework for clinicians to use in everyday general psychiatric practice and discusses how psychoanalytic ideas can be of great value when used in the treatment of seriously disturbed and disturbing psychiatric patients with psychoses, including both schizophrenia and the affective disorders.

In this book Richard Lucas suggests that when clinicians are faced with psychotic patients, the primary concern should be to make sense of what is happening during their breakdown. He refers to this as tuning into the psychotic wavelength, a process that allows clinicians to distinguish between, and appropriately address, the psychotic and non-psychotic parts of the personality. He argues that if clinicians can find and identify the psychotic wavelength, they can more effectively help the patient to come to terms with the realities of living with a psychotic disorder.

Divided into five parts and illustrated throughout with illuminating clinical vignettes, case examples and theoretical and clinical discussions, this book covers:

- the case for a psychoanalytical perspective on psychosis
- a historical overview of psychoanalytical theories for psychosis
- clinical evidence supporting the concept of a psychotic wavelength
- the psychotic wavelength in affective disorders
- implications for management and education.

*The Psychotic Wavelength* is an essential resource for anyone working with disturbed psychiatric patients. It will be of particular interest to junior psychiatrists and nursing staff and will be invaluable in helping to maintain treatment aims and staff morale. It will also be useful for more experienced psychiatrists and psychoanalysts.

**Richard Lucas** was a consultant psychiatrist at St Ann's Hospital, London. He was also a fellow at the Royal College of Psychiatrists and a member of the British Psychoanalytical Society. In 2003 he received an OBE for his services. This is his only book.

# THE NEW LIBRARY OF PSYCHOANALYSIS
## General Editor Dana Birksted-Breen

The New Library of Psychoanalysis was launched in 1987 in association with the Institute of Psychoanalysis, London. It took over from the International Psychoanalytical Library which published many of the early translations of the works of Freud and the writings of most of the leading British and Continental psychoanalysts.

The purpose of the New Library of Psychoanalysis is to facilitate a greater and more widespread appreciation of psychoanalysis and to provide a forum for increasing mutual understanding between psychoanalysts and those working in other disciplines such as the social sciences, medicine, philosophy, history, linguistics, literature and the arts. It aims to represent different trends both in British psychoanalysis and in psychoanalysis generally. The New Library of Psychoanalysis is well placed to make available to the English-speaking world psychoanalytic writings from other European countries and to increase the interchange of ideas between British and American psychoanalysts.

The Institute, together with the British Psychoanalytical Society, runs a low-fee psychoanalytic clinic, organises lectures and scientific events concerned with psychoanalysis and publishes the *International Journal of Psychoanalysis*. It also runs the only UK training course in psychoanalysis which leads to membership of the International Psychoanalytical Association – the body which preserves internationally agreed standards of training, of professional entry, and of professional ethics and practice for psychoanalysis as initiated and developed by Sigmund Freud. Distinguished members of the Institute have included Michael Balint, Wilfred Bion, Ronald Fairbairn, Anna Freud, Ernest Jones, Melanie Klein, John Rickman and Donald Winnicott.

Previous General Editors include David Tuckett, Elizabeth Spillius and Susan Budd. Previous and current Members of the Advisory Board include Christopher Bollas, Ronald Britton, Catalina Bronstein, Donald Campbell, Sara Flanders, Stephen Grosz, John Keene, Eglé Laufer, Juliet Mitchell, Michael Parsons, Rosine Jozef Perelberg, David Taylor and Mary Target, Richard Rusbridger, and Alessandra Lemma, who is Assistant Editor.

# ALSO IN THIS SERIES

# THE NEW LIBRARY OF PSYCHOANALYSIS

General Editor: Dana Birksted-Breen

# The Psychotic Wavelength

A Psychoanalytic Perspective for Psychiatry

Richard Lucas

Routledge
Taylor & Francis Group

LONDON AND NEW YORK

First published 2009
by Routledge
27 Church Road, Hove, East Sussex BN3 2FA

Simultaneously published in the USA and Canada
by Routledge
270 Madison Avenue, New York, NY 10016

*Routledge is an imprint of the Taylor & Francis Group, an Informa business*

© 2009 Lynne Lucas

Typeset in Bembo by RefineCatch Limited, Bungay, Suffolk
Printed and bound in Great Britain by TJ International Ltd, Padstow, Cornwall
Paperback cover design by Sandra Heath

This publication has been produced with paper manufactured to
strict environmental standards and with pulp derived from
sustainable forests.

*British Library Cataloguing in Publication Data*
A catalogue record for this book is available from the British Library

*Library of Congress Cataloging-in-Publication Data*
Lucas, Richard, 1943–2008.
The psychotic wavelength : a psychoanalytic perspective for psychiatry /
Richard Lucas.
p. : cm.
Includes bibliographical references and index.
ISBN 978-0-415-48468-8 (hbk) – ISBN 978-0-415-48469-5 (pbk.)
1. Psychoses. 2. Psychoanalysis. I. Title.
[DNLM: 1. Psychotic Disorders–diagnosis. 2. Psychotic Disorders–therapy.
3. Affective Disorders, Psychotic–diagnosis. 4. Affective Disorders, Psychotic–
therapy. 5. Psychoanalytic Theory. WM 200 L933p 2009]
RC512.L83 2009
616.89′17–dc22

2009003522

ISBN 978-0-415-48468-8 (hbk)
ISBN 978-0-415-48469-5 (pbk)

Dedicated to the memory of Richard Lucas, OBE
2nd April 1943 – 28th July 2008

# Contents

# Contents

# Contents

# Preface

In this admirably lucid book Dr Richard Lucas demonstrates that psychoanalysis has much to contribute to the treatment of seriously disturbed and disturbing psychiatric patients. Dr Lucas's aim is 'to provide clinicians with a psychoanalytically based framework of understanding to help them in their work with the major psychotic disorders encountered in everyday psychiatric practice.' He strongly believed that only by immersing themselves in general psychiatric settings would psychoanalysts be able to exert a favourable impact on the treatment of psychoses and develop psychoanalytic theories with a proper focus on the very daunting problems found there. This book is based on his forty years of work in the National Health Service with patients suffering from major psychotic disorders and demonstrates his deep involvement as a psychoanalyst and psychiatrist. He applied psychoanalytic thinking in general psychiatric settings in a way that no other psychoanalyst has managed to date. Dr Lucas distils practical lessons derived from his life's work, condensing and elucidating his long and rich experience in a captivating way.

His justified refrain is that when clinicians are faced with patients suffering from psychoses, they must tune into the psychotic wavelength. He means by this that, in order to best understand one's encounters with such patients, one must discern whether one is addressing the psychotic or the non-psychotic part of the personality. Dr Lucas emphasises that the book illustrates the 'vital role that applied psychoanalytic thinking can play within general psychiatry to help staff, relatives and patients adjust to the realities of living with long-term psychotic disorders.' He felt strongly that psychoanalysis could not and should not be peddled as a cure-all for psychosis. Clinicians will feel reassured that their apparently faltering attempts to 'cure' long-suffering patients are not failures at all but part and parcel of the long-term management that such stressful disorders demand. Here, Dr Lucas shows how psychoanalytic approaches to multidisciplinary team work can be invaluable in helping maintain realistic treatment aims and staff morale.

In the 1970s, as a junior psychiatrist and psychoanalyst in training, Dr Lucas experienced a psychiatric world markedly different from the one he departed upon his premature death in 2008. In that era Rosenfeld, Bion, Sohn and other eminent psychoanalysts routinely read papers on psychosis at the British Psychoanalytical Society, where he was training for membership. Psychiatric patients treated at the Maudsley Hospital, where he worked within the National Health Service (NHS) as it was then, could be seen up to five times per week for psychoanalytic sessions. Later on, when based at Claybury Hospital and as a young consultant psychiatrist, Dr Lucas took charge of the ward for psychotic patients where his applied psychoanalytic work was not only welcomed but also strongly supported. His dedication to patients, and to the clinical teams caring for them, was apparent from the beginning, as was his supple application of psychoanalysis within these psychiatric settings. This experience is reflected in chapters that clearly link psychoanalysis historically, theoretically and clinically with his everyday experiences as a psychiatrist and psychoanalyst, a balance of identities he maintained throughout his working life.

Over the ensuing decades, though, he became dismayed by the fact that within the NHS, patients suffering from psychoses were deprived of therapeutic resources which had been made available earlier. The rift widened between professionals in psychiatry who were organically inclined and those who were more psychoanalytic in approach, to the former group's advantage, and he detected that the patients had become the main victims of this rift. This arose following the changes in the 1980s to a more neo-Kraepelian approach to psychiatric classification and diagnosis, a shift to emphasise phenomenology in mainstream psychiatry and a decline in the meaning-based approach. Patients suffering from psychotic disorders came to be treated mainly with medication and in a mechanistic fashion, with few professionals prepared to try to think about their symptoms as meaningful and understand their predicaments. Dr Lucas was also critical of 'classical' psychoanalysts who complained of a dilution of psychoanalysis when applied in settings other than five sessions per week on a couch, as though this was the only 'real' form of psychoanalytic treatment. He challenged those professionals in psychiatric settings who had contempt for psychoanalysis and who insisted on their own treatment methods as being the only worthwhile ones. In this polarised climate of conflicting treatment methods, the large psychiatric hospitals were being shut down to offer so-called community treatments, shorter and supposedly less expensive treatments (in the short term anyway) were being sought, and patients assuredly became the victims, not only of their psychotic illnesses but also of the system. Dr Lucas's friendly, approachable personality and diplomatic skills ensured that he was always heard. Dr Lucas persevered in maintaining that there was a place for both of the main approaches to treatment, ensuring that patients received the most comprehensive and up-to-date treatments available in a setting that provided understanding for them, their relatives and their carers.

The book, written in a wonderfully accessible style, is divided into five parts. Part One makes the case for a psychoanalytic perspective on psychosis, emphasising the need to integrate the medical model with a dynamic approach, the aim being to gain the views of all involved professionals in patients, especially those who specialise in projecting and disowning their disturbance. Part Two provides an excellent historical review of the main psychoanalytic theories on psychoses, including areas of overlap and differences in opinion between main theoreticians. These chapters could be said to offer the reader everything you ever wanted to know about psychoanalytic theories of psychoses but never quite understood before! The four chapters contained in Part Three are perhaps the most important part of the book's structure, functioning as the pivot by providing key clinical evidence to show why clinicians must tune into the psychotic wavelength of their patients. This is where the book's mantra is amplified and exemplified: 'when approaching major psychotic disorders, we have always to think in terms of two separate parts of the personality, the psychotic and the non-psychotic, and ask ourselves which part we are being confronted by at any particular moment in time'.

If only one chapter was chosen as representing the core of the book, this would have to be Chapter 11, with its instructive cases illustrating how to tune into the psychotic wavelength. In my view, this chapter is essential reading for anyone working in general psychiatric settings or involved professionally with patients suffering from major mental disorders. This also applies to those professionals who, for example, may sit on mental health review tribunals and make crucial judgements based on a patient's manifest presentation, which may be loaded with denial and rationalisations but behind which the active psychosis can often remain camouflaged.

While the emphasis in Part Three, including several fascinating and informative clinical vignettes, is on schizophrenia, Part Four focuses on the major affective disorders, including those that arise in the puerperium. Again these chapters are illustrated with informative and clinically impressive vignettes providing the evidence for the need to keep in mind the psychotic part of the patient in any encounter with the patient, direct or indirect. Part Five is dedicated to the implications of this psychoanalytic framework in relation to highly topical issues such as risk management. Dr Lucas emphasises the importance of attempting to reach a realistic understanding of any patient's psychotic and non-psychotic parts in managing risk, rather than relying on the 'forms and tick-box' approach to risk management, which is more of an anxiolytic for overburdened staff who have to deal with critical inquiries when an incident arises, such as an episode of self-harm, suicide or harm to another. Precious time wasted in completing forms can provide beautifully comprehensive patient files, which bear little relation to the patient him or herself and have not contributed to sound patient care. Dr Lucas provides plenty of moving clinical evidence that a psychoanalytic perspective can support staff and relatives when tragic events happen. Clinicians might feel relieved to read so succinctly the reality that when one is involved with such patients, some tragic events cannot be prevented, no matter how excellent the care and understanding. Risk cannot be eradicated, despite the pressure from uncomprehending authorities to do so. Risk can, however, be managed as effectively as possible using the integrated approach to psychiatric care espoused by Dr Lucas. Part Five also includes a section on education, a subject of great importance to Dr Lucas, who was also a highly active and passionate trainer of clinicians from different disciplines and, in particular, junior psychiatrists.

Dr Lucas often alluded to Freud's awareness of the tensions between the two disciplines of psychiatry and psychoanalysis and his wish to bridge this gap. In my view, Dr Lucas here has demonstrated to the reader his own remarkable capacity to do just that. He also has shown the reader why this bridge is so important for patients, staff and relatives. Throughout the volume, Dr Lucas's deep compassion for patients and his concern for staff and relatives pours through. He was an inspirational colleague who is sorely missed. We can be very grateful that he left us with such a splendid legacy, which I sincerely hope will be read by a wide, professional, national and international audience involved with disturbed and disturbing patients and will become essential reading for junior psychiatrists and nursing staff in particular.

Carine Minne
October 2008

Dr Carine Minne is Consultant Psychiatrist in Forensic Psychotherapy at the Portman Clinic, Tavistock and Portman NHS Foundation Trust and at Broadmoor Hospital, West London Mental Health Trust. She is a psychoanalyst and associate member of the British Psychoanalytical Society.

# Acknowledgements

Sadly, this book is published posthumously and Richard Lucas will not have the pleasure of seeing his work in print. Knowing how ill he was gave him the impetus to move forward on this project and we were grateful that he wanted to make this effort at the end of his life to transmit the ideas which were dear to him.

Before he died, Richard Lucas was able to discuss his ideas and the draft of the book with Liz Allison and she has done a wonderful job of putting the draft into publishable form. I am sure that he would have wished to express his warmest thanks to her for her outstanding work as editor of his papers.

Richard would have also wished to thank Priscilla Roth and Carine Minne for their constructive comments on the draft, and it is also clear in his writings that he felt he owed a debt to his teachers.

Dana Birksted–Breen
Series Editor

## PART ONE

# Making the Case for a Psychoanalytic Perspective on Psychosis

# 1

## Introduction

This book aims to provide clinicians with a psychoanalytically based framework of understanding to help them in their work with the major psychotic disorders encountered in everyday psychiatric practice. It is written for both an analytic and general psychiatric audience. It provides theoretical and clinical discussion material for junior doctors starting in psychiatry, nurses undergoing postgraduate psychodynamic courses, social workers, psychologists and students of other disciplines related to psychiatry, as well as analytic psychotherapists in training who are striving to make sense of their psychiatric placements. It is also intended for the wider professionally experienced analytic and psychiatric audience, since it raises for consideration the important and often controversial issues that arise from encounters with psychotic states of mind.

The current trend in psychiatry, based on a stress–vulnerability model, is for psychoanalysts to work in early onset psychosis settings, with associated favourable outcome figures linked to relapse prevention, avoidance of admission and with medication kept to a minimal dosage (Cullberg 2001; Martindale 2001).

There is a danger of a split developing between those running early onset services and those running the general psychiatric services. The latter have responsibility for many patients at the severe end of the spectrum of psychosis, who may require significant amounts of medication and repeated or protracted admissions. In working with this group of patients, who will at times require containment on the ward when in a state of relapse, avoidance of admission is clearly not an issue. The cause of the psychosis, whether viewed theoretically as constitutional or as a consequence of early trauma, is not the pressing issue, neither is the level of required medication. The primary

3

problem is to make sense of what is happening in a psychotic breakdown.

The lament that psychoanalytic perspectives are no longer taken account of in the area of psychosis (Grotstein 2001) may be a consequence of analysts positioning themselves on the periphery rather than being prepared to share in the everyday experiences of general psychiatry. Only work within the general psychiatric setting can enable psychoanalysts to have a meaningful impact on psychosis, by developing ideas that they and their fellow professionals can make use of in this most demanding of areas. Without this vital engagement, although psychoanalytic theories of psychosis may have their own academic coherence, they will not resonate for those who are working at the coal-face.

This book is based on my forty years of experience of working with major psychotic disorders in the NHS. While also informed by individual analytic experiences, its primary concern is the role of applied analytic thinking in a busy psychiatric setting. Though the theoretical framework outlined here is based on my work in the UK, in an NHS setting in a deprived area of North London, it is hoped that a wider international audience will find that they can make use of it to inform their work in other contexts.

Psychoanalysts have understandably grown fond of referring to the pure gold standard of individual psychoanalysis. Any application of analytic thinking outside of an individual analytic setting has come to be regarded as a dilution of the pure situation. In consequence, applied analysis, such as that undertaken by many practising analysts who also work in an NHS setting, has not always received the support and appreciation that it merits.[1]

In thoughtfully presented individual case studies, analysts have more often than not chosen to focus on the early infantile traumas behind the generation of schizophrenia (e.g. De Masi 2001). However, addressing the psychoses unavoidably confronts us with the need to integrate a consideration of constitutional or biological factors (Yung and McGorry 2007). We cannot rely solely on an analytic explanation in terms of early childhood trauma. Pioneers of individual psychological approaches, which include cognitive as well as analytic therapists, have tended to be optimistic about the treatability of psychosis, but the question of whether it is possible to achieve lasting change remains controversial. Pursuit of this elusive goal can detract from the requirement to provide an effective containment that addresses the psychotic patient's intense dependency needs (Steiner 1994).

The focus of this book is not primarily on the feasibility of inducing lasting change, but rather on the vital role that applied psychoanalytic thinking can play within general psychiatry to help staff, relatives and patients adjust to the realities of living with long-term psychotic disorders.

In relation to the place for the analytic study of psychoses, Freud (1925) had the following to say:

> The neuroses were the first subject of analysis, and for a long time they were the only one. No analyst could doubt that medical practice was wrong in separating those disorders from the psychoses and in attaching them to the organic nervous diseases. The theory of neuroses belongs to psychiatry and is indispensable as an introduction to it. It would seem, however, that the analytic study of the psychoses is impracticable owing to its lack of therapeutic results. Mental patients are as a rule without the capacity for forming a positive transference, so that the principal instrument of analytic technique is inapplicable to them. There are nevertheless a number of approaches to be found. Transference is often not so completely absent but that it can be found to a certain extent; and analysis has achieved success with cyclical depressions, light paranoic modifications and partial schizophrenias. It has at least been a benefit to science that in many cases the diagnosis can oscillate for quite a long time between assuming the presence of a psychoneurosis or of a dementia praecox; for therapeutic attempts initiated in such cases have resulted in valuable discoveries before they have had to be broken off. But the chief consideration in this connection is that so many things that in the neuroses have to be laboriously fetched up from the depths are found in the psychoses on the surface, visible to every eye. For that reason the best subjects for the demonstration of many of the assertions of analysis are provided by the psychiatric clinic. It was thus bound to happen before long that analysis would find its way to the objects of psychiatric observation.
>
> (Freud 1925, p. 60)

Many points of interest are raised here by Freud. First, does therapeutic success matter in relation to the analytic study of psychoses; or is it more important to ask whether analytic insights can help those who have to manage the most difficult of patients on a long-term basis? How do we evaluate transference? Do we see it as only coming from the vestiges of a healthy part of the patient, as Freud implied?

One day, as I was walking down a hospital corridor, a long-stay patient passed me and said, 'Hello, Dr Lucas'. She made me feel like a benevolent and important father figure, with her as one of my cared-for flock. I felt full of this warm feeling, until she brought me back to earth by adding as she went by, 'You stupid old fucker.'

Both transference and countertransference phenomena were clearly in evidence here. The episode reminded me of the baby who builds a column of bricks only to knock them down again. The lesson is that events which can be illuminated by analytic thinking, linked to transference and countertransference phenomena, are ever-present throughout the hospital and its corridors. The challenge is what we do with them.

While we might not be able to change the habits of a lifetime in patients with chronic psychoses, we can learn a great deal from them. While Freud noted that seeing patients individually in the early stages of a developing psychosis may lead to valuable analytic discoveries, seeing patients in general psychiatry while keeping an analytic perspective in mind can also inform the clinician's thinking in a creative way.

An underlying theme of this book is that the major psychotic disorders present different challenges from borderline and non-psychotic disorders. Since projective processes predominate in psychosis, we need to decipher the emotional meaning contained in delusions by attending not only to their content, but also to our countertransference experiences – exploring what the patient makes us feel at the time.

Using one's ordinary sensitivities is not sufficient in trying to make sense of major psychotic disorders. One needs to learn to tune into a different wavelength, what I have termed *the psychotic wavelength*, hence the title for the book.

In approaching the major psychotic disorders, both schizophrenia and affective disorders, it is vital that we always think not in terms of one person but in terms of two quite separate parts to the personality, the psychotic and non-psychotic parts. Whenever we listen to the patient we have to ask ourselves whether we are listening to a straight-forward communication from a non-psychotic part or hearing a rationalisation from the psychotic part that is covering up an underlying psychosis.

Bion was reported anecdotally to have said that as a non–German speaker, he had an advantage listening to Hitler on the radio before the war. As a result, he was not seduced by the words, but heard only the sounds of a raving madman. Hitler's seductive words thus did not blind him to the dangerousness of the man.

Professionals often remain unaware of the commonest presenting symptom of psychosis and its diagnostic implication. If one consults a standard psychiatric textbook, one will find that the commonest symptom is not, as one might have expected, persecutory delusions (64 per cent) or auditory hallucinations (74 per cent), but lack of insight (97 per cent) (Gelder et al. 1998). This lack of insight typically presents as denial of any problems with associated rationalisations. In other words, if we are not aware that denial and rationalisation are the commonest presenting features of psychosis, we are in danger of succumbing to the rationalisations and missing the underlying psychosis.

This fundamental dynamic is not generally appreciated or taught within the realm of psychiatry. It remains a controversial issue even within the field of psychoanalysis, where there is a preference for thinking in the more familiar terms of defence mechanisms and the need for reintegration of split-off parts of the personality. However, the concept of the two parts is of crucial importance in everyday general psychiatric practice, for example when approved social workers (ASWs) have to decide whether a patient, who is reported by relatives to be in a dangerous state of mind, but who presents in an apparently calm and compliant state, needs to be formally admitted under the Mental Health Act 1983. Similar problems arise when mental health review tribunals have to decide whether it is safe to release a patient from a detention order.

The following serves as a striking example of denial and rationalisation:

A patient came into hospital on a section, having smashed up the contents of his flat. On admission he was in such a disturbed state that he was placed on the locked ward. I saw him for evaluation the next day. He presented in a perfectly calm state and denied having any problems. However, he asked how he could be sure that I was really Dr Lucas and not an impostor, and said that he therefore intended to call the police.

Here we can see that it is the patient who is the impostor. He behaves in an apparently calm way despite the fact that he had been brought into hospital by the police in a severely disturbed state only the previous evening. By the next day, he masquerades as reasonable, while projecting his awareness of this action into me. Through the process of projection and reversal into the opposite, I become the impostor for whom the police are needed.

With a physical illness, the patient goes to the doctor with symptoms and the doctor makes the diagnosis. With psychotic disorders, especially in relapse of chronic disorders, it is the nearest relative, not the doctor, who makes the diagnosis. It is then a question of whether the professional workers will believe the relative's account. If the professionals succumb to the patient's rationalisation, they may fail to take the beleaguered relative's concerns seriously.

However experienced we are as professionals, we will often be fooled by patients' rationalisations. It is therefore crucial to be aware of the phenomenon and be open to changing one's mind on receiving additional information, rather than inflexibly standing by one's initial opinion. The following incident is a typical experience.

> The patient was a woman with a long-documented history of manic depression, though I previously had not known her before being asked to see her on a domiciliary visit. The community psychiatric nurse (CPN) had requested the home visit because the patient had been defaulting from her outpatient appointments. When I saw her she denied that she had any problems, and said that she would keep her next outpatient appointment and take any prescribed medication. I did not feel that there were grounds for a formal admission.
>
> She subsequently did not keep the hospital appointment, and I saw her again at home, but this time armed with more information, which a close friend had passed on to the CPN. The friend told the CPN that while at times she presented as perfectly reasonable, at other times she would start shouting, and this was disturbing her downstairs neighbour, who was terminally ill with cancer. The CPN noted that while the patient insisted that she would cooperate with treatment, this was not the case. When I again found her in a seemingly rational state the second time I visited, I changed my view and completed my part of a compulsory admission order. It was the patient's denial of any problems – the rationalisation – that was indicative of the psychosis.

In the following vignette, an ASW is faced with an understated psychotic state.

A patient with a history of chronic schizophrenia had stopped his depot medication (medication given by injection and slowly released into the body over a number of weeks), and was becoming more disturbed in the community. It was known that when he had relapsed in the past, he had become violent. This time, not wanting to be sectioned, he accepted voluntary admission at the last moment, so the ASW did not complete his part of the section. In hospital the next day, without provocation or warning, the patient suddenly attacked a nurse with a broom handle, and it took several nurses to restrain him.

The ASW was called to the ward to complete a compulsory treatment order, in view of the patient's unpredictable state. The ASW saw the patient before speaking to the nursing staff and was therefore unaware that an assault had occurred. Since the patient appeared calm and said that he was willing to stay and cooperate with treatment, the ASW decided that the patient did not need sectioning. When the ASW later met with the nurses, they described the patient's unpredictable outbursts, but having made his original decision, he felt unable to change it, although he was willing to be called back if a further incident occurred.

As patients in psychotic states of mind tend to project out and disown their disturbance, when case reviews take place, whether in hospital or in the community, it is essential to gather together all the involved professionals and the close relatives. The work of the review is like assembling the pieces of a jigsaw puzzle, and we cannot know in advance who might be bringing the most important piece.

Psychotic disorders represent the most extreme and difficult end of the spectrum of human behaviour. Patients may remain in seemingly intractable states of mind for lengthy periods. The work can be very demanding and stressful.

To manage the situation without acting out to the detriment of the patient, one must not be too rigid in one's approach, and it is necessary gradually to develop and acquire clinically relevant frameworks of understanding. Acquiring these frameworks is a lifelong personal process and one is always looking for additional insights to deepen the frameworks of reference. No single framework is comprehensive enough to cover all situations; each has its limitations. We are continually challenged to find new and meaningful understandings and to integrate them.

Throughout this book, different theoretical frameworks for understanding psychosis will be examined and related to clinical examples.

Part One of the book introduces the case for a psychoanalytic perspective on psychosis. Chapter 2 considers the strengths and limitations of the medical model of psychosis. The medical model is based on the concept of phenomenology, the attempt to be scientifically objective over subjective experiences, for example defining hallucinations and delusions and relating them to the diagnosis of psychotic disorders. The positive aspect of the medical model is that it introduces an element of diagnostic precision, but it has its limitations, as it allows no room for a dynamic understanding.

Rather than falling into the trap of extolling one approach as superior to the other, it is necessary to integrate the medical model, with its concentration on classification and physical treatments at the biological level, with a dynamic approach focused at the psychological level. We then need to ask ourselves what is the most appropriate measure to be taken at a particular time, within an integrated model of understanding. Sometimes medication may be the priority to aid a process of containment. At other times the priority will be the achievement of a psychological understanding, while both measures can be used in conjunction with each other.

The subject of psychosis raises many controversial questions, which require continued debate. Some of these issues are considered in Chapter 3, including the question of whether there is a continuum between normality and psychosis and whether analytic theorising and input is irrelevant in relation to conditions now perceived by many as predominantly organically based disorders. Contrasting approaches to delusions from the medical model, cognitive behaviour therapy (CBT) and analytic perspectives are also reviewed.

Part Two of the book provides a selective historical overview of psychoanalytic theories of psychosis. In Chapter 4, Freud's contribution is reviewed starting with his seminal ideas emanating from the Schreber case. Particular consideration is given to his ideas on narcissism, the death instinct, defence mechanisms and the structural model. Freud thought that patients with psychosis lived predominantly in a narcissistic world of their own creation, thereby rendering themselves inaccessible to influence by the classical analytic method of interpretation through the transference. Nevertheless, he made a plea for future generations to become conversant with both psychoanalysis and general psychiatry for analysis to make a contribution to psychosis.

In Chapter 5, the Kleinian contribution is considered. Following a brief review of fundamental concepts on psychosis as described by Melanie Klein, some contributions by others on psychosis from the Kleinian school are noted. These include the contributions from Rosenfeld, who introduced the concept of the psychotic transference, and Segal, Sohn, Rey, Steiner, O'Shaughnessy and Britton.

Chapter 6 is devoted to Wilfred R. Bion's unique contribution to psychoanalytic thinking about psychosis. In his book *Second Thoughts*, Bion introduced an entirely new way of viewing schizophrenia. He described in detail the separate functioning of the psychotic and non-psychotic parts of the personality and the genesis of hallucinations and their relation to delusions. He also introduced an original theory of thinking. Bion's work is not easy to follow, especially for those not already familiar with analytic theory, so I have taken particular care to relate his concepts to clinical material in order to make them more easily comprehensible, as they are of fundamental relevance to informing our thinking in everyday psychiatric practice.

Chapter 7 considers the work of Tom Freeman by way of a contrast to the Kleinian approach. Freeman worked closely with Anna Freud, and developed his own theoretical framework for thinking about psychosis. After a lifetime working in general psychiatry in Scotland, he retired to Northern Ireland, where he single-handedly set up the Northern Ireland Institute for Analytic Studies. Like Freud in the early days, he provided candidates with both individual analysis and supervision for their cases, before involving other analysts from London in expanding the teaching programme.

Chapter 8 discusses the important lessons to be drawn from the history of Chestnut Lodge in Rockville, Maryland, near Washington DC, where an entirely psychoanalytic approach to the treatment of psychosis was used for many decades. Since Freud had reported the lack of transference in psychosis, the procedure was called intensive analytic therapy rather than classical analysis, with sessions held four times rather than five times weekly to maintain a distinction. While important contributions were made on psychosis by eminent analysts working at Chestnut Lodge, the story illustrates the need for a more flexible attitude, including incorporation of medication where indicated, when approaching psychosis. For patients treated with a solely psychoanalytic approach, the outcome figures were favourable for more borderline patients but not those with schizophrenia, opening up the debate as to the relevance of psychoanalysis to psychosis.

In Chapter 9, Laing's criticism of the psychiatric approach to psychosis is briefly reviewed. Laing's work raises the fundamental question of whether psychosis should be viewed primarily in terms of society's intolerance of difference, or whether there are persisting conditions to be studied in their own right. This is a debate that continues to this day.

Part Three turns to the development of a psychoanalytic framework for psychosis that can be of assistance to clinicians working in general psychiatry. Such a framework needs to allow for incorporation of other modalities of treatment within an integrated approach.

In developing a framework for working with the psychoses, it is important to differentiate psychotic processes in borderline states from major psychotic disorders. This is the subject of Chapter 10. It is necessary to tune into what I have referred to as the psychotic wavelength to address the specific needs of a patient in a psychotic state, and this is the subject of Chapter 11. Tuning into the psychotic wavelength, as already emphasised, requires us to continually bear in mind the two separate parts of the personality, the psychotic and non-psychotic.

In Chapter 12, dreams are contrasted with delusions. Within psychiatry, dreams can provide important clues during assessment interviews, provide markers for progress in psychotherapy, and provide important teaching for trainees on the working of the unconscious when arising in their supervised cases. In schizophrenia, typically delusions replace dreams and the challenge becomes to decipher the meaning to the delusion.

Since patients in psychotic states tend to predominantly use projective processes, our countertransference reactions become crucially important in deciphering the meaning behind delusions. Involved professional staff need help to familiarise themselves with this process and gain confidence in processing and using their own feelings, when exploring presenting material. This is the subject of Chapter 13. Introducing this perspective not only stimulates interest in the staff working with psychotic patients, but also adds humour, warmth and humanity to what would otherwise be unremittingly demanding work and can help to protect staff against burnout.

Part Four is concerned with tuning into the psychotic wavelength in working with the major affective disorders, including bipolar disorder, puerperal psychosis and depression – the forgotten psychosis. As with schizophrenia, we cannot rely solely on empathy in relating to affective disorders. We again need to tune into the psychotic wavelength and identify the psychotic part of the patient with its own belief system, agenda and autonomy of action.

In Chapter 14, I describe a psychoanalysis conducted in the NHS with a patient with a severe recurrent manic depressive psychosis. Although I made little impact on the process, the analysis enabled me to appreciate the underlying dynamics to the cycle. The psychotic part of this patient would submit to a tyrannical superego in the depressive phase but her resentment would silently build up like the tightening of a clockwork spring, until it would unwind in a manic rebellious stage and then the process would repeat itself. I learned to appreciate that no one was to be blamed for the repeated admissions and to respect the non-psychotic part of the patient that had to live with the recurring cycle. The experience taught me that many times one may need to remain supportive and tolerant of a patient going through a protracted psychotic state in hospital with seemingly no end in sight and let the process run its natural course, without becoming preoccupied with searching for an ideal physical treatment.

The puerperium is the most vulnerable time for developing a depressive psychosis in someone with an underlying propensity. Psychiatrists continue to search for hormonal changes to account for this special vulnerability. In Chapter 15 an alternative dynamic explanation is proposed via consideration of some clinical material. It is suggested that cases that require admission to hospital are only the tip of an iceberg; that the condition with its underlying psychopathology is much more common than is realised, and that community workers need alerting to the underlying psychodynamics in order to provide the most effective support for these mothers and their babies.

We use the term depression in several different ways and they need to be differentiated. There is the Kleinian concept of the depressive position, a state of tolerating painful feelings, reactive depression, states of mourning and what is now termed major depressive illness, previously referred to as endogenous or psychotic depression. In Chapter 16, the psychodynamics operating behind major depressive illnesses are explored, starting from the insights of Freud (1917) as described in his classical paper 'Mourning and melancholia'.

A spectrum of treatments is available for major depression; some patients receive psychotherapy, some receive a mixture of psychotherapy and medication, and some are treated solely with antidepressant medication. However, even in the latter cases, psychodynamics underlie their presentation. An experienced consultant psychiatrist once said to me that in training he was taught to prescribe antidepressant medication for outpatients, but not how to talk to them. Being made aware of the dynamics underlying major depressive illness can help the clinician to find new ways to think about and talk to their patients, even in busy outpatient clinics, enlarging the interaction with the patient beyond just the prescribing of antidepressant medication.

Part Five of the book turns to the implications of the psychoanalytic framework elaborated in Parts Three and Four for management, including risk management, and education. Chapter 17 discusses a patient in the early stages of a severe schizophrenic illness arising in late adolescence in order to make the case for the overriding need to develop a supportive exoskeleton that can enable the patient to function in the community. The development of the exoskeleton requires collaboration of the psychiatric services with the nearest relatives. In severe cases this can take up to five years to develop, with relatives as well as the patient needing full support during the early turbulent period. The role for psychoanalysis in this setting is reviewed.

Chapters 18 and 19 examine the risks that are an inevitable consequence when managing psychotic patients prone to impulsive actions. With the closure of the asylums and reduction in beds, anxiety arose about the containment of disturbed states in the community. Tragic episodes of violence increased the anxiety leading to the introduction of the Care Programme Approach (CPA). Patients regarded as at special risk of violence or self-neglect were placed on enhanced CPA, requiring close supervision by a care coordinator. Risk assessment forms were also introduced by management, with great importance placed on them, which created a climate of blame when forms were found to be incomplete at the time of an untoward incident. Completed forms, of course, do not prevent incidents from occurring; we still have to live with risk and each case will require its own clinical assessment.

In Chapter 18, a psychoanalytic perspective is provided on risk assessment. Both acts of harm to others as well as acts of self-harm are considered, linked to the underlying psychopathology. Even if it is not always possible to prevent a destructive act from occurring, one can learn from the experience and it can help in the management in other cases. Maintaining an analytic perspective can help the psychiatrist to provide meaningful support to staff and relatives when tragic events happen.

In Chapter 19, a patient with recurrent manic depressive episodes, but with much less severe psychopathology than the patient described in Chapter 14, is considered. In this case analytic psychotherapy was able to have a significant impact once the therapist was able to identify and tune into the agenda of the psychotic wavelength, thereby reducing an initially significant suicidal risk.

In Chapter 20, different forums for education on psychosis are considered. For junior doctors new to psychiatry, weekly psychosis workshops where problems can be presented in an informal atmosphere provide a setting to introduce related psychoanalytic concepts, make sense of psychotic communications and help the doctors to explore their countertransference feelings. At the specialist registrar level, whether training for general psychiatry or psychotherapy, there is no substitute for deepening one's clinical experience through treating a case individually under supervision, ideally augmented by a personal analytic experience.

Finally, experienced analytic therapists, in charge of supervising others, can gain from shared discussion of patients with psychosis who have been referred to them for management. In a changing climate within the NHS, psychotherapy departments are coming under increasing pressure to become more involved within the community health centres in helping in the management of psychotic patients and this needs further thought.

The concluding chapter provides a summary of the framework of approach developed throughout the previous chapters. It is hoped that this book will show how much psychoanalytic perspectives can contribute to the world of psychiatry. I hope to succeed in demonstrating that in an area often regarded as the most arid for a psychoanalytic input, applied analysis paradoxically has a centrally important role to play.

# 2

# The medical model

## Introduction

In this chapter I will review both the positive aspects and the limitations of the medical model of psychosis, arguing that the medical model has an important contribution to make within an overall framework that also needs to incorporate an analytic dimension. Readers are referred to comprehensive psychiatric textbooks for detailed descriptions of classification in psychiatry, and guidance on the conduct of the clinical interview and the mental state examination (Gelder et al. 2001; Goldberg 1997).

## The rationale behind classification

All medical models relate to a background system of classification. In psychiatry there are two main classifications, the International Classification of Diseases (ICD-10: World Health Organization (WHO) 1994) and the American *Diagnostic and Statistical Manual of Mental Disorders* (DSM-IV: American Psychiatric Association (APA) 1994). The use of an agreed international nomenclature allows for research and comparison studies of the incidence of mental illness in different cultures and different continents.

A classical example of the need for a mutually agreed classification arose many years ago from a UK–US study on cases of depression. In England, videos shown of depressed patients were all diagnosed by psychiatrists as depression. In the East Coast of the United States they were similarly diagnosed, but as one moved to the West Coast the diagnosis altered to pseudo-neurotic schizophrenia, a locally used nomenclature. Such incidents highlighted the need for an internationally agreed nomenclature (Cooper et al. 1972).

As well as national and international classifications, used for research purposes, psychiatrists carry with them their own more simplistic classification for everyday practical purposes. For some this may include headings of neuroses, psychoses, personality disorders, learning difficulties, psychosomatic and adjustment disorders, though in the formal classifications terms like neurosis have been dropped in favour of more specific categorisation.

When we turn to psychoses, practically speaking they can be divided into the organic psychoses and those that were once known as the 'functional psychoses', schizophrenia and affective disorders, where the underlying organic aetiology has yet to be fully established.

Individuals suffering from organic psychoses exhibit a demonstrable cognitive impairment on mental state examination, related to an identifiable physical cause. Organic psychoses may be divided into acute and chronic disorders. The former, also described as acute toxic confusional states, could relate to infections, drug abuse or metabolic disorders. They are characterised by confusion, often with visual hallucinations, and have a more favourable prognosis than the dementias.

The need for doctors to have a classificatory system of the psychoses in mind is very important at the everyday clinical level, as illustrated by the following gross examples. Many years ago, I worked as liaison psychiatrist in a general hospital. At the time, the referring medical doctors often had no system of classifying mental disorders in their minds.

> One day when I was asked to see a young man in casualty, the message I received was that he was 'as nutty as a fruit cake, call the psychiatrist!' When I saw this young man, he was in a confused state with visual hallucinations, but without presenting any neurological signs. Clearly, he was in an acute toxic confusional state and I suggested that he was admitted as a medical emergency. He was later found to have meningo-encephalitis.

In another case, no distinction was made between a reversible toxic confusional state and dementia.

> I was asked to see a 92-year-old woman, who had been admitted the day before and was in a confused state. All it said on the referral note was, 'For senile disposal!' When I took her history, it turned out that only a few days

previously her mind had been quite clear, and her confused mental state was the result of acute bronchitis. With antibiotics she made a full recovery.

The general psychiatric viewpoint on classification in psychosis is interesting, as described in the *Oxford Textbook of Psychiatry* (Gelder et al. 2001). The authors advocate the need for an agreed system of classification to enable clinicians to communicate about their patients' symptoms, treatment and prognosis and for research purposes. They point out that the main critics of classification have tended to be psychotherapists who are concerned more with neurotic and personality disorders than with the more severe disorders. The critics of the medical model complain that attempts at classification ignore the individual patient and their unique characteristics, while the psychiatrist's response is that it is possible and important to consider an individual's response to treatment and its prognostic implications, as providing additional information to work with, complementary to the classification that they use.

Like neurosis, psychosis is no longer used as an organising principle in either the ICD-10 or DSM-IV, with the aim nowadays being to describe individual disorders in more precise terms. Gelder et al. (2001) note that in modern usage, the term psychosis refers broadly to severe forms of mental disorder such as organic mental disorders, schizophrenia and affective disorders. However, since it is difficult to define what is meant by lack of insight or identify criteria to assess the patient's ability to distinguish between subjective experiences of reality and hallucinations or delusions, the term psychosis is unsatisfactory for classificatory purposes. Further, different conditions placed under the rubric of psychoses have little in common, so that it is better to concentrate on the different conditions such as schizophrenia.

They do note that the adjectival use of the term psychotic will remain in clinical parlance, thus hallucinations and delusions are commonly referred to as psychotic symptoms (Gelder et al. 2001).

The logic and rationale behind the approach outlined by Gelder and colleagues is clear and well stated. However, at an everyday clinical level, the term psychotic carries far more weight than merely an adjectival term recognised as shorthand for certain symptoms. It is therefore important to think carefully about what we mean when we use the term psychosis. Recognising a psychotic state is the first step towards arriving at the understanding that enables the prognosis and appropriate management to be determined, and this in itself is not always an easy task, let alone then identifying a more precise diagnosis. Where a psychotic state is recognised, a wholesale reorientation in considering the approach to the presenting situation may be required. For example, we will approach a patient who we understand as simply overreacting to stress differently from someone who we see as covering up an underlying psychotic state with all its implications for understanding and management, even though the presenting situations may be superficially similar.

Nevertheless, it is important to fully appreciate the rationale behind the medical approach, if one is to feel comfortable in integrating its contribution within a dynamic approach to psychosis.

## Diagnosing schizophrenia

In 1896, Kraepelin separated the organic psychoses, such as general paralysis of the insane (terminal syphilis), from manic depressive states and what he called dementia praecox (Kraepelin 1896). Dementia implied an irreversibility and praecox meant of the young. In 1911, Bleuler's term schizophrenia gained acceptance. The use of this term implied a fragmentation of the mind, that there was more than one disorder under the overall heading, that the prognosis was not necessarily poor and that the condition did not necessarily occur only in the young (Bleuler 1911).

Schizophrenia remains very difficult to define. One tends to fall back on a textbook description of the most characteristic symptomatology and areas of dysfunction. Such a description would include symptoms under general headings such as disturbance of thinking, disturbance of mood, loss of drive or volition (the so-called negative symptoms of social withdrawal), disturbance of movement including catatonia, and delusions and hallucinations. These symptoms would occur in the absence of an associated organic disorder.

If a patient presents with all the classic textbook symptoms, then there may be no difficulty in making the diagnosis. However, problems arise if only a withdrawn state is present or just a thought-disordered, vague state of mind. Then the diagnosis becomes harder to make.

When it comes to diagnosis in medical terms, there are different levels of precision (Scadding 1967). We can diagnose through a cluster of symptoms forming a syndrome, the method advocated by Hippocrates. We can use diagnostic biochemical tests, or we may be able to isolate the specific cause. For example, taking syphilis as a model, it may present as a genital sore. Yet there are many other causes for such a venereal infection. One could then look for a positive Wasserman Reaction, a biochemical test, but a positive result is not specific only to syphilis. One may then identify the responsible organism, the spirochaete, Treponema Pallidum, and one has then reached a precise diagnosis.

In the case of schizophrenia, we remain at the level described by Hippocrates, namely diagnosing at the syndrome level. The aetiology of schizophrenia remains a mystery despite all the research with its suggestions of structural changes to the brain. Many conditions with differing aetiologies can present with a picture that resembles schizophrenia, such as temporal lobe epilepsy, amphetamine psychosis, porphyria, Huntingdon's chorea, in addition to stress-induced states and bipolar disorder. There may be many more conditions, as yet unclassified, all presenting in similar ways and all currently labelled schizophrenia. Thus we can see the limitations of our current knowledge.

Returning to the textbook descriptions of schizophrenia, one might use migraine as a parallel example to illustrate the problems with diagnosing at the syndrome level. A visual aura followed by a unilateral throbbing headache with nausea and vomiting is called classical migraine. If the aura is absent it is called common migraine. If the headache is bilateral or is not throbbing should one describe it as a 'forme fruste' of migraine or no longer call it migraine? There is no clear answer to this question. The same problem applies to diagnosing schizophrenia. This uncertainty accounts for the dominating preoccupation in general psychiatry with phenomenology and eliciting so-called first-rank symptoms in the mental state examination.

## Phenomenology

Phenomenology, as originally applied to psychology by the German psychologist Jaspers, is concerned with the objective description of abnormal states of mind (Jaspers 1967). The phenomenological approach aims to be objective and scientific in describing subjective experiences in psychosis, through defining and classifying psychic phenomena as the first step. Thus a delusion might be defined as a false belief held in the face of contrary evidence and not amenable to reason or logic acceptable to someone of a similar cultural background.

A sudden appearance of a firmly held delusion in the absence of an organic illness may be strongly suggestive of a schizophrenic illness.

In Jasperian terms, if a voice is experienced as coming from outside one's head this is termed an auditory hallucination and would be regarded as pathological. If it is felt to be coming from inside the head, it would phenomenologically speaking be termed a pseudo-hallucination and be viewed as non-pathological. Eliciting psychopathology indicative of schizophrenia is seen from the medical position as the preliminary task in interviewing all patients. Only then can the elicited symptoms be grouped together to form a recognised syndrome.

In this exercise, theoretical views of causation have no place; indeed they would be felt to interfere with the aim of achieving an objective description of the patient's subjective experiences. The advantage of the phenomenological approach is to build up descriptions of psychopathology where there is a clear and agreed understanding of the terminology being used.

Nevertheless, the question remains how to make optimal use of the phenomenological approach in defining schizophrenia. Schneider (1959) tried to make the diagnosis more reliable by viewing certain symptoms as carrying more weight, the so called 'Schneiderian first-rank symptoms'. These include hearing your thoughts spoken out loud, voices talking about you, believing that you are being made to feel things or having thoughts inserted into your mind, or having thoughts withdrawn and broadcast, as well as delusional perceptions. However, some 25 per cent of patients with manic depressive states show first-rank symptoms, while some 25 per cent of patients with established schizophrenia do not. While standardised interview techniques have arisen from this dilemma for research purposes, such as the present state examination (Wing et al. 1974), in everyday clinical practice the diagnostic difficulties remain.

## The mental state examination

Junior psychiatrists in training spend a great deal of time on the mental state examination, developing their ability to elicit first-rank symptoms using the phenomenological approach. The first part of the mental state examination concentrates on this area, describing appearance, speech, mood, thought disorder and abnormal beliefs and perceptions. The second part turns to the cognitive state, looking for organic pathology such as evidence of disorientation and memory impairment. After evaluating the patient's insight into his or her condition, a diagnostic formulation is made with a differential diagnosis, based in the UK on the ICD-10 classification system (WHO 1994).

While the aetiology of schizophrenia continues to be investigated, primarily through neurological studies of the brain, and through the psychopharmacological action of drugs and neurotransmitters, general psychiatry recognises that emotional factors have a part to play in relapses.

It is recognised that as well as defaulting from medication, living in an emotionally over-pressurising environment, described as an environment where there is high expressed emotion (EE), can lead to relapses. Educating the family to lower their expectations of the patient can alter this pattern (Leff 1994). However, though the potential of emotional stresses to precipitate relapse is recognised, the general psychiatric approach to schizophrenia is firmly focused at the phenomenological and psychopharmacological level. Once the diagnosis has been made through the phenomenological approach, the focus is treatment through medication.

This approach seems to leave little room for a psychoanalytic contribution. Indeed patients diagnosed with schizophrenia are felt to be too unwell for any psychotherapeutic intervention other than a general supportive approach or a cognitive-behavioural approach that reinforces reality.

The mental state examination is a snapshot taken at a particular moment in time and as such it lacks a dynamic element. A patient with a schizo-affective disorder may present a picture that resembles schizophrenia one day, and a few days later looks more like depression. Also, when taken in isolation, a purely phenomenological approach is not necessarily reliable diagnostically in distinguishing schizophrenia from hypomanic states.

## Clinical implications

The importance of the formal mental state examination is over-emphasised in psychiatric training. This may encourage junior doctors to develop a somewhat one-sided, rigid, organically based approach to psychosis, lacking a dynamic touch. The following serves as an illustrative example.

A young man in his twenties already had a protracted history of severe chronic schizophrenia. As well as failing to take his medication, he would also drink, and when he ran out of money would go round to his mother and demand money from her in a threatening manner. His mother could not stand up to him. His father, who worked as a long-distance lorry driver and was away much of the time, was the only one who stood up to him.

The patient was in such a disturbed state on his latest admission that he required initial containment on the secure ward. After spending a lengthy period on the secure ward and receiving a large dose of depot medication to calm down his aggressive paranoid state, which had been accompanied by persecutory voices, it was felt that he might finally be ready for transfer to our open ward. My junior doctor saw him and said that the persecutory voices had all gone apart from one: he was still troubled by hearing his father's critical voice. The doctor asked whether he should increase the patient's medication further prior to his return to an open ward, as it seemed that his psychosis had not yet quite resolved.

I replied in the negative, pointing out that his father's voice represented his sanity, the only part in his mind standing up to his disruptive lifestyle. When I saw him the patient also complained about hearing his father's voice and said that he wanted it removed. However, when I pointed out its positive significance as a representative of the only person who stood up to him, he smiled in a way that seemed to acknowledge that a meaningful exchange was taking place, rather than an approach centred solely on phenomenology and concern with the appropriate level of medication to the exclusion of all other considerations.

## Incorporating an analytic perspective

Organic psychiatrists draw attention to the difference between patho-genesis and pathoplasty. In other words, conditions have their under-lying organic causation, although the presenting clinical picture may be influenced by the individual's culture and social circumstances.

The danger with this approach is the development of a false degree of confidence in relation to psychotic states. The clinical procedure becomes straightforward and predictable. One simply diagnoses the type of psychosis through the mental state examination and establishes the appropriate drug regime, while reviewing any concurrent social stresses and rehabilitation needs. Tom Freeman, a psychoanalyst who also spent his career in general psychiatry, once said to me at a meeting that 'The difference between us and the organically orientated psychiatrists is that they know what is going on. We haven't the faintest idea so we have to listen to our patients to see if they can teach us!' (see Chapter 7 for his contributions).

I have found that incorporating an analytic perspective when listening to the patient's history opens up a whole new way of relating to the patient. In the following chapters I will show how this approach can deepen our understanding of our patients. It offers a way to move on from the necessary preliminary phenomenologically based diagnostic approach, into an affectively more relevant and meaningful way of relating to our patients.

## Summary

The medical model has both positive aspects and limitations. Through a phenomenological approach, the medical model takes an objective stance towards subjective symptoms in order to arrive at a diagnostic and classificatory system for psychotic disorders. This is valuable for cross-cultural research and for legal purposes, when a medical diagnosis is required. However, the model is limited by its lack of accommodation of a dynamic perspective. It is this aspect that will be explored in the chapters that follow.

# 3

## Controversial issues in psychosis

### Introduction

This chapter will consider some ongoing controversies in psychosis. These include the questions of whether the differentiation of psychosis is stigmatising, what psychoanalysis has to offer if the roots of schizophrenia are biological, the role of the inpatient ward and how medical, CBT and psychoanalytic perspectives differ.

### Should we differentiate psychosis?

In 2003 Richard Bentall, who was then Professor of Clinical Psychology at Liverpool University, wrote a book entitled *Madness Explained*, in which he expressed the view that there was no clear dividing line between what he termed sanity and madness, and that the use of diagnostic labels was therefore stigmatising (Bentall 2003). In his preface he wrote:

> Scientists, like ordinary folk and psychiatric patients, are flawed, emotional and excitable human beings who are sometimes wise and sometimes stupid, sometimes lovable and sometimes bloody irritating. By talking about my own experiences, both positive and negative, I have attempted to highlight an important theme of this book, which is the vanishingly small difference between them the 'us' who are sane and the 'them' who are not.
>
> (Bentall 2003, p. xiv)

He later cited his own experience of distress following the break-up of his first marriage, as anecdotal evidence in support of this assertion.

Bentall (2003) argued that experiences such as delusional beliefs and hearing voices are exaggerations of mental foibles to which we were all vulnerable, and which in some cultures were not seen as abnormal at all. He continued:

> In these pages, I have tried to demonstrate that the difference between those that are diagnosed as suffering from a psychiatric disorder and those who are not amounts to not very much. This is an important insight because of its application for psychiatric care. As I hope to demonstrate in a later publication, the dreadful state of psychiatric services is not only a consequence of muddled thinking about the nature of psychiatric disorders, but also a consequence of the way in which psychiatric patients have been denied a voice by being treated as irrational and dangerous, like wild animals in a zoo.
>
> (Bentall 2003, p. xiv)

Bentall emphasised that he approached psychosis from the position of an experimental psychologist. For example, he described how he investigated the relationship between mania and depression and the concept of the manic defence by exploring patients' attitudes to words presented to them in these two states. This was regarded as a scientific and measurable approach, in contrast to the analytic approach. Bentall entitled a chapter on mania 'A colourful malady', in support of which he quoted Virginia Woolf saying: 'As an experience madness is terrific' (Bentall 2003, p. 271).

From a CBT perspective, Kingdon and Turkington (1994) proposed a general framework for working with psychotic patients, which they described as a *normalising strategy*. Bentall observed:

> The idea behind this approach is to demystify psychotic experiences and make them seem less frightening, for example by pointing out the similarities between hallucinations or paranoia and more mundane mental states, or by explaining to patients that these experiences are much more common than is often realised.
>
> (Bentall 2003, p. 508)

Bentall concluded with the view: 'Why not help some psychotic patients just to accept that they are different from the rest of us? Fear

of madness may be a much bigger problem than madness itself'
(Bentall 2003, p. 511).

Bentall's views are representative of an important attitude to psychosis from a predominantly non-medical cognitive psychological
perspective.

In his foreword to the book, Aaron T. Beck, the father of cognitive
therapy for delusions, observed that Bentall 'has endeavoured to slay
the monster – mental illness – and in this volume he has shown that
he has trapped it, if not finished it off', giving his support to the view
that the idea of mental illness as a diagnostic entity can be discarded
(Bentall 2003, p. xii).

Despite the title of Bentall's book, he does not define madness or
specify whether it is to be distinguished from psychosis. The *Oxford
Dictionary* (1990) does make this distinction. It gives several different
ways we use the term madness, from insane to wildly foolish, excited,
angry or light-hearted, while in contrast psychosis is described as a
severe mental derangement, especially when resulting in delusions
and loss of contact with external reality.

Bentall's refusal to differentiate the major psychotic disorders from
moments of temporary aberration enables him to argue that the
approach of differentiation taken by mental health care services
dehumanises their patients and denies them a voice.

Bentall (2003) emphasised the limitations of the solely medical
model of psychosis, with its preoccupation with classification, phenomenology and the biological approach, without considering its
positive aspects with respect to diagnosis and classification.

For example, the manic states that characterise bipolar disorders are
linked with a denial of the underlying severe depression with potential self-harm, with associated statistics of a 15 per cent risk of suicide.
Thus Virginia Woolf's manic states would alert the clinician to her
possible underlying vulnerability to suicide, as tragically occurred.
Here diagnostic labels matter because of the associated prognostic
concerns that they can raise.

The view that fear of madness may be a much bigger problem than
madness itself is an interesting proposition. If it is correct, then we
have to consider it from all angles. First, madness, or here I would
prefer to use the term psychotic disorders, leads to frightening states of
mind for all those involved with them. We cannot easily grasp and
understand these states of mind, which challenge all our belief systems.
The challenge is for us to learn to accept these conditions, however

ignorant we may be about their aetiology, and try to study them on their own terms. If we cannot meet this challenge, we will fall back on imposing views and theories with which we are already familiar.

Many non-psychiatrists try to minimise the condition of schizophrenia, pointing out that each person is different and unique and that a diagnosis of schizophrenia is stigmatising. When this view is adopted, the psychiatrists and nursing staff who have primary responsibility for containment and management of very difficult states may come in for particularly harsh criticism.

However, it is unlikely that strategies such as changing the name of schizophrenia to 'integration disorder', or even abolishing the concept, would affect the root cause of the stigma – the public's ignorance and fear of people with mental illness. Renaming might even have the unintended consequence that the individual, rather than their illness, would be blamed for their symptoms.

As Lieberman and First (2007) have written:

Ultimately, we must gain a more complete understanding of the causes and pathophysiological mechanisms underlying schizophrenia. Only then can we replace the way we characterise schizophrenia with a diagnosis that more closely conforms to a specific brain disease. In the meantime, we can be confident and grateful that the benefits conferred by the concept of schizophrenia far outweigh any perceived disadvantages.

(Lieberman and First 2007, p. 108)

## Is psychoanalysis relevant to schizophrenia?

When the *International Journal of Psychoanalysis* decided to run a series of articles on current psychoanalytic controversies, they chose to begin with the relationship between psychoanalysis and schizophrenia (Lucas 2003a). I was invited to put the case for analysis, while Robert Michels, an analyst from New York, put the counterview. Michels began by referring to the work of Martin S. Willick as an example of the prevailing and in Michels' view appropriate attitude among North American analysts to the question of the relation between psychoanalysis and schizophrenia.

In an article entitled 'Psychoanalysis and schizophrenia: A cautionary tale', Willick (2001), an American analyst, had cited the history of psychoanalysis and schizophrenia as an example of psychoanalytic theories that have not stood the test of time.

Analysts had imposed their theoretical views of aetiology, attributing schizophrenia to early trauma linked with an emotionally unresponsive mother, rather than accepting an underlying biological causation. This was supported by the outcome figures from Chestnut Lodge (see Chapter 8), where a purely analytic approach had been taken to borderline states and schizophrenia. While outcome figures were favourable for an analytic approach to borderline states, they were not for schizophrenia (McGlashan 1984b).

In a review of British object relations theorists, with the exception of Rosenfeld, Willick held that he was unable to find a single well-documented case of schizophrenia in the work of Klein, Winnicott, Fairbairn, Guntrip, and Bion. Without any clinical supportive evidence, they had all lumped together schizophrenia, schizoid personalities and the more severe character disorders as examples of failures adequately to overcome the paranoid-schizoid position.

In response to my argument that psychoanalysis still has a unique contribution to make in relating to psychosis, Michels (2003) wrote:

> The history of the relationship between psychoanalysis and schizophrenia is complex. So-called psychoanalytic theories of aetiology have not only been of little scientific value, their application to the psychotherapy of schizophrenic patients or in discussion with their families has often been demoralising and counterproductive. In the empiric arena of evidence and science, they have largely lost out to biologic and psychosocial models. Most North American psychoanalysts, exemplified by Willick, see the important aspect of the story of psychoanalysis and schizophrenia to be an example of how analysis can go so far astray, with the hope of preventing misadventures in the future.
>
> (Michels 2003, p. 9)

In my article I gave several vignettes in support of the psychoanalytic framework that I have developed in relating to schizophrenia, which this book will elaborate. I take the view that in working with patients with schizophrenia, as Bion suggested, we always need to think in terms of two separate parts, the psychotic and the non-psychotic, not one person (Bion 1957a; Lucas 1992). The psychotic part is intolerant of frustration and attacks the thinking arrived at by the work of the non–psychotic part. Hence the need to tune into the psychotic wavelength: whenever we are dealing with a patient with a major psychiatric disorder, we need to ask ourselves whether we are receiving a communication from a non–psychotic part or a psychotic part masquerading as normal (Bion 1957a). As discussed in Chapter 1, the commonest symptoms of schizophrenia are not auditory hallucinations or paranoid delusions, encountered in some 60 per cent of cases, but denial and rationalisation, found in over 95 per cent of cases (Lucas 1993). One vignette was the example of a young woman who had jumped out of a window (see Chapter 11, Case 4 for full details). I suggested to this woman that she had not jumped out but rather had been pushed out by an intolerant (psychotic) part of her; this led to a dramatic change in her mental state. Michels thought this intervention was 'highly theoretical, confusing and potentially misleading – not the kind of thing I would say to a schizophrenic patient who might have difficulty interpreting metaphor or thinking abstractly' (Michels 2003, p. 12). He also felt that a model incorporating issues of conflict was inappropriate for a condition with an organic aetiology.

Michels was very critical of the lack of any evidence-based material to support the belief that psychoanalytic treatment was relevant to schizophrenia, for without applying this standard: 'examples of how psychoanalytic concepts can enhance our understanding of experiences with patients with schizophrenia won't simply be unconvincing, they will be seen as irrelevant to the dialogue concerning the treatment of schizophrenia' (Michels 2003, p. 12).

Michels recognised that psychoanalysis helped people to cope with stress and so helped caretakers to experience the humanity of their patients or clients, but however valuable this was: 'psychoanalysis had no more special relevance to schizophrenia than it does to multiple sclerosis or cancer or homelessness' (Michels 2003, p. 10). Michels went on to question the claim that psychoanalysis has a unique relevance in the area of schizophrenia, arguing that 'most psychoanalytic claims in this area have been based on professional narcissism rather than clinical evidence' (Michels 2003, p. 11).

He concluded:

I suspect that psychoanalytic treatment has little relevance to schizophrenia, or to its so-called 'primary' psychopathological features. Psychoanalytic treatment is most helpful for individuals whose core problems are largely related to mental conflicts and experiences that can be understood psychoanalytically, and who have the capacity to participate in the process of enquiry and treatment. Unfortunately, neither is true of most schizophrenic patients [. . .] In brief, schizophrenia is a relative contraindication to psychoanalytic treatment.

(Michels 2003, p. 11)

Michels' critique highlights some central controversial issues in a clear way that requires responses. First, it is crucial to distinguish between psychoanalysis as a curative treatment, a method of study of the mind and a theoretical framework that can inform our work with patients in general psychiatry.

Given our current ignorance of the aetiology of schizophrenia, the criticism that the relationship history of psychoanalysis and schizophrenia is complex applies to all approaches to schizophrenia, not just psychoanalysis.

Michels highlights the risk for all practitioners of becoming over-enthusiastic about their particular line of approach. He argued that thinking about the behaviour and communications of schizophrenic patients from a psychoanalytic perspective was comparable to the use of applied analysis in interpretation of a work of art, and suspected that while taking this approach might make the practitioner feel more comfortable and engaged in his difficult work, other equally plausible explanations could equally well be proffered.

It is certainly true that a consideration of the symbolic meaning behind communications can make practitioners feel more comfortable and humanise their work, since it helps them to see the patient as an individual with his or her own particular way of responding to a crisis, rather than viewing the patient in a cut-off way as purely a representative of a diagnostic category.

Many years ago, I heard Professor Roger Higgs, a Professor for General Practice at London University talking about the training of general practitioners (GPs) and the feelings related to their work. I was struck by his descriptions, which resonated with my own feelings working as a psychoanalyst in general psychiatry.

When he sent trainees to his practice, he did not expect them to see all the patients in a busy clinic, but rather take one patient and see them for as long as they liked in order to come to understand them. He felt this experience could later be transposed into running the busy clinics. Similarly, the experience I gained from analytic training

31

where I had time to learn from seeing patients individually, informed my work in busy outpatient clinics and ward reviews, which at times can involve seeing over twenty patients at a time, including several new admissions.

Higgs highlighted GPs' worries about coping and fears of burnout if they had to fit an emergency into an already busy clinic; feelings one could readily identify with in the role of general psychiatrist.

Higgs then made the interesting point that GPs often regarded their work as trivial in comparison to specialists. A similar attitude can prevail in psychoanalysis, where applied analysis can be devalued compared to individual analysis. However, Higgs drew attention to the Latin root of the word trivial, meaning where three roads met and where people would stop to gossip.

In subsequent chapters, clinical examples will be given to show that incorporating an analytic perspective can enrich the psychiatrist's work and help to bring clarity and direction, as for example when helping the judge arrive at a decision in 'A tale of a wig' (Chapter 11, Case 2). Incorporating an analytic perspective can also bring interest and humour into very demanding work, thereby reducing the risk of burnout and indifference.

If we now consider the lifelong management of patients with chronically disabling psychotic disorders, then one could take issue with Michels' view over the relevance of psychoanalysis in this area. While recognising that psychoanalysis provides overall frameworks for helping people cope with stresses, Michels suggests that psycho-analysis has 'no more special relevance to schizophrenia than it does to multiple sclerosis or cancer or homelessness' (Michels 2003, p. 10).

However, individuals with the latter conditions do not require continual risk assessment. Their communications do not require us to ask ourselves whether they are straightforward communications from a non–psychotic part of the personality or denials and rational-isation from the psychotic part, which may be harbouring dangerous intentions (see Chapters 11, 18 and 19).

Michels questions the technique of interpreting in a confronta-tional way to the patient about the functioning of their psychotic part, due to the cognitive difficulties present in schizophrenia and the lack of capacity for symbolic thinking. However, in the case of the patient who jumped out of the window, my interpretation produced a dramatic response, and a shift in emphasis, after months of stasis. It brought the patient's murderousness into the open. I believe that her frightened non–psychotic part felt supported and was grateful for my intervention. This was also true for her involved and caring mother (Chapter 11, Case 4).

With regard to technique, if one thinks in terms of the psychotic and non–psychotic parts of the personality, one has to deal with the problem of the behaviour of the psychotic part first. Inevitably, this may at times take the form of a confrontational style.

An example would be the case of a patient with a thirty-year history of chronic schizophrenia, who was placed in a group home when his previous asylum, Claybury Hospital, closed. In the home he became aggressive, hit other patients and stubbed cigarettes on the carpet until he was readmitted, now to the district hospital. In hospital, he repeatedly claimed in a tirade that he was not Mr X, but Mr Y, born six years before Mr X. He said that he owned Claybury Hospital, was owed £80 million pounds and that Dr Lucas had stolen his Ford Granada!

In the end I found a way of speaking to him. I told him that I was not talking to Mr Y but Mr X. We had a big problem with Mr Y. He was infantile, did what he wanted and if he couldn't get his way all the time he would do things like stubbing cigarettes on the carpet and hitting other residents in the group home; and he lived in a grandiose world of his own making, believing that he owned Claybury Hospital and that I had stolen his Ford Granada.

This intervention took the wind out of his sails. When I saw him later in the hospital corridor, he said to me in a rather sulky voice, 'All right, Dr Lucas, there are two of me!' He was transferred in time to the rehabilitation ward. I always knew when he had been misbehaving, as on such occasions if we bumped into each other in the corridor, he would say, 'I'm Mr Y not Mr X!' Invariably the rehab staff would subsequently confirm my suspicions.

While it is important at times to stand up to the psychotic part of the patient, there are many other situations where a consideration of the delusions they describe together with one's countertransference can help one to become empathic to the patient's current predicament. Michels (2003) questions the ability of the patient with schizophrenia to understand metaphors. The challenge is rather for us to get onto the patient's wavelength and find a way to understand the meaning conveyed within their delusional communications.

Michels referred to psychoanalysis as providing a framework for conversations about human experiences, but only one among many others. He is correct that there are other approaches, such as cognitive behavioural or narrative styles. However, psychoanalysis differs fundamentally from other psychological disciplines in its recognition of an unconscious internal world and its influence on the individual's life and behaviour.

Finally, Michels emphasises the importance of controlled outcome studies and the fact that while they have shown the efficacy of psychoanalysis as a treatment for borderline states, this has not been the case for schizophrenia. However, by focusing solely on the research outcome of controlled trials, one is in danger of moving away from seminal insights gained through individual case studies, and throwing the baby out with the bathwater.

Moreover, within the context of audit, there are in fact operational research outcome data to support the effectiveness of applied analysis as part of an overall integrated approach to schizophrenia.

## The role for hospital–based services within an integrated approach

Robbins advocated an integrated approach to schizophrenia, thinking in terms of interlocking hierarchical systems – intrapsychic, interpersonal, family, social and cultural and neurobiological – to remedy a reductionistic approach in the United States, which some decades ago was dominated by a psychoanalytic approach (Jackson 2001a; Robbins 1993).

Based on forty years of psychotherapeutic involvement with patients with schizophrenia in Finland, Alanen (1997) advocated the development of what he termed a 'need-adapted' approach to treatment. While all approaches to treatment were recognised, including biomedical, individual, familial, therapeutic community and rehabilitation, Alanen held that decisions about which approaches are most appropriate should be made on a case-specific basis. For this to happen, Alanen argued for the central importance of an overall psychoanalytically informed assessment.

Input from a consultant supervisor with analytic experience is required to make the need-adapted evaluation. As Alanen (1997) described, the consultant should promote a non-authoritarian attitude, in which each team member is encouraged to develop his/her own skills in a creative way. Caring family members also have a crucial role to play in the initial assessments and ongoing treatment. This approach led to shorter admissions, lower levels of medication and improved rehabilitation figures compared to other districts in Finland.

When I moved out from the asylum to a district setting, the introduction of a sector team afforded the opportunity to make this sort of integrated approach available to a local area. The community workers, the day hospital and the inpatient unit were now able to function together as parts of one cohesive service. The sector ward was designed by the ward manager to maximise the size of a centrally supervised area for day activities, while allowing for separate-sex sleeping quarters.

Regular ward reviews three times a week, availability of access to move out easily to the day hospital and other community support were vital ingredients. However, a psychoanalytically informed framework of approach to assessments was at the core of the approach.

This framework of approach encompassed a basic philosophy of accepting psychosis, tuning into the psychotic wavelength, differentiating the psychotic from the non-psychotic personality, exploring the meanings of hallucinations and delusions, utilising the team's countertransference experiences and an appreciation of the importance of the function of the ward admission for containment and assessment.

The adoption of this approach led to annual bed occupancy figures of 100 per cent compared to 150 per cent levels for the other acute wards, with associated lower drug expenditure figures and shorter length of stay in hospital (Lucas 2004).

Unfortunately, a policy was subsequently introduced to make each ward single sex, leading to the loss of the integrated model and six consultants sharing beds on one ward. This led to bed occupancy running at 150–170 per cent, with sleeping out in the private sector. The response has been the creation of crisis resolution home treatment teams and early intervention services to reduce the stress on the ward and contain patients in the community wherever possible away from hospital based services (Johannessen et al. 2006).

Brian Martindale (2007) described setting up such an early intervention service in North England, based on Cullberg's Swedish 'stress–vulnerability model' (Cullberg 2001; Martindale 2007). He noted that 'In the UK, perhaps because of the separation of specialist training for psychotherapy from adult and community psychiatry, psychodynamics is rarely integrated into the psychiatry of psychosis' (Martindale 2007, p. 34).

Nowadays, there is less emphasis on developing a seamless service that incorporates inpatients, day hospital outpatients and community services, and admission to hospital is often viewed in negative terms. The closure of the asylums resulted in a drastic reduction of inpatient beds and the acute wards became overburdened, leaving the nurses little time to relate therapeutically to their patients. The wards became depressing, unsafe places, with easy access to drugs (Fagin 2001, 2007; Mind 2000). This problem remains, though attempts are being made to address the crisis (Firth 2004; Holmes 2004; Kennard et al. 2007).

However, the important role played by the acute ward in containment and assessment needs recognition. Within this context, nurses need support and training to gain confidence in what is most demanding work (Evans 2006).

There is also controversy about the role of day hospitals. Some of us would argue strongly that having a professionally run day hospital at one's disposal is a real asset. It can be used to prevent admissions and facilitate early discharge. It can help people to work through adjustment reactions. It can also help young patients facing the early stages of a schizophrenic illness to combat social isolation. It provides individual therapy, groups and occupational therapy.

Apart from the economic cost of running a professionally staffed day hospital, there is a view in some quarters that the name alone of day hospital carries the stigma of institutionalisation and that like the inpatient ward, it is a place best avoided. The aim, after early onset psychotic breakdowns, would be to 'normalise' the situation by getting people back in the community as soon as possible and receiving their support away from hospital settings. Our day hospital recently only just survived a threat of closure within a climate of economic austerity, thanks to powerful representations to management from the users. Nevertheless many such day hospitals have been closed in recent years.

## Contrasting approaches to delusions

### *The medical model*

Classical psychiatric teaching, based on phenomenology, the eliciting of symptoms for purposes of diagnostic classification, does not look for dynamic explanations for delusions. This approach distinguishes between obsessional symptoms, overvalued ideas and delusions.

Obsessional or compulsive symptoms are characterised by a subjective sense of compulsion overriding an internal resistance from the healthy part of the patient. If the whole of the patient identifies itself with the idea (e.g. of contamination), then we are dealing with a delusional idea rather than a compulsive one. Overvalued ideas fall in between these two forms of symptoms; they are accepted by the patient but not without doubts.

In relation to delusions the idea of 'incomprehensibility' is not an absolute one. For example, a markedly sensitive premorbid personality who develops delusional jealousy could partly be understood in terms of their previous background (Slater and Roth 1969).

In modern day psychiatry,

> A delusion is a belief that is firmly held on inadequate grounds, is not affected by rational argument or evidence to the contrary, and is not a conventional belief that the person might be expected to hold given their educational, cultural and religious background.
>
> (Gelder et al. 2006, p. 9)

Partial delusions are those that are held with some degree of doubt. The phenomenological approach also classifies delusions in relation to onset, distinguishes primary and secondary delusions, and considers them according to theme, discriminating between paranoid (persecutory) delusions, delusions of reference, grandiose delusions, delusions of guilt, nihilistic, hypochondriacal, religious, jealous, sexual or amorous, delusions of control, delusions concerning possession of thought, thought insertion, thought withdrawal and thought broadcasting. There are also shared delusions (Gelder et al. 2006, p. 10).

*The cognitive-behavioural approach to delusions*

From a CBT perspective, Turkington et al. (1996) recommended that the definition of delusion be revised as follows:

> A delusion is a false belief at the extreme end of the continuum of consensual agreement. It is not categorically different to overvalued ideas and normal beliefs. It is held in spite of evidence to the contrary but it may be amenable to change when that evidence is collaboratively explored. In that case, the belief may come to

approximate closely to ideas in keeping with the patient's social, educational, cultural and religious background.

(Turkington et al. 1996)

CBT treatment involves assessment of delusional beliefs in terms of pre-existing beliefs, and linked emotional reactions. First and foremost, a therapeutic alliance is established through sensitivity. The clinician avoids being drawn by the patient into a confrontational stance by using responses such as 'Well, that is a possible explanation, but could it be something else?' or 'Let's explore the evidence and see if your ideas are right' (Turkington and Siddle 1998).

There appear to be two differing approaches to working with delusions. The first uses normalisation strategies including peripheral questioning and Socratic questioning to encourage the patient to relinquish his or her delusion. The second recognises when there is a defensive nature to delusions, linked to strong affects ('hot cognition'), protective of underlying low self-esteem, where a different approach is advocated using 'inference chaining' and 'schema focused' work.

Techniques include 'peripheral questioning' about how the delusion might work. 'Socratic questioning' involves using a line of questioning to lead the deluded patient to an entirely different conclusion. For example, if a patient said that she was the Queen of Spain, one might respond by saying, 'Let's presume for a moment that this belief is completely true. In that case you must have had a coronation, speak good Spanish and you must have made many state visits.'

Socratic discussion is regarded as a penetrating and challenging form of questioning only to be attempted later in cognitive therapy when the patient is beginning to be doubtful of their beliefs.

The second scenario recognises where the delusion serves as protection for underlying low self-esteem, the clue being its link to strong affects ('hot cognition'). Here a different approach is advocated using 'inference chaining' and 'schema focused' work.

'Inference chaining' is a method of working beneath the delusion, in particular with grandiose or systematised delusions, which are often resistant to other techniques because of their protective function in relation to self-esteem.

If a patient said that she was the Queen of Spain, but on being questioned about why she held on to this belief, said it meant that she was admired by everyone, and then became tearful, this would be explored further. The patient might disclose that she no longer wished to take abuse from anyone and just wanted to be her normal self, without criticism. The tears are indicative of a 'hot cognition', a cognition which carries with it a powerful affective charge that indicates an important arena for further investigation, through 'schema focused' work.

Work at the schema level would focus on issues of approval demands and underlying low self-esteem. Schemas include core maladaptive beliefs, for example 'I am unlovable', and compensatory beliefs such as 'I must be approved at all costs'. Techniques involve articulating the evidence, positive and negative, logging of approvals, acting against the belief in imagery and in real-life situations, and direct disputation. CBT does not contraindicate concurrent use of medication.

Turkington and Siddle (1998) concluded that all available evidence points towards the fact that delusions, at least in certain of their parameters, can be expected to shift along the spectrum towards normality when a cognitive therapy approach is used.

I was fortunate on 10 July 2006 to share a session on 'Psychosis – Dreams and Delusions' with Douglas Turkington, a leading authority on the application of CBT to delusions. The session was part of a day event in celebration of Freud's 150th birthday held at the Royal College of Psychiatrists' annual meeting. Turkington took the Schreber case to illustrate common ground between Freud's analytic approach and Beck's CBT approach to delusions, showing that both agreed that the emergence of delusions is linked to stress and that symptom formation and content was replete with meaning.

Turkington outlined the CBT treatment that he would have instigated for Schreber. This included ten sessions each of the following:

## 1 Scaffolding

This involves 'containing', affect reduction, scheduling activities and healthy living exercises. This input can by provided by other involved staff as well as the CBT therapist, who would typically visit a patient with a persistent severe psychotic disorder at home, or group home. Scaffolding plays a very important role in patients lacking in motivation and without it nothing else is possible, although in Schreber's case, Turkington thought that the aim would be to engage his keen intellect.

*2 Systematised delusional level work*

*3 Schema level work*

In Schreber's case this would involve noting his background history: his abusive father and the fact that he was a second son whose elder brother had committed suicide, which probably resulted in laying down early schemas of core weakness and inferiority, expressing views that 'I am not man enough'. His desperation for achievement and approval then led to the progression of his illness. He developed severe hypochondriasis from overwork but, as his anxiety levels rose, this led to a delusional mood and the emergence of grandiose delusions of being mankind's redeemer and the passive recipient of God's attentions. This protected him against his schema vulnerability.

*4 Consolidation*

*5 Relapse prevention*

In the same presentation, Turkington described being asked to visit and treat a man with chronic paranoid schizophrenia, at his residential home. This man had never lived independently, abused cannabis and had a forensic history of assaulting people. He harboured chronic delusions.

Following CBT he became initially a lot less preoccupied with his delusional system, reduced his cannabis intake, was compliant with his medication and started living for the first time in his life in a supported flat. The professionals involved in his treatment paid a lot of attention to the scaffolding work on befriending and challenging his schema of low self-esteem.

Midway through the interventions, however, the patient became panicky and his conviction rate increased again. On review, the 'containing' scaffolding work was felt to have played a very important role and without it nothing else would have been possible, but his chronic delusional beliefs remained essentially unaltered.

*CBT and psychoanalytic approaches: similarities and differences*

Commenting on the CBT approach, Martindale (1998) wrote:

> It is a very welcome development that cognitive therapists are now finding effective techniques to work with people with problems relating to psychosis. It is clear that their approaches involve a very special attention to the therapeutic relationship. Though there are radical differences, it is also striking that their approaches are leading to a rediscovery of some important features long familiar to those with a psychodynamic perspective who have worked with such patients.
>
> (Martindale 1998, p. 242)

Murray Jackson went further in his comment: 'I think that the long-term future of cognitive behavioural work with psychotic patients without a psychoanalytic input is uncertain' (Jackson 2001b, p. 51).

Certainly the rediscovery and incorporation of psychoanalytic concepts within CBT, including an appreciation of defence mechanisms and the complexity of the therapeutic relationship, is evident in the work of CBT therapists. One example of this would be the development of Anthony Ryle's cognitive analytic therapy (CAT). The Royal College of Psychiatrists in the UK requires its psychotherapy trainees to have experience of three approaches, psychoanalytic, CBT and CAT. CAT is an integrative model of psychotherapy (Ryle and Kerr 2002). It is a brief time-limited procedure, expanded from an initial range of neurotic disorders to more difficult groups of patients. CAT understands abnormal development as due to the internalisation of dysfunctional reciprocal role procedures (RRPs). The aim is to create with the patient both narrative and diagrammatic reformulations of their difficulties. Advocates of the procedure feel that CAT could be helpful in extending the repertoire of individual approaches to psychosis (Kerr et al. 2006).

### An analytic understanding of the cognitive approach

Cognitive techniques have an advantage over the analytic approach in that changes in attitudes are easily measurable, but the patient's responses may be more complex than might at first appear to be the case. Britton (2009) suggests that believing is something that we do from birth, like breathing. He distinguishes between beliefs that have merely been surmounted and those that have been worked through and relinquished. The relinquishment that is necessary for psychic

41

change takes time and contrasts with CBT strategies of generation of alternative explanations, normalisation and behaviour reattribution (Morrison 2004).

Britton (2009) writes:

> A belief that has been surmounted is simply overlaid by another belief and its quiescence remains dependent on the prevailing context of rationality and the authority of a parental transference figure; the surmounted belief meanwhile bides its time. It is like believing one thing when in company in daylight and another when alone in the dark. It is those lurking beliefs of the night that most interest us as analysts, those ghosts that vanish when we subject ourselves to the sharply focussed light of educated reason. In contrast to the attempt to overcome beliefs that I take to characterise CBT, the aim of analysis is to find the hidden beliefs of our patients and to help to relinquish them.
>
> (Britton 2009)

The suggestion here is that CBT works through identification in the transference with a desired authoritarian parental figure. Patients are guided in how to think and do task-related exercises. Of course at a time of crisis some patients may find it a relief to be directed how to think and may prefer to be offered such an approach.

Those who wish to identify with a parental authority figure might prefer a CBT approach, while those wishing to free themselves from parental values and develop a mind of their own might favour an analytic approach. Of course both attitudes can be present in the patient at the same time, adding to the complexity.

Patients tend to nudge their therapists to act out their unconscious wishes, something an analyst has to consider prior to their formulation of an interpretation (Joseph 1985). Perhaps in response to the patient's ambivalence about whether to be interested in or dismissive of their delusional experiences, CBT practitioners have formulated two approaches that seem otherwise to be contradictory. The first approach is 'normalisation', trying to remove the delusion through logical argument, while in the second approach patients convey through their affect ('hot cognition') that their delusion has a meaning that needs to be understood.

In psychiatry, it is interesting to observe how many psychoses resolve through a flight into health by identification with an idealised parental figure. This is particularly apparent with the resolution of episodes of psychotic depression. Up to one-third of cases of puerperal psychoses seem to spontaneously click back into place, often after the patient has been in a severely dysfunctional state for a long period. If one studies the process, as in the first case reported in Chapter 15, it becomes apparent that it is through forming identification with an idealised parental figure that the psychosis is resolved. To others this patient may have seemed to undergo a spontaneous cure, but she herself knew better, remaining aware of what Britton might refer to as her former beliefs lurking in the night, with her recognition of her vulnerability to a further psychotic episode with her next pregnancy.

Psychoanalysts recognise the effects that transference and countertransference phenomena can have on the nature of the therapeutic alliance. In psychotic states, the patient may initially attribute special therapeutic powers to the therapist, which later becomes unsustainable, leading to relapse, as perhaps was the case in Turkington's description of the case of the man with a severe chronic psychosis.

This underlines the need to differentiate between relating to delusions as acute stress reactions and relating to an underlying longstanding psychosis. The latter condition will not go away, whatever therapeutic approach is used. It will fluctuate in intensity depending on whether the degree of support being provided is commensurate with the patient's needs.

Not all cases are receptive to treatment. I could imagine that whatever intervention strategy might have been employed with Schreber, in his case there would have been a strong probability of an underlying psychotic state with its own autonomy.

If we provide appropriate environments in the community for patients with persisting psychoses, whether this is described in CBT terms as scaffolding or in my terms as building an exoskeleton (see Chapter 17), the patients are less likely to act out in alarming ways. This may appear self-evident, but its importance is by no means always appreciated (see Chapter 17).

## Summary

In this chapter I have reviewed some controversial issues in the treatment of psychosis, including the question of whether considering a diagnostic label is necessarily stigmatising, whether psychoanalysis has anything to contribute to schizophrenia if its origins are biologically determined, and whether hospital admission should always be regarded as a negative outcome. I have also considered similarities and differences between the cognitive and analytic approaches to psychosis.

Despite views expressed to the contrary by both psychoanalysts and some cognitive psychologists, I have argued that psychoanalytic perspectives have a central role to play within the world of psychosis. In Part Three, on tuning into the psychotic wavelength, I will develop this argument, showing how a consideration of counter-transference phenomena is of crucial importance, and how exploration of meaning and developing dialogues with patients can replace normalisation strategies as the way forward. From an analytic perspective, one also needs to differentiate psychotic processes from major psychotic disorders.

Part Two will set the scene for this development with a review of psychoanalytic perspectives on psychosis.

# PART TWO

# Psychoanalytic Theories about Psychosis

## A Selective Review

# 4

# Freud's contributions to psychosis

## Introduction

Any review of psychoanalytic thinking about psychosis must begin with Freud's contribution. He produced many seminal ideas, inviting their further elaboration by succeeding analysts. Here I will consider the relevance of some of his ideas.

## The Schreber case

Freud inaugurated our psychoanalytic thinking on psychosis in 1911, with his analysis of the memoirs of Daniel Paul Schreber. Schreber was a judge who had a psychotic breakdown. He wrote a memoir of his experiences on recovery before succumbing to a further and final hospitalisation. In a very rich paper, Freud (1911a) introduced three major concepts in relation to psychosis – projection, narcissism and delusional formation as pathological attempts at recovery.

After a breakdown associated with multiple hypochondriacal symptoms, Schreber perceived the world as being in a state of primitive catastrophe. He believed that his mission was to restore the world to its former state of bliss. This was to occur through his delusional experience whereby God transformed him into a woman, and then as a result of direct impregnation from God, Schreber produced miraculous rays that restored the world.

Freud's approach to Schreber's memoirs draws attention to many aspects to be explored in psychosis, beyond the conventional psychiatric question of clarification of diagnosis. Although Freud spent much time in his paper explaining analytically how he arrived at his own formulation for Schreber's delusions, his approach encourages the development of a whole new way of viewing psychotic experiences.

Implicit in Freud's description is the notion that Schreber has an unconscious internal world, with its own rich content. This world has its own specific characteristics, and functions according to its own rules, separate from external reality but with links to real life experiences. Although this internal world may be largely unconscious, external manifestations periodically present themselves.

Freud described processes of displacement and symbolisation, splitting and condensation in Schreber's delusions (processes first described in relation to dreams). For example, Freud suggested that Schreber's primary conflict with his father was displaced onto a God figure, which was then split into anterior and posterior realms.

At the time of writing this paper, Freud emphasised the importance of unconscious homosexual conflicts with a perceived powerful father figure in the genesis of Schreber's paranoid states. In fact, Schreber's father was a well-known doctor and a powerfully influential figure, the founder of Schreber health clinics throughout Germany, who had his own strong ideas about mental illness. He designed models of penile clamps with spikes for babies to wear to stop them from masturbating, since he regarded masturbation as the cause of insanity (Niederland 1974).

Freud did not claim that his understanding of Schreber's delusions was the only possible explanation, but the strength of his paper lies in the invitation to the reader to consider different possible explanations. Indeed at the end of his paper Freud wrote:

> It remains for the future to decide whether there is more delusion in my theory than I would like to admit, or whether there is more truth in Schreber's delusion than other people as yet are prepared to believe.
>
> (Freud 1911a, p. 79)

On recovery from his psychotic episode, Schreber was aware of the separateness of his psychic experiences from the real world and was even able to convince a tribunal that he was fit for release from hospital and competent to resume his former work as a judge. It was at this point that he wrote his memoirs.

Freud's central point, namely that we should listen with care to the content of psychotic experiences rather than dismissing them merely as manifestations of underlying organic pathology, remains equally pertinent today. As such, this paper remains the inspiration and starting point for all further analytic explorations in the field of psychosis.

## Projection

Freud viewed Schreber's unconscious homosexual conflict with his powerful father as central to his psychopathology. The conflict was transferred first on to his eminent psychiatrist Flechsig and then on to God, whom he would openly taunt for having sexual needs to be satisfied through turning Schreber into a woman.

Schreber's delusions of persecution were seen as arising through projection of his disowned homosexual feelings. Love is denied by turning the feelings into hatred – 'I love him' becomes 'I hate him'. The hatred is then projected, taking the final form – 'I do not love him, I hate him because he hates me' (Freud 1911a, p. 63).

Here Freud gives an explanation of the mechanism underlying the creation of paranoid delusions, that is the denial of unconscious anxieties through reversal into the opposite followed by projection into an external object.

## Delusions as attempts at recovery

Freud invites us to consider delusions as attempts at recovery, albeit pathological ones. Freud understood Schreber's idea that the world was at an end as a projection of a catastrophic internal mental state. His subsequent delusional formation, the belief that he was being turned by God into a woman, was seen as 'an attempt at recovery, a process of restoration' (Freud 1911a, p. 71).

Freud later described the restorative function of delusional formation as 'like a patch where originally a rent had appeared in the ego's relation to the external world' (Freud 1924, p. 151).

Analytic understanding of delusions has not remained static since Freud's time. The contribution of Wilfred Bion (1957a), who introduced a new way of approaching delusions, has been particularly striking. Bion's contribution on psychosis will be the subject of Chapter 6.

## Narcissism

Freud regarded narcissism as a central concept to be considered in all cases of major psychotic disorders. In the Schreber case, Freud had postulated theoretical stages of the development in object relationships, from a stage of primary narcissism, in which one takes one's own body as one's love object, to a homosexual relationship, and finally a heterosexual object relationship. Freud viewed Schreber, in his paranoid psychosis, as regressing from a homosexual object relationship to a primitive state of primary narcissism.

The concept of primary narcissism remains controversial and has engendered much debate among different schools of thought. For classically orientated analysts primary narcissism describes a primary oceanic feeling, before object relationships start. By contrast, analysts in the Kleinian tradition (see Chapter 5), see all our phantasies as object-related from the start, and this implies that all states of narcissism involve a denial of the presence of another, a two–person object relationship. For classical analysts this would be termed secondary narcissism. Leaving aside the academic argument, from a clinical perspective the problem in psychosis is how powerfully the narcissistic forces are operating at any given moment in time in terms of denial of the need for help from others.

In his paper 'On narcissism: an introduction', Freud (1914) contrasted two fundamentally different types of object choice:

1. The anaclitic (attachment) type, where object choice is determined by early experiences of satisfaction with the infant's caregivers and their later substitutes, such as teachers.
2. The narcissistic type – individuals whose model for later love objects is their own selves. Such individuals may love what they themselves are, were, would like to be, or someone who was once part of themselves.

(Freud 1914, p. 90)

Freud noted a predominance of the narcissistic mode of relating in psychotic disorders, especially schizophrenia. As a result, at this juncture, Freud referred to the psychoses as the narcissistic neuroses, in contrast to the transference neuroses (anxiety hysteria, conversion hysteria and obsessional neurosis). Freud held that psychoses were not amenable to treatment by classical analytic technique, since the narcissistic self-centredness of these patients meant that transference phenomena were generally lacking.

In his metapsychological paper on the unconscious, Freud was to write:

> In the case of schizophrenia, on the other hand, we have been driven to the assumption that after the process of repression the libido that has been withdrawn does not seek a new object, but retreats into the ego; that is to say, that here the object-cathexes are given up and a primitive objectless condition of narcissism is re-established. The incapacity of these patients for transference (so far as the pathological process extends), their consequent inaccessibility to therapeutic efforts, their characteristic repudiation of the external world, the appearance of signs of hypercathexis of their own ego, the final complete apathy – all these clinical features seem to agree excellently with the assumption that their object-cathexes have been given up.
>
> (Freud 1915, pp. 196–197)

David Rosenfeld, an analyst from Argentina, pointed out that Freud did not entirely dismiss the concept of transference in psychosis: at a later date, Freud wrote, 'Transference is often not so completely absent but it can be used to a certain extent' (Freud 1925, p. 60; D. Rosenfeld 1992, p. 5). Nevertheless, the prevailing view among most classically trained analysts remained that transference was relatively absent so that analytic technique had to be modified with psychosis. The American analysts at Chestnut Lodge who became involved with schizophrenia consequently described their approach as 'intensive psychotherapy' rather than psychoanalysis, as reviewed in Chapter 8 (Fromm-Reichmann 1950).

It was many decades after Freud that Herbert Rosenfeld, a Kleinian analyst, was to refute the notion of an absence of transference phenomena in psychosis (H. A. Rosenfeld 1954). Rather, in patients with psychoses, there was a particularly concrete nature to the transferences, which lacked the usual 'as if' quality; for example, Schreber concretely viewed his psychiatrist as a persecutory father figure. Rosenfeld, therefore, thought that the analytic technique of interpreting the transference did not require modification for patients with diagnoses of schizophrenia.

Segal and Bell (1991) have argued that Freud's notion of narcissism

51

implies the idea of an innate destructiveness, an idealisation of death and a hatred of life. In their review of the concept of narcissism, they bring this out by returning to the original Narcissus myth:

> Narcissus is trapped gazing at something that he subjectively believes is a lost object but it is the idealised aspect of his own self. He believes himself to be in love. He dies of starvation, however, because he cannot turn away towards a real object from whom he might have been able to get what he really needed.
>
> (Segal and Bell 1991, p. 172)

It is not difficult to relate this to patients with chronic schizophrenia who have turned their backs on life to live in a world of their own making in an asylum. Freud was later explicitly to develop the idea of an innate destructiveness when he introduced the concept of the death instinct.

## Melancholia (psychotic depression)

In 'Mourning and melancholia', Freud (1917) emphasised the predominance of the narcissistic type of object choice as the key to understanding melancholia. Freud's brilliant paper, in conjunction with Abraham's (1924) paper, cannot be bettered as a description of what is nowadays called major depressive illness. Freud related depression to a disease of an internal critical agency or conscience, as he had not yet introduced the term superego. The need for an appreciation of the hidden psychosis underlying what is now termed major depressive illness will be addressed in later chapters (see Part Four).

## The structural model and psychosis

Freud's earlier model of the mind was called the 'topographical model', the word topography coming from the Greek, meaning theory of places (Laplanche and Pontalis 1973, p. 449). In that model, Freud differentiated the psychical apparatus into a number of sub-systems, namely the conscious, preconscious and unconscious. Conflict occurred between the system unconscious, which was dominated by the pleasure principle and the conscious, which was dominated by the reality principle. Censorship occurred between one subsystem and another, through the operation of repression, with return of the repressed in disguised forms as evidenced in hysterical states and in dreams.

From 1920 onwards, Freud introduced a new framework, the id, the ego and the superego, to describe the personality and its mode of functioning. This has sometimes been referred to as 'the second topography', but more commonly as 'the structural model' (Laplanche and Pontalis 1973, p. 452). The id represents the storehouse of primitive instinctual feelings demanding gratification. The ego, viewed as partly operating unconsciously, has to cope with demands from the id, but also from the superego and external reality (Freud 1923).

The introduction of the structural model did not entail a rejection of the earlier notions described under the topographical model, but the new structure allowed for more precise descriptions. For example, the earlier concept of the ego being faced with a conflict due to the incompatible demands of the pleasure principle and the reality principle could now be reconsidered in terms of the demands placed on the ego by the id, superego and external reality.

Similarly, many previous concepts were brought together in the role of the superego. The functions of the superego include the sense of a conscience, a self-observer and also the representative of ego ideals. The superego was also seen as the heir to the Oedipus complex. The child gives up its wish to take the place of one of the parental couple with the other and instead incorporates their values in the superego. Freud thought that this internalisation occurred, with the resolution of the Oedipus complex, at around 3 years old. Melanie Klein (1945) was later to introduce the idea of an earlier, more primitive and severe superego that came into existence within the first year of life, as a forerunner to the later more mature superego.

Following the introduction of the structural model, Freud amended his theoretical formulations on the psychoses. Transference neuroses (anxiety, hysterical and obsessional states) now corresponded to a conflict between the ego and the id. Narcissistic neuroses, by which Freud now meant melancholia, corresponded to a conflict between the ego and superego; while the psychoses, i.e. schizophrenia, related to a conflict between the ego, under the dominance of the id, and the external world (Freud 1923).

## Defence mechanisms

The introduction of the structural model invited further consideration of how the ego develops defence mechanisms against psychic stress (A. Freud 1936). A defence mechanism is an automatic unconscious mental operation, taking place in the ego, which has the function of helping the individual to retain a state of psychic equilibrium (Milton et al. 2005). The aim of the ego is to maintain psychic equilibrium under conflicting pressures from the id, the superego and external reality.

Repression lies at the centre of the defence mechanisms. If repression fails, there are many other defence mechanisms including projection, denial, negation, identification with the aggressor, reversal into the opposite, rationalisation and intellectualisation.

The following vignette illustrates the power of repression and the consequences when the patient is no longer able to maintain it.

> Years ago, while I was in training, I was working in a psychiatric rehabilitation day unit. The unit consisted of a detached house on several floors. This arrangement made it hard to cope with a patient who was in a disturbed state. A patient was admitted with a diagnosis of paranoid schizophrenia. He had been referred from an inpatient unit where he had required over a thousand milligrams of chlorpromazine, a large dose of antipsychotic medication, to settle him sufficiently for his discharge. In the day hospital, he would fall asleep in groups. However, the staff were afraid to lower his medication dose in case he relapsed into a paranoid aggressive state. On the other hand, it was felt that he needed to be in a less soporific state in order to benefit from the rehabilitation programme.
>
> However, after the groups, he played badminton without showing any of the tiredness or stiffness that would be the expected side-effects of his medication. It was then noticed that in therapy groups, the patient would fall asleep whenever the psychologist raised any emotional topic. Here we can see the effects of massive repression, mimicking the physical side-effects of medication. Unfortunately, this repression was not sustainable, leading to an aggressive eruption with the need for a further admission.

Historically the introduction of the structural model was of enormous importance for the subsequent development of the ego-psychology that became the prevailing school of thought particularly in the United States (Hinshelwood 1989, pp. 286–295).

Differences of analytic approach to psychosis emerged between the ego psychology school in the States, with its emphasis on encouraging the development of more mature defence mechanisms than projection and denial, and the Kleinian school in London, where the focus centred on interpretation of the transference (H. A. Rosenfeld 1969).

## The death instinct

In *Beyond the Pleasure Principle,* Freud (1920) introduced the concept of the death instinct or drive. In a detailed review of the death instinct, Laplanche and Pontalis (1973) summarised Freud's view as follows:

> [T]he death instincts, which are opposed to the life instincts, strive towards the reduction of tensions to zero-point. In other words, their goal is to bring the living being back to the organic state.
> The death instincts are to begin with directed inwards and tend towards self destruction, but they are subsequently turned towards the outside world in the form of the aggressive or destructive instinct. The notion of a death instinct [. . .] has not managed to gain the acceptance of [Freud's] disciples and successors in the way that the majority of his conceptual contributions have done – and it is still one of the most controversial of psycho–analytic concepts.
>
> (Laplanche and Pontalis 1973, p. 97)

A problem is that the concept embraces more than one idea. For example, at an intellectual level many have questioned the notion that human beings have an inbuilt drive to return to an organic, lifeless state.

While the concept of the death instinct somewhat belatedly introduced aggressive drives into Freud's conceptualisations, thereby enriching them, many would argue that aggressiveness is an understandable reaction to frustration and does not require the hypothesis of a death instinct. The human wish to live makes it difficult to accept the concept of an innate self–destructive drive.

Laplanche and Pontalis (1973) point out that a dualistic tendency is fundamental to Freudian thought, and the introduction of the death instinct, in opposition to the life instinct, added another dimension in thinking about the ambivalent nature of communications from people in very disturbed states of mind.

Classical analysts argue that Freud conceptualised the death instinct at a purely theoretical (metapsychological) level, putting it forward as a speculative idea that had no basis in clinical practice. In reviewing the concept, Black (2001, p. 195) wrote: 'the death drive, as such, probably merits no future in psychoanalytic thinking'. Schwartz (2001, p. 199) endorsed this view: 'We should stop thinking of a death drive but directly in terms of destructiveness', forcefully adding, 'We should stop teaching the death drive in our training'.

In contrast, Klein viewed envy directed towards the breast as the earliest direct externalisation of the death instinct, since it attacked the source of life (Klein 1957; Segal 1973a).

However, Britton (2003), as a post-Kleinian, has also questioned Freud's concept. He observes that Freud was much more diffident about his thoughts on the 'destructive instinct' than about his thoughts on the libido (i.e. the life instinct), and writes:

> It seems to me to make more sense to see the original destructive-ness directed outwards and in the course of development internal-ised, rather than the other way round. For this reason I prefer to call this a destructive instinct, and not the death instinct as it is more usually referred to.
>
> I believe that both the desire for a love object and hostility to objects outside the self is primary. It is the sort of thing that experience in the consulting room cannot settle, and for that reason will remain debatable. Some of my colleagues who are convinced of the action of the 'death instinct' will differ from me on this and point out the effects on some individuals' own mental appar-atus of a deadly internal force. I think that can be accounted for by supposing that the anti-object relational force acts on any attachment to an object.
>
> (Britton 2003, pp. 3–4)

In *The Ego and the Id*, Freud described how the superego can come to be committed to the death of the ego, with a part of the ego that is opposed to another part becoming entrenched in the superego: 'the destructive component has entrenched itself in the super-ego and turned against the ego. What is now holding sway in

the super-ego is, as it were, a pure culture of the death instinct'
(Freud 1923, p. 53).

Klein also refers to the conflict in the ego between the two
instincts, with splitting of the ego and location of the bad object
within the superego, leading to the formation of an early harsh
superego. Britton notes how:

> Melanie Klein repeatedly stresses that this original hostile internal
> object is only modified and mitigated by love. In her model,
> therefore, the introjection of a loving mother and father is *abso-*
> *lutely necessary* in order to modify the potentially ego-destructive
> super-ego. . . .
>
> If the actual parent is hostile and envious, it becomes the
> external location for the projection of this malignant internal
> object and this becomes its incarceration.
>
> (Britton 2003, pp. 119, 128).

We are left with the question of why, in the face of sustained criticism,
Freud ended up so strongly endorsing the concept of the death
instinct, given its original speculative foundations. To quote:

> To begin with, it was only tentatively that I put forward the views
> that I have developed here, but in the course of time they have
> gained such a hold upon me that I can no longer think in any
> other way.
>
> (Freud 1930, p. 119)

In my view, differences in opinion over the usefulness of the concept
of the death instinct can be resolved only at the clinical level. Those
analysts who are critical of the concept of the death instinct are
relating to their experience in the consulting room with neurotic
and borderline states, where Freud's concept does not seem to
consider aggression as an understandable expression of the frustration of not being understood within the parent–child relationship
(Winnicott 1960).

I see Freud's conceptualisation of an innate destructive force
directed towards the self as aimed at addressing the area of psychosis.
It may have been the suicide of his psychoanalytic colleague Victor
Tausk in 1919 that first alerted him to consider the concept in
relation to depression (Roazen 1973).

In relating to patients with major psychotic disorders, namely schizophrenia and affective disorders, we need to develop a quite different psychoanalytic framework from that applied to neuroses or borderline states. For the framework to be clinically meaningful, it will have to incorporate recognition of a separate psychotic part of the personality and deadly internal forces.

How are we to relate to incidents where patients kill themselves out of the blue in spite of all the love and support being given to them by their relatives and staff? Awareness here of the operation of the death instinct, acting in envious rivalry to the life instinct, can help relatives, professional staff and management to understand the dynamics behind such events and to grasp why blame should not be apportioned when unavoidable tragedies occur (see Chapter 18).

While debate over the death instinct will no doubt continue at an academic level, the need remains to assess the extent of powerful anti-life forces in all cases of major psychotic disorders. Years of daily involvement with psychotic states of mind leads one to an appreciation of the power and autonomy of destructive forces and of why Freud should have said, once he had discovered the death instinct, that he could no longer think in any other way.

## Psychoanalysis and psychiatry

Freud was aware of the tensions between the two disciplines and wished to bridge the gap:

> Psychiatry does not employ the technical methods of psycho-analysis; it omits to make any inferences from the content of the delusion, and, in pointing to heredity, it gives us a very general and remote aetiology instead of indicating first the more special and proximate causes. But, is there a contradiction, an opposition in this? Is it not rather a case of one supplementing the other? Does the hereditary factor contradict the importance of experience? Do not the two things rather combine in the most effective manner? You will grant that there is nothing in the nature of psychiatric work which could be opposed to psycho-analytic research. What is opposed to psycho-analysis is not psychiatry, but psychiatrists. Psycho-analysis is related to psychiatry approximately as histology is to anatomy: the one studies the external form

of organs, the other studies their construction out of tissues and cells. It is not easy to imagine a contradiction between these two pieces of study, of which one is a continuation of the other. Today, as you know, anatomy is regarded by us as the foundation of scientific medicine. But there was a time when it was forbidden to dissect the human cadaver in order to discover the internal structure of the body as it now seems to practise psycho-analysis in order to learn about the internal structure of the mind. It is to be expected that in the not too distant future it will be realised that a scientifically based psychiatry is not possible without a sound knowledge of the deeper-lying unconscious processes in mental life.

(Freud 1916–1917a, p. 254)

Freud was also aware of the lack of a psychoanalytic presence in general psychiatry and the need for such a presence to make an impact and further our means of relating to patients with psychotic disorders:

There are difficulties in addition that hold up our advance. The narcissistic disorders and the psychoses related to them can only be deciphered by observers who have been trained through the analytic study of the transference neuroses. But our psychiatrists are not students of psycho-analysis and we psycho-analysts see too few psychiatric cases. A race of psychiatrists must first grow who have passed through the school of psycho-analysis as a preparatory science. A start in that direction is now being made in America.

(Freud 1916–1917b, p. 423)

## Summary

In this chapter, I have reviewed some of the basic analytic concepts described by Freud that are relevant to psychosis, commencing with his exploration of Schreber's memoirs. These concepts include an appreciation of the power of the unconscious inner world, the meaning of delusions, narcissism and defence mechanisms and the introduction of the structural model of the mind. Particular attention has been paid to the notion of the death instinct, with its clinical implications.

While Freud did not personally analyse psychotic patients, he provided many seminal insights and issued a challenge to future generations of analysts to work with patients in such states in order to further our clinical understanding of them.

# 5

# The Kleinian contribution to psychosis

## Introduction

Melanie Klein introduced many basic concepts that have proved crucial to the psychoanalytic understanding of psychosis. This chapter will highlight some of these concepts in order to illustrate their relevance within the sphere of general psychiatry. I will also draw attention to some relevant post-Kleinian contributions. This will not constitute a résumé of the works of Klein and her followers. The interested reader is referred to Hanna Segal's (1973a) *Introduction to the Work of Melanie Klein* and Robert Hinshelwood's (1989) *Dictionary of Kleinian Thought* for a fuller exposition.

## The internal world

In her work with little children, Klein was impressed by the richness of their unconscious phantasy life. Her observations of babies and small children led her to argue that from earliest infancy all of us have an internal world as well as an external world. This internal world arises as

> the result of the operation of unconscious phantasy, in which objects are introjected and a complex internal world is built up within the ego, in which the internal objects are felt to be in dynamic relationship to one another and the ego.
>
> (Segal 1973a, p. 127)

Patients with schizophrenia may renounce the external world in favour of an internal world of their own making, dominated by their unconscious phantasies. In all cases of psychoses, part of our task is to come to grasp the underlying dynamics operating within the patient's internal world.

## The paranoid–schizoid position

Klein went on to describe, theoretically speaking, two basic constellations of anxieties, defences and characteristic object relations, which she called positions: the paranoid–schizoid position and the depressive position. Throughout life we shift back and forth between these positions, although the paranoid–schizoid position appears before the depressive position in infantile development. In describing the paranoid–schizoid position, Klein chose the word schizoid to evoke splitting, rather than the more common meaning of social withdrawal, while paranoid referred to the fact that the leading affect or mood was a persecutory one. In the paranoid–schizoid position the internal world was characterised by part-object relationships, predominantly to the breast, with another important part-object being the penis. At the stage of infantile development where the paranoid–schizoid position dominates, because of the immaturity of the ego, in order to maintain a relationship with a good object the infant is forced to use the primitive defences of splitting and projection of the bad object, along with idealisation to preserve the good object. In the older child and adult idealisation may be seen as part of a manic defence against underlying depressive anxieties (see below).

Klein was struck by the similarity between the internal world of children in the paranoid–schizoid position and patients with psychotic disorders. In schizophrenia, the patient may be living in an internal world of part-objects dominated by paranoid ideation. For example, in the case of a patient who carries a knife for protection against imaginary assailants, the knife, symbolically speaking, might stand concretely for a penis that is protecting an identification with an idealised breast from attack.

When we come across patients in a psychotic breakdown, it is useful to ask ourselves whether they are functioning in their internal world at a part-object level dominated by a persecutory affect, with little or no insight at the time.

## Envy and gratitude

A particularly important internal factor affecting the infant's experience of the paranoid-schizoid position is envy. Envy is a destructive projective process, operating in the paranoid-schizoid position, through which the good qualities of the external object are denied and destroyed in phantasy. Envy aims to spoil the object's goodness. Since it attacks the source of life (the breast), Klein saw envy as the earliest externalisation of the death instinct. If envy is particularly strong and predominating, as is the case in major psychotic disorders, this may seriously hamper emotional development since the individual is unable to preserve a good object. The hostility of the projective attack on the good object leads to persecutory anxiety of a retaliatory nature. The gratitude towards the good object that arises as a result of good experiences can reduce the negative effects of envy.

## The depressive position

At the time of weaning, the baby comes to recognise the mother as a whole person. The bad breast and the good breast experiences come together and the baby feels guilty and frightened that his or her aggressive phantasies may have damaged the mother. If the guilt becomes unbearable, then defences come into play, such as manic defences or regression to the splitting associated with the paranoid-schizoid position. The depressive position is never fully worked through and is linked to our varying capacities to stay with psychic pain.

## Regression to the paranoid-schizoid position

As noted above, Klein described the paranoid-schizoid and depressive states of mind as positions rather than stages. Although they can be thought of as descriptions of stages of development, Klein thought that throughout life we continue to oscillate between these two positions, at times operating in a more integrated, reflective way and at other times functioning in a paranoid way.

For example, I used to work in a situation where the hospital beds were divided between two sites. When we were not under pressure it was possible to reflect on the way the sites functioned together as a service. However, if we felt overworked and our beds were full to over-flowing, then we would complain that the other site was not doing its fair share of the work. When the pressure of external demands makes it very difficult to maintain the more reflective state of mind associated with the depressive position, one way to gain relief is to regress to a paranoid-schizoid mode of functioning, blaming the other site and turning it into the bad object.

While we can see such psychotic processes at work in everyone at times of stress, a more persistent paranoid-schizoid mode of functioning predominates in patients with underlying major psychotic disorders.

## The superego

Reaching the depressive position involves a painful realisation of having damaged one's love object. At this stage the ambivalently loved parental objects are introjected to form the core of the superego. Freud originally linked the formation of the superego with the resolution of the Oedipus complex, aged 3 to 5, when the child incorporates parental values to form his or her conscience. Freud (1917) later understood melancholia or psychotic depression as a disease of the 'critical agency' or superego.

Melanie Klein (1945) introduced the concept of an earlier, more primitive and persecutory superego operating at a part-object level in the paranoid-schizoid position. This persecutory superego emerges in consequence of attacks on the good object and is particularly harsh and severe. It can dominate the mind of patients in a psychotic breakdown. For example, on admission in a psychotic state, patients in their confusion may feel that the staff are criticising them and may respond violently (M. Klein 1945).

## Persecutory, depressive and castration anxiety

Segal (1973a) summarised the different forms of anxiety that arise when the death instinct is deflected outwards. In the paranoid anxiety that is characteristic of the paranoid-schizoid position, the projection results in an experience of objects as persecutors that are trying to annihilate the ego and the ideal object. Depressive anxiety is the concern that one's own aggression has annihilated one's own good object. Castration anxiety is a paranoid anxiety linked to a fear that one has lost one's penis as the organ of reparation.

Freud highlighted the intimate relationship between the mind and body with his statement that 'The ego is first and foremost a bodily ego' (Freud 1923, p. 26). This means that the organs of the body are intimately connected to the acting out of unconscious phantasies. Young children in their play will speak freely in terms of bodily functions, and Klein would relate to children in those terms in her interpretations. We are less likely to interpret in bodily terms with adults unless patients are expressing themselves in this way. However, psychoanalysts familiar with the inner world of unconscious phantasy may be at ease in thinking in these ways, even if they might not speak to their adult patients in such terms.

Schizophrenic patients may be particularly concrete in their projection of their aggressive phantasies into bodily organs, and may well present their problems and the solutions that they find for them in these terms.

> For example, a patient with his first breakdown, which subsequently developed into a chronic schizophrenic illness, changed his name to 'Johnny Nothing' and came along to see me in outpatients, asking to be castrated, as he felt that his penis was a dangerous organ with which he would attack women.

## Projective and introjective identification

Projective identification is a key Kleinian concept. It is the process by which parts of the self are projected into an object. Klein originally saw projective identification as a means for the infant to communicate with the mother, who by taking in the projection would become aware of the child's needs. Since then the concept has been thought about and expanded in many other ways, becoming an umbrella term for many different processes ranging from normal modes of communication to violent types of fragmentation in psychotic states (Sodre 2004; Steiner 2008).

Klein (1959) wrote:

> By projecting oneself or part of one's impulses and feelings into another person, an identification with that person is achieved. . . .

On the other hand, in putting part of oneself into the other person (projecting), the identification is based on attributing to the other person some of one's own qualities. Projection has many repercussions. We are inclined to attribute to other people – in a sense, to put into them – some of our own emotions and thoughts; and it is obvious that it will depend on how balanced or persecuted we are whether this projection is of a friendly or a hostile nature. By attributing part of our feelings to the other person, we understand their feelings, needs, and satisfactions; in other words, we are putting ourselves into the other person's shoes. There are people who go so far in this direction that they lose themselves entirely in others and become incapable of objective judgement. At the same time excessive introjection endangers the strength of the ego because it becomes completely dominated by the introjected object.

(M. Klein 1959, pp. 252–253)

If the aim of projective identification is to rid oneself of troublesome feelings, the object may be perceived as having acquired the characteristics of the projected part, or the self may become identified with the object of its projections. If both good and bad feelings are projected into the same object, this will result in ambivalent feelings towards the object.

In introjective identification the object is introjected into the ego, which then identifies with it. Throughout development there is a constant to and fro of projective and introjective processes in the building up of internal objects in one's inner world.

Projective identification as a means of communication is particularly striking in patients with borderline states.

> I was once asked to see such a patient who, after being physically treated for taking an overdose, was referred on to the psychiatric emergency clinic. In the emergency clinic, the patient told me his whole life history. He then became extremely anxious when I went to leave the room. He had felt that he had concretely projected the whole of himself into me, and was then worried about where I was going with him.

O'Shaughnessy (1992) emphasised that Klein approached psychosis via anxiety and that the baby's earliest anxieties are psychotic in origin, that is a dread of primitive projected terrifying figures. If the infant is unable to bind, work through and modify his or her primitive anxieties about these terrifying figures that threaten to dominate the psyche, then the ego is driven to excessive use of the otherwise normal defence of splitting and projective identification.

In other words, Klein understood psychoses in terms of an excessive use of normal projective processes in relation to persecutory anxieties, and located the pathology in the paranoid–schizoid position.

## Pathological projective identification

This is the term used by Segal for the process that Bion later described as operating in schizophrenia. Pathological projective identification is characterised by fragmenting and disintegration of the self, which is projected into external objects to create what Bion called 'bizarre objects' (Segal 1973a, p. 127). Bion's contribution will be examined in Chapter 6, but it is important to note here that Bion disagreed with Klein's view that schizophrenia arose out of an excessive use of normal projective processes in the paranoid–schizoid position. Bion (1957a) thought that those individuals who would subsequently develop schizophrenia negotiated the paranoid–schizoid position in a markedly different way from others, due to a fragmentation of the psyche, resulting in the formation of a psychotic part of the personality that was left functioning quite differently from the non-psychotic parts.

## Manic defences

This is a concept of fundamental clinical importance. In Segal's account of Klein's work manic defences are described as arising to protect the individual from the experience of depressive anxiety, guilt and loss. In manic defences psychic reality and object relations are omnipotently denied. Manic defences are characterised by feelings of triumph, control and contempt (Segal 1973a, p. 127).

Clinical practice reveals manic defences as a universal phenomenon that can arise to protect the individual from experiencing any severe underlying anxiety or psychic pain, whether predominantly persecutory or depressive in nature. Manic states can be encountered in patients with schizophrenia as well as in manic depressive states. Wherever one encounters manic states, it is important to consider what underlying unbearable states of mind are being warded off. Sometimes the answer is readily apparent, as in the following vignette.

A 49-year-old woman was admitted in a manic state. She was cheerful and infected those around her with her jollity when she was seen for review. She felt persecuted when I did not join in the laughter. Her manic defence broke down and she became tearful. Underneath her apparent cheerfulness was a feeling that everything important in her life had been lost. She had recently been made redundant, a long-term relationship had broken down, and she was now menopausal, too old to have children. Her manic defence was an attempt to avoid facing up to her underlying depression about the bleakness in her life.

Short-lived manic defensive states need to be distinguished from protracted manic states in recurrent manic depressive disorders, which will be considered later in the book.

## Reparation and manic reparation

In working through the depressive position, the ego is preoccupied with restoring the loved and injured object, through an active reparative drive. This means facing up to underlying depressive anxieties and guilt, not denying them. Klein drew attention to unconscious reparative drives as a basic human trait. We can appreciate how reparative drives contribute to the choice of work within the caring professions, at the same time as obliging us to face the fact that we cannot always cure but must sometimes make the best of a bad job in our therapeutic efforts to help others.

If one's internal objects are felt to be unforgiving, then persecutory or depressive anxieties can be so overwhelming that guilt cannot be faced and no working through can occur. Instead, manic reparation occurs, characterised by feelings of triumph, control and contempt linked to a denial of dependency. The object is magically restored to its previous state, prior to the breakdown, without the patient having to face up to and work through their underlying feelings of guilt.

Time and time again, one can observe patients with severe psychotic disorders, whether of a schizophrenic or depressive nature, recover from relapses through manic reparation, by means of which they appear to magically get better, suddenly recovering and leaving hospital none the wiser about the reasons for their admission. The following example taken from everyday general psychiatry is a gross example of manic reparative mechanisms in operation.

A patient with a diagnosis of recurrent manic depression was admitted in a severely disinhibited state. He kept taking baths on the ward with all his clothes on. Every time he was confronted with his behaviour, he promised not to do it again, but did. His action could be seen as a very concrete attempt to wash away feelings of persecutory guilt. He then threw his wedding ring in the bin in occupational therapy. His wife was very angry, so he tried to repair the damage by leaving the hospital to put a deposit on a car for her, regardless of the fact that she did not drive.

He then took to picking up elderly ladies walking in the asylum corridors and frog-marching them to the hospital church. It was as if the old women represented the attacked and denigrated internal mother figures that God was to magically restore to their former state of health. This example illustrates the characteristic triad of feelings of triumph, control and contempt towards the needed object, acted out here initially towards his wife and then the elderly patients.

This patient was living entirely in an internal phantasy world of his own making. As with so many severe cases in general psychiatry, while it may not be possible to influence the behaviour patterns of such individuals, working with them offers the opportunity to gain first-hand experience of the operation of some fundamental mechanisms of the mind, which can help the practitioner to understand similar and less severe cases. If one can understand the way the mind deals with psychic pain in psychosis, one can share this experience with the nurses, stimulating a more involved and human response among the staff to the patient's suffering. This would help to address Hinshelwood's concern that nursing staff are nowadays becoming overwhelmed by the projection of deadening forces from patients with psychosis, and need an 'external consultant' to help revive the reflective function of the 'internal consultant' within them (Hinshelwood 2004).

## Post-Kleinian contributions

Following on from Klein's seminal work, Kleinian analysts have continued to contribute to our understanding of psychosis, through their own detailed analytic work with borderline and psychotic patients. This section of the chapter offers an overview of some key concepts emanating from their work.

*Hanna Segal*

### Symbolism and symbolic equation

The capacity for symbolism, projecting phantasies into objects and using them to convey our deepest feelings, is a basic feature of the human mind and is intimately linked to all artistic expression. Segal distinguished between symbolism proper and what she termed the 'symbolic equations' that operate in psychosis. Symbolism proper depends on the capacity to differentiate psychic reality and external reality:

> If psychic reality is experienced and differentiated from external reality, the symbol is differentiated from the object; it is felt to be created by the self and can be freely used by the self.
>
> (Segal 1973a, p. 76)

Segal contrasted symbolism proper with 'symbolic equation' in which the symbol is equated with the original object, giving rise to concrete thinking. Segal gives two contrasting examples to illustrate the distinction. In the first one, a young man dreams of playing a violin duet with a young girl and has associations to fiddling and masturbation, conveying his recognition of the symbolic meanings in this dream. In the second case, a concert violinist has a psychotic breakdown during which he says that he will never play the violin again as that would be masturbating in public. Here the violin is concretely equated with the genitals, so that touching it in public becomes impossible (Segal 1981a, p. 49).

The following example from my work in general psychiatry serves as a striking illustration of concrete thinking and symbolic equation.

> A patient was admitted for the first time to hospital. He told me that the Devil was good and God was bad and that he was going to Africa to preach about it. I felt that I had better inform his father that his son was suffering from a severe schizophrenic illness with all its long-term management implications. However, the father endorsed his son's view and I realised that

70

they were both psychotic. Some time later a situation arose where the son took to banging all the doors in the house. His father, lacking the ability for symbolic thinking, dealt with the situation by removing all the doors, including the front and back doors. One was left feeling sympathy for his wife having to cope with it all.

*Herbert Rosenfeld*

### The psychotic transference

Rosenfeld refuted Freud's suggestion that no transference could occur in psychotic disorders, since such patients had withdrawn into a narcissistic world of their own making where they remained unavailable for transference interpretations. Rosenfeld (1954) maintained that transference indeed occurred but that, as with symbolic equations, it was of a concrete nature. Rosenfeld argued that since transference did occur, patients with psychotic disorders were open to an analytic interpretive approach. Psychotic transference phenomena of a concrete nature occur all the time in the psychiatric wards. For example, a patient who hits a nurse for no apparent reason may do so because he is concretely experiencing her through projection as a persecutory parental figure. In a similar vein, a patient who smashes up the ward's television may do so because he feels persecuted by the newsreader on the screen due to a hostile projection of his own perceptual apparatus onto the newsreader.

Rosenfeld's insight into the nature of the psychotic transference opened the door to further development of psychoanalytic approaches to the mind in psychosis.

### Confusional states

In schizophrenia, Rosenfeld emphasised that instead of the normal clear splitting of good and bad experiences that occurs in the paranoid–schizoid position, hostility towards the good object leads to confusion about the nature of what is being reintrojected. This in turn leads to further hostile projective splitting and still more confusion about the nature of the object. The patient ends up not being able to distinguish self from object or good from bad, and as a result stays stuck in a confusional state within the paranoid–schizoid position (H. A. Rosenfeld 1950).

71

## Destructive narcissism

Freud posited an instinctual dualism between positive libidinal forces emanating from the life instinct and destructive forces associated with the death instinct. Rosenfeld described how in certain character structures, the libidinal forces can come to be subjugated to the more powerful destructive narcissistic forces. The result is that pleasure is obtained from destructive behaviour: Rosenfeld termed this destructive narcissism. In their internal world, such patients often look to similarly minded others to support their destructive internal organisation, and typically the mafia or similar types of gangs may feature in their dreams (H. A. Rosenfeld 1971).

In this state destructiveness is idealised, with propaganda that it is macho to drink or take drugs rather than face emotional needs with help from others. The destructive narcissistic part of the personality perversely distorts and feeds off any positive intercourse. If a patient with this underlying character structure were to overdose on alcohol or drugs and require hospital admission, we would then try to find ways of helping them to change their behaviour, but the dominating destructive narcissistic organisation in the patient may have a different intention, namely, simply to recover as quickly as possible in order to return to their former state of denial of their problems. Any concerns that such patients feel are projected into the carers, who are then left feeling guilty that they should have done more. Those working in addiction centres are only too well aware of having to face up to such difficult dynamics.

If the destructive organisation breaks down as a defence, then the patient may temporarily feel extremely vulnerable, experiencing something akin to the feelings undergone during a drug withdrawal state, and may experience paranoid psychotic states. Temporary paranoid states, including hearing voices, can occur in patients with so-called personality disorders, especially when the picture is complicated by drug abuse, and such symptoms do not necessarily mean that one should revise the patient's diagnosis to one of schizophrenia.

### Betty Joseph

I have had the privilege of attending Betty Joseph's clinical workshops for some twenty years, where leading analysts have presented clinical material for discussion (Hargreaves and Varchevker 2004). Her contributions have related primarily to psychoanalytic technique, especially the need to be aware of the nudge from the patient for the analyst to act out to relieve the patient's anxieties, rather than stay with the problem. Among her contributions has been the notion of the 'total transference situation' where everything occurring in the session needs to be taken into account in arriving at the picture before formulating an interpretation (Joseph 1985). She has also described patients who remain 'addicted to near death' in their psychopathology, refusing to allow movement to occur (Joseph 1982). The title of her book *Psychic Equilibrium and Psychic Change* points to her exploration of the question of when a patient's response is defensive against anxiety linked to change, or when it may be more perverse in its intention (Joseph 1989).

### Leslie Sohn

I was very fortunate to have Leslie Sohn as my training analyst. Sohn has taken a lifelong interest in the application of analytic thinking to the world of psychosis as encountered in NHS settings. Following the days of Cooper and Laing, he took over Villa 21 at Shenley Hospital. During his time there he offered his inpatient beds for patients in analysis, provided the analyst came to see the patients for their sessions.

Sohn had a unique ability to provide understanding in the area of psychosis. My first experience of his clinical acumen came while I was still in analysis.

> For a year as a senior registrar, I was delegated to work in liaison psychiatry at a general hospital. I vividly recall visiting one woman on a dialysis machine in the renal unit who was mute. She had a past history of manic depression, but was not on lithium due to the dialysis. She was uncooperative and when she went home for the weekend, her husband had difficulty in bringing her back.
>
> Sohn's response was that she was obviously in envious rivalry with the dialysis machine. In my early naivety, I saw no evidence for this. However, the next time I went round the dialysis unit, I approached the mute patient, and asked her what she thought of the dialysis machine. It was as if I had pushed the magic button.

73

She responded: 'What machine, the machine does nothing', and pointed to the clips on the blood lines as proof of this.

Clearly her envious rivalry with her mother as a person who was able to detoxify her feelings had been concretely projected on to the machine. Unfortunately, in the end her lack of cooperation led to her death. Nowadays I would see a situation like this as raising the challenge of how to start a meaningful dialogue with such a patient.

Sohn's work has illuminated many areas linked to psychotic thinking over the years, and these analytic insights can then be taken and applied within the world of general psychiatry.

## The narcissistic identificate

Sohn described a particular highly organised quality to destructive narcissistic processes in schizophrenia. Rather than speaking of identifications in such cases, Sohn preferred the term 'identificate' to highlight the relative permanence of the narcissistic organisation in the ego brought about by projective identification in psychosis. Parental qualities were taken over in a controlling and triumphant manner. The identification had a callow, cynical and plastic quality. Thus Sohn extended Rosenfeld's concept of destructive narcissism into the world of psychosis (Sohn 1985b).

A patient who I once had in analysis would immobilise the analytic work by maintaining a sitting-on-the-fence state of mind. He used his own awareness of this to openly mock me. He pointed out that the analysis was all a charade and that he was merely going through the motions in the session.

Clearly, with such a patient one is asked to contain an enormous amount, reaching the very limits of endurance, until the patient can allow himself to be in a more reflective state. Awareness of these highly organised and enduring narcissistic organisations can be taken into general psychiatry where an appreciation of the underlying dynamics can help the nursing staff to tolerate periods of unbearable behaviour by patients, which may often be protracted in duration.

*Anorexic and bulimic states of mind*

Sohn described a peculiar appetite-less disinterested facade encountered in the analysis of anorexic patients, which conceals secret greedy
demands on their objects that can never be satisfied. He described a
patient who exhibited these states of mind to an extreme degree.

> She would throw all the food she was given on the floor. When a ward sister
> gave her a magazine to read, she only became interested in it when she
> had torn it into pieces and urinated on the bits. She then ate the bits of paper
> with relish. This obliteration of difference was also manifest in the way she
> treated interpretations in her analytic sessions (Sohn 1985a).

The attack on difference in anorexia nervosa was forcibly brought
home to me by an anorexic patient whom I saw for a number of years
for analytic therapy in the NHS.

> She wore grey, nondescript clothes and always wore trousers. She was
> delighted when she took her motorbike for petrol, and the petrol pump
> attendant was unable to tell if she was male or female. This did not stop her
> having a boyfriend and being insanely jealous if there happened to be a
> blonde-haired girl in the pub.
>     She reported a dream, where she had stuffed herself with cream buns so
> that when I made an interpretation there was no room left for her to take
> it in and she vomited. Perhaps the most striking lesson I learned from her
> was regarding the anorexic part of the personality's hatred of appetite. This
> was an intelligent young woman attending university. Yet she reacted quite
> bizarrely when a friend accompanied by her 3-year-old daughter came to
> tea at the patient's mother's house. The patient's mother offered the 3-year-
> old girl a bar of chocolate. When the child accepted it, the patient swore at
> the child and stormed out of the room.

Sohn followed Bion's distinction between the separate psychotic and
non-psychotic parts of the mind, and emphasised the need to be mindful of which part of the mind is receiving one's interpretation and
responding. Analogously, it is helpful to think about the anorexic
and non-anorexic parts of the mind in approaching anorexia nervosa,
and study the anorexic part in its own right. This concept is applied to
the second case described in the discussion of the psychosis workshop
in Chapter 20.

*Murderous assaults on strangers*

In his later work with patients in the maximum security hospital prison at Broadmoor, Sohn (1997) explored the psychotic processes underlying murderous assaults on strangers. I recall him describing what was going through the mind of a patient, suffering from chronic schizophrenia, who pushed a stranger on to a railway line.

> The patient needed money, but when he had gone to the benefit office the previous day he was confronted with a notice saying that it was closed and instructing visitors to come back tomorrow. When he arrived the next day, the office was closing and he was left with no money. He then saw a woman standing on the station platform, seemingly on holiday and carefree. He projected all his wishes to be free from problems, and his murderous hatred of experiencing himself in a needy helpless state into her and then felt that she was mocking him, so he pushed her on to the railway line.

Sohn's insights help to make sense of similar events as they occur in the general psychiatric setting.

> During a relapse, a patient with a diagnosis of paranoid schizophrenia threw bleach in the face of a stranger, a young woman, who had come to collect her young child from a school opposite to where he lived. Fortunately no lasting damage was done, but afterwards in hospital he said that his intention had been to scar her.

To the patient, this woman seems to have represented part of a hated couple of a mother giving all her love and undivided attention to her child. This forced the non-psychotic part of the patient to be aware of his own similar needs and wishes. The psychotic part wished to disown any awareness of this. His murderous state of mind towards this self-awareness led, through projection into the mother, into the wish to scar her as if to make sure the disownment was complete.

*Henri Rey*

When training in psychiatry, I had the privilege of working under Henri Rey in the psychotherapy department at the Maudsley Hospital. Rey described many seminal ideas, especially in relation to borderline psychopathology. Borderline psychopathology will be given detailed consideration in Chapter 10.

Rey was fond of emphasising the centrality of object relations in our inner world and their re-enactments in the transference. He summarised the information needed to characterise the analytic interchange with a patient in one sentence by asking 'What part of the subject is in what state, situated where in space and time, with what consequences for the object and subject?' (Rey 1994a, p. 7).

Rey graphically described the inner world of the borderline patient. The only safe position for such patients was sitting on the fence avoiding unbearable affect from the depressive position on one side and the paranoid–schizoid position on the other, hence the term borderline states. Borderline patients can teach the clinician a great deal about the use of psychotic mechanisms. At the same time, it is important to be aware that they pose different psychotherapeutic and management problems from patients presenting with schizophrenia (see Chapter 10). Rey saw the differences as being due to the fact that in schizophrenia the container has been destroyed and schizophrenics are living in a delusional world entirely of their own making; schizophrenics do not concern themselves with external reality but delusionally believe whatever they wish. In contrast borderline patients remain very concerned over the functioning of the container.

## The claustrophobic-agoraphobic dilemma

Rey described the claustrophobic–agoraphobic dilemma as a basic universal organisation of the personality. This organisation is especially prominent in borderline states and schizophrenia. Patients seek space to breathe by projecting internal excessive demands into the outer world. They then feel the effects of their projected unbearable feelings coming back at them. This leads them to oscillate between reclusive states and attempts to escape from this restricted state of mind. Due to the concrete thinking that characterises both borderline states and schizophrenia, this may lead such individuals to make constant adjustments to their environment in order to avoid projected persecutory feelings. This can be especially marked in schizophrenia, as illustrated by the following example.

A patient had managed to avoid facing up to her paranoid psychotic experiences by constantly keeping on the move in her life. Every few months she would feel that she had to move accommodation. After some twenty years of this, the council gave her permanent accommodation. Consequently, she began to experience a persecutory delusion that she could hear a couple having non-stop intercourse in the flat above. In reality, there was no flat above. Finally she went round to an elderly male neighbour, attributing the cause of the persecution to him, and attempted to stab him with her kitchen scissors. As long as she had kept on the move, the problem of facing her concretely projected delusional world was avoided. Interestingly, she later attempted to rationalise away her disturbed behaviour, drawing on knowledge originating from a nursing background to claim that she had developed a steroid psychosis through using ointment for eczema.

*Repair versus reparation*

Rey distinguished between repair and reparation. With concrete thinking, true reparation in Kleinian terms cannot occur, only a concrete repair. The original object is restored in such a way that no acknowledgement and working through of conflicts is possible. Repair without working through of conflict can occur in borderline states and schizophrenia and it also accounts for the repetitive cycle in recurrent manic depressive states, as illustrated in Chapter 14.

Rey added a new dimension to our understanding of manic depressive states. In depression, the maternal breast, as a part object, represents the destroyed mother. In contrast, in mania the penis is identified with as the means of reparation, imagined as able to recreate the mother's attacked babies and breasts, through a phantasy of making her pregnant and refilling her empty breasts with milk. However, in the manic state, Rey argued that 'we have a pseudo-penis which repairs nothing.' It denies the reality of the destroyed objects and presents itself as the universal substitute, while the aggressive impulses continue to destroy the object. Since no reparation proper takes place in the manic phase, the subject returns to their depression without any progress in maturation having occurred. Rey cites a dream related by a very schizoid patient to illustrate the immeasurably grandiose quality of the manic penis. In the dream, the patient was balancing a baby on the tip of an enormous penis. He found that he was saying to himself: 'this fucking penis is good for nothing, it's so big that it's useless' (Rey 1994b, p. 18).

## John Steiner

*Psychic retreats and pathological organisations: the retreat to a delusional world in psychotic organisations of the personality*

Steiner's concept of psychic retreats describes pathological organisations of the personality that offer protection from anxiety and pain. These organisations are conceptualised both as a grouping of defences and as a highly structured, close-knit system of object relationships. They can occur in psychotic, neurotic and borderline patients. In psychosis such organisations represent the most extreme end of the experiences with which the psychotic patient has to contend, a retreat to a delusional world in defiance of reality:

> Psychotic organisations are rarely completely successful or stable, and the anxieties which threaten the individual as the organisation begins to break down are usually conspicuous. The catastrophic nature of such anxiety underlies the desperate dependence on the organisation, the loss of which implies the return of uncontrolled panic associated with experiences of fragmentation and disintegration of the patient's self and his world.
>
> (Steiner 1993a, p. 64)

Even though the patient may recognise that the retreat he has created is mad, he idealises his delusional world because of the protection it affords against psychotic ordeals of disintegration and annihilation. 'True integration and security are felt to be impossible and, despite its delusional foundation, the retreat offers a measure of stability as long as the psychotic organisation is not challenged' (Steiner 1993a, p. 65). Within this context delusions have a restorative function.

In a review of the Schreber case, Steiner emphasised a depressive core, and saw Schreber's delusional system as a form of psychic retreat, with Schreber's subsequent projection of omnipotence in search of further relief leading to his descent into paranoia and humiliation (Steiner 2005).

Steiner also considers the complexity of the relationship between the psychotic and non-psychotic parts of the personality, as described by Bion, within the functioning of the psychotic organisation. The non-psychotic part can learn to face mental pain and guilt and introduce reparative drives in defiance of the psychotic part, disturbing the status quo:

> The patient's sanity and his respect for the analytic work may survive the psychotic attacks and become sufficiently strong that they cannot simply be overwhelmed by brute force. It is then that perverse mechanisms are likely to become operative and the sane parts of the patient have to be seduced, threatened, and invited to collude with the psychotic organisation.
>
> (Steiner 1993a, p. 68)

A patient I saw for analysis with a diagnosis of schizophrenia would become intimidating and turn to alcohol when threatened by insight. The complexity of his psychotic organisation was summarised in correspondence from his long-suffering father:

> It is a half-and-half thing, a battle, no side has the ultimate grip. Both sides have their victories and defeats. With my son, somehow, it's like the life force has joined up with the dead force and the life is in service of the dead. That is why there is triumph about. It's like Mother Theresa making a pact with the devil to provide him with the nourishment to continue his ambitions.

Steiner questioned how much progress can be made through analysis with such powerful psychotic organisations of the personality, but took the view that where the psychotic process had not totally destroyed the patient's capacity to feel depression, some useful analytic work still seems feasible. Nevertheless, there may be limits to the progress that can be made, with the patient having to face the psychic reality of his state.

Steiner's description of the usefulness of what he calls analyst-centred rather than patient-centred interpretations was an important technical contribution to work with the acute sensitivity of borderline patients (Steiner 1993b). His approach is considered in some detail in Chapter 10 on borderline states.

## Edna O'Shaughnessy

Edna O'Shaughnessy has made her own original observations on the functioning of the pathological ego-destructive superego in psychotic depression and the problem it poses for treatment, as well as providing a clear review of the contribution of Klein and Bion to psychosis. Her contribution is considered further in Chapter 16 (O'Shaughnessy 1992, 1999).

## Ron Britton

Ron Britton's wide-ranging writings have deepened our appreciation of preceding psychoanalytic contributions from Freud, Bion, Winnicott and others. Britton has also provided insights into the minds of famous creative writers, poets and scientists. To appreciate the depth of his work one has to turn to his writings (Britton 1989, 1998 2003). Here I will briefly review some aspects of his work that are relevant to our thinking on psychosis.

### Belief and psychic reality

Phantasies are generated and persist unconsciously from infancy onwards. Britton drew attention to the way that some of our unconscious phantasies can be favoured over others, becoming beliefs; our favourite beliefs can then be treated as if they were facts.

Giving up favoured beliefs can be a disturbing and painful process, and counter-beliefs may usurp the place of disturbing beliefs, as in mania. The function of belief may be suspended as in the 'as-if' syndrome; or the apparatus for belief may be destroyed or dismantled, as may occur in some psychotic states (Britton 1998).

### Oedipal illusions

Britton invites a different emphasis in approaching beliefs that are held to a delusional intensity in hysteria and borderline states, compared with schizophrenia.

While we all have oedipal illusions, some may live their entire life in such a world, as in the case of Anna O (Bertha Pappenheim), where an erotised transference dominated her treatment with Breuer (Britton 2003). As well as our individual relationships with each parent, Britton underlines the importance of being able to allow the parental couple to have their own privacy in order to establish the triangular space that is necessary for thinking. The parental relationship comes to represent the third position, one for reflection. If this third position has not developed, as in borderline states where there are unresolved issues with the maternal object, the dominating feeling can be that one is constantly being misunderstood (Britton 1989).

Erotised transference relationships can occur in psychoses as well as in hysteria and borderline states, making it difficult at times diagnostically to differentiate between the onset of a major psychotic disorder and borderline states. This area will be considered further in Chapter 10.

## The ego's relation to the superego, and the ego-destructive superego

In relation to the superego, Britton concludes: 'self-observation is an ego–function and not a superego function' (Britton 2003, p. 72). The ego observes itself in a realistic light, the superego in a moral light. He sees the position of self-observation as vulnerable to being usurped by the superego with self-depreciation and reproach, the language of morality, taking over from non–judgemental self-observation.

Thus, the emancipation of the ego from the superego becomes a task for analysis. Britton's description of the internal struggles of Job, as a believer, when challenging the calamities imposed on him by God, provides a very vivid background for the theme (Britton 2003). Britton also considers further the characteristics of the ego-destructive superego, as noted first by Freud in the case of melancholia, and enlarged on by Bion. Here the superego is committed to the death of the ego. Britton highlights its envious qualities, and links this to Klein's comment 'creativeness becomes the deepest cause of envy' (Britton 2003, p. 120; M. Klein 1958, p. 202).

The nature of the ego-destructive superego and its attempt to usurp the place of a more benign superego in psychotic depression will be explored in some detail in later chapters relating to depression.

## Summary

Klein provided many basic analytic concepts that are relevant to understanding psychosis. In this chapter, I have described and illustrated some of them. I have highlighted some of the leading theoretical contributions from members of the Kleinian school, following on from Klein, including the work of Segal, Rosenfeld, Joseph, Sohn, Rey, Steiner, O'Shaughnessy and Britton. Bion, a follower of Klein, introduced a new theoretical approach to psychosis, and this is the subject of Chapter 6.

# 6

# Bion and psychosis

## Introduction

Edna O'Shaughnessy has written of Bion's ideas: 'For me they are that truly rare thing – new scientific ideas. They have thrown light on the obscure territory of psychosis, and they will. I feel sure, illuminate it still further in the future' (O'Shaughnessy 1992, p. 101).

While many articles and books have reviewed Bion's overall ideas, fewer have focused specifically on his contribution to psychosis (Meltzer 1978; O'Shaughnessy 1992; Segal 1979), and none has considered their application within general psychiatry.

In his book *Second Thoughts*, arising from his analytic involvement with patients in psychotic states, Bion (1967) introduced a new approach to understanding the functioning of the mind in schizophrenia, which has profound implications for clinical practice. This new approach is outlined in the chapters: 'Differentiation of the psychotic from the non-psychotic personalities', 'On hallucination' and 'A theory of thinking'.

These chapters are densely written, with much theoretical analytic content. Although they are not always easy to follow, they amply repay detailed attention. In this chapter I have endeavoured to extract some of the essential concepts and demonstrate how they relate to the world of everyday psychiatry. I will refer to each of the chapters in turn.

## Differentiation of the psychotic from the non-psychotic personalities

Most therapists, whether of an analytic or a cognitive persuasion, do not think in terms of the functioning of a separate psychotic part in major psychotic disorders, but prefer to view each person on a continuum basis, locating their functioning on a spectrum from projecting mental pain in psychotic states of mind to taking ownership of feelings in more neurotic states.

In his chapter on differentiating the psychotic from the non-psychotic personalities, Bion invites us to consider a different approach in schizophrenia and schizophrenia-like states of mind in those who may not be diagnosed as schizophrenic, where in his view the individual is dominated by a separate psychotic part that needs to be studied in its own right. In my view fruitful opportunities for such study can present themselves within everyday general psychiatry, as well as within an analytic setting. In later chapters I will argue that the notion of the separate psychotic part has profound implications for work in everyday psychiatry and that it is just as important to think in these terms in approaching affective disorders as it is with schizophrenia.

Bion characterised the difference between the psychotic and non-psychotic personalities as follows:

> The theme of this paper is that the differentiation of the psychotic from the non-psychotic personalities depends on a minute splitting of all that part of the personality that is concerned with awareness of internal and external reality, and the expulsion of these fragments so that they enter or engulf their objects.
>
> (Bion 1957a, p. 43)

From early on in life, Bion suggests that there exists a separate psychotic part that attacks all the aspects of the mind that have to do with registration of awareness of internal and external reality. In consequence of this attack, the individual's developing awareness of sense impressions, attention, memory, judgement and thought are fragmented and projected into objects outside of the self. The projected fragments engulf the objects so that they take on the characteristics of the projections. Bion called these creations 'bizarre objects', and saw them as developmentally early examples of delusional formations.

85

The psychotic part of the personality lacks the ability for balanced assessment that is available to the non-psychotic part, and is unable to evaluate emotional issues. Instead, it functions as a muscular organ to fragment and evacuate troublesome feelings.

### *Intrinsic features linked to the development of schizophrenia*

Bion lists four characteristic features of an individual who is likely to develop schizophrenia, in whom the psychotic part of the personality will be the dominating force. The four features are:

1   A preponderance of destructive impulses so great that even the impulse to love is suffused by them and turned to sadism.
2   A hatred of reality, both internal and external, which is extended to all that makes for awareness of it.
3   A dread of imminent annihilation.
4   A premature and precipitate formation of object relations.

This premature, precipitate formation of object relations is marked in the transferences made by such individuals. Bion writes of these transferences that

> [their] thinness is in marked contrast with the tenacity with which they are maintained. The prematurity, thinness and tenacity are pathognomonic and have an important derivation, in the conflict, never decided in the schizophrenic, between the life and death instincts.
>
> (Bion 1957a, p. 44)

The attack by the psychotic part of the personality on the individual's capacity for reflective thinking leaves individuals very dependent on others for answers to all their emotional problems: hence the precipitateness, prematurity, thinness and tenacity of the transferences they make. It can be a bewildering experience for junior doctors starting life in psychiatry and finding themselves in the emergency clinic on their own at night for the first time to be confronted with a patient with a chronic psychotic disorder, who arrives from nowhere in a dependent state demanding all manner of decisions and answers.

Bion's description of 'the conflict, never decided in the schizo-phrenic, between the life and death instincts' refers to an internal conflict between the non-psychotic part of the patient, which seeks help, and the psychotic part, which tries to negate this need. In practical terms this irresolvable conflict explains why, in psychiatry, lifelong monitoring of patients with chronic schizophrenia is neces-sary in order to combat social withdrawal.

The need for constant monitoring of schizophrenic patients was vividly illustrated in a classical rehabilitation study on patients with chronic schizophrenia who were residing in mental hospitals. It was observed in occupational therapy that patients with learning difficul-ties, or with organic brain damage recovering from strokes, retained the new skills they were taught. In contrast, as soon as patients with schizophrenia were no longer being supervised they rusted up, did not retain the new skill and returned to their former state of inertia (Wing and Brown 1961).

## The nature of bizarre objects

As already described, the psychotic part of the personality attacks, minutely fragments and projects all the aspects of the mind needed for emotional assessments. This pathological splitting and projective iden-tification differs from normal splitting and projective identification where the projected parts remain relatively unaltered by the project-ive process and can subsequently be reintegrated into the ego. In pathological splitting and projective identification the splitting that takes place is a splintering and disintegration into minute fragments which are then violently projected in such a way that containment, reintegration and reintrojection become extremely difficult. In the psychotic individual's phantasy, once they have been expelled, these fragments encyst the objects into which they are projected, which swell up in angry reaction to the projection into them to form 'bizarre objects' that then suffuse and control the projected piece of personality (Bion 1957a, p. 48).

Bizarre objects are characterised by the part of the mental apparatus that has been projected into them. If a part of the mind concerned with sight was projected into a gramophone to form a bizarre object, then the gramophone would be experienced as spying; if related to hearing then the gramophone when played would be experienced as listening to the patient. If the projection contained a fragment to do with judgement, then the experience would be one of being judged. Bion therefore recommends paying careful attention to determine the sensory modality that has been projected and has given rise to a delusional experience.

## The non-psychotic part

The psychotic part of the personality attempts to impose a total withdrawal from reality by fragmenting and projecting the sense impressions that are the precursors to the development of thinking, and attacking the links between different thoughts. However, contact with reality is never entirely lost, due to the existence of a non-psychotic part of the personality that functions in parallel with the psychotic part, though it is often obscured by it.

Therefore, the psychotic part can never succeed in totally negating reality and completely cutting itself off from psychic pain. Importantly, this means that there is always a part of the patient that we can try to talk to about the way that their psychotic part is operating, even if at times it feels as though all the sanity has been projected into the carers and professionals, so that the capacity for thinking has to reside in them until the patient has settled into a more receptive state.

While total withdrawal from reality remains for the patient an illusion not a fact, this may not stop the psychotic part from trying to actualise total withdrawal from reality. Religion is often used for this purpose.

> For example, one patient on admission to hospital complained bitterly that when baptised as a child one of his feet had not been submerged in the holy water. If he had been totally submerged, then by identification with God he would have been immune to all problems, without this Achillean vulnerability.

## Thinking: putting thoughts into words

According to Freud, thinking was originally an unconscious process that became 'perceptible to consciousness only through its connection with memory traces of words'. Freud argues that a thing becomes

88

preconscious 'by coming into connection with verbal images that correspond to it' (Freud 1923, p. 20).

Putting thoughts into words puts us in touch with our underlying feelings. In psychosis, through the functioning of the psychotic part, the link with words may be attacked in order to annihilate the possibility of a connection to underlying thoughts and feelings.

I recall a patient with schizophrenia who was completely silent when he first came into hospital, just twitching his extended arms. As he settled down he started to speak. At first his utterances were an incomprehensible word salad, but later he began to speak comprehensibly. The psychotic part had attacked links between thinking and words, first evacuating his feelings non-verbally through twitching, then later in a mutilated form of speech, word salad.

An NHS patient whom I unsuccessfully tried to engage in analytic treatment illustrated how persecutory linking thoughts to words could feel because the result of this was to make his thoughts more conscious. He spent all his time criticising the notices on the ward or articles in the newspaper, pointing out that they were unreliable as every word had a double meaning. He argued that you could not therefore rely on words. I realised that this was his way of attacking the links that would have enabled him to be in touch with thoughts and feelings that would threaten his current state of mind.

When I put this to him, he initially became quite paranoid and defensive. He then said that if I was right then he was in a terrible state and really needed twenty years of analysis. However, he said that he did not have time for this and instead cajoled his mother to finance him to go on a trip to the United States to learn to be a film director. Relieved at the prospect of a temporary respite, his mother agreed, but he later returned to London and was readmitted after trying to baptise her in the bath. He had experienced the voice of an old man persecuting him from across the road, making one think of the absence of an effective father figure in his case. He then turned to the neighbours for help, but experienced sexually taunting voices coming through their walls, so he daubed 'Christian?' on their walls, as if questioning their response. He then went to church to request an exorcist to remove the evil spirit from next door. He said that this was like going to one side for help and being told to join the enemy, as they told him that what he needed was not a spiritualist but a psychiatrist! On admission, he apologised for his behaviour, saying that there had been a voice in his anus controlling him. However, when he was ready to leave hospital, he refused all offers of involvement in therapeutic activities, adding that his intention now was to become a professional comedian.

While many aspects of the working of this patient's mind are fascinating, his case aptly illustrates how attaching thoughts to words makes for much more conscious awareness, which leads to paranoid reactions as Freud suggested.

## Ideographs and origins of thinking

Bion regarded the linking of thoughts to words as an advanced stage of development that was preceded by an earlier pre-verbal stage. He wrote:

> My experience has led me to suppose some kind of thought, related to what we should call ideographs and sight rather than to words and hearing, exists at the outset. This thought depends on a capacity for balanced introjection and projection of objects and, a fortiori, on awareness of them. This is within the capacity of the non-psychotic part of the personality.
>
> (Bion 1957a, p. 49)

Therefore, according to Bion, the earliest development of thought is visual rather than verbal in nature. In my view, the psychotic part collects visual memories, or ideographs, which are accumulated through the working of the non-psychotic part. These memories are stored and retrieved when required. They are then used for the purpose of communication through what we commonly refer to as delusions.

Bion (1957a, p. 56) gave the example of a patient who said, 'My head is splitting; maybe my dark glasses', without giving any associations. This statement was a response to Bion's interpretation that he had got rid of his capacity to see in order to avoid the pain that seeing can cause. In interpreting this statement, Bion recalled that he himself had worn such glasses many months previously. Although the patient had made no comment on this at the time, Bion thought that this had provided him with an ideograph which he had stored up for possible use in communication if needed later.[2] For the patient, Bion in the dark glasses had been a bizarre object formed as a result of the patient's projection of his capacity to see. His reference to 'my dark glasses' was an attempt to take back his ability to see. He made use of the ideograph of the dark glasses as part of an attempt to repair the damage to his ego caused by his excessive projections so that he would be able to cope with the coming weekend break. In schizophrenia the priority is to address the needs of the psychotic part to repair the ego before turning to any other concerns.

## The functioning of the psychotic part

From the outset, the psychotic part of the personality has attacked all the mental functions that lead to consciousness of external and internal reality, the development of ideographs and the linking of ideographs in developing new thoughts. The capacity to bring objects together while leaving their intrinsic qualities unimpaired, symbolic thinking, is not available to the psychotic part.

The psychotic part cannot think; it can only fragment and expel. If the expelled parts come back, individuals experience this as an assault by actual objects. The more they aggressively fragment the particles coming back at them, the more they experience them as being increasingly hostile as they try to take them back in an attempt at restitution.

The following clinical vignette serves as a marked example of this:

> The wife of a patient in a severely psychotic state left him, resulting in his experiencing, through hallucinatory projection, a witch in his bedroom. He dealt with this by setting his room on fire. He then massively fragmented the persecutory experience coming back at him from the witch, creating hostile particles to be evacuated as far away as possible. By the time he came into hospital, he felt that rays coming from the outer planets were causing painful pin-pricks on his skin. He dealt with this by covering his skin with Vaseline and sleeping under the bed. He said that he did not need to see a psychiatrist but an astrologer! It took some nine months in hospital before this state subsided.

According to Bion, since the psychotic part lacks the capacity for symbolic thinking, the patient is apt to confuse primitive mental functioning with the laws of natural science. In other words, the psychotic part has no resources other than logical thinking by means of which to comprehend matters that belong to the emotional sphere. The following vignette vividly illustrates this point:

91

A patient with a diagnosis of chronic schizophrenia decided that he wanted to leave hospital in order to have sex, so he wrote to the head of the YWCA (a women's youth hostel association) asking for a place there. He signed the letter 'Mr X, educated to "A" level standard, the world's best logician'. I received an irate phone call from the head of the YWCA asking me to speak with the patient and telling me that she was not amused by the letter. When I spoke to the patient, he replied with no trace of emotion, 'I can't see the problem; if I went there it would be a mixed hostel!' Clearly the patient's logic was impeccable, but he demonstrated a complete incapacity to consider emotions and their effects on others.

### The divergence between the psychotic and non-psychotic parts of the personality

The fragmentation of the ego and its expulsion into objects by the psychotic part of the personality takes place at the onset of the patient's life.

> The sadistic attacks on the ego and on the matrix of thought, together with projective identification of the fragments, make it certain that from this point on there is an ever-widening divergence between the psychotic and non-psychotic parts of the personality until at last the gulf between them is felt to be unbridgeable.
>
> (Bion 1957a, p. 51)

Bion thought that

> real progress with psychotic patients is [not] likely to take place until due weight is given to the nature of the divergence between the psychotic and non-psychotic personality [. . .] The patient's destructive attacks on his ego and the substitution of projective identification for repression and introjection must be worked through. Further, I consider that this holds true for the severe neurotic, in whom I believe there is a psychotic personality concealed by neurosis as the neurotic personality is screened by psychosis in the psychotic, that has to be laid bare and dealt with.
>
> (Bion 1957a, p. 63)

Bion's conclusion is that, in major psychotic disorders in particular, we have always to think in terms of two separate parts of the personality and identify the needs of the psychotic part as the priority. Later chapters will illustrate the profound implications of this insight for work in everyday psychiatry.

## On hallucination

### *Genesis of hallucinations*

In this chapter, Bion writes about his detailed observations of hallucinatory processes and the theory that follows from these. The chapter centres round clinical material from a patient in analysis.

In the patient described, over a period of time, Bion had discerned a pattern whereby as a result of an envious reaction by the psychotic part, a good session was inevitably followed by a bad session. Following one such good session, the patient came in and the way that he then lay down on the couch made Bion feel that the two of them had become parts of a clockwork toy denuded of life. Before lying down, the patient glanced at Bion, stared into the far corner of the room, gave a shudder and then when he lay down continued to look at the corner of the room as though he saw something hostile there. He then said 'I feel quite empty. Although I have eaten hardly anything, it can't be that. No, it's no use; I shan't be able to do any more today', and lapsed into silence (Bion 1958, p. 66).

Bion was able to arrive at a quite remarkable formulation of the patient's behaviour, which he derived from the patient's subsequent comment that 'I seem to hear things all wrong'. Bion thought that this statement indicated that the patient had taken in Bion's interpretations in a way that he felt 'all wrong', that is cruelly and destructively. The patient had taken in Bion's helpful interpretations through his ears, experienced his ears as chewing them up and consequently expelled them out through his eyes to distance himself as far as possible from them, thereby creating the frightening figure in the corner of the room. Here we can clearly see the psychotic part of the mind at work. It takes in Bion, linked with his interpretations, through his ears, chews him up, and then acts as a muscular organ in projecting the attacked Bion through his eyes, resulting in a frightening visual hallucination.

## Psychotic and hysterical hallucinations

Bion distinguished between two types of hallucinations, psychotic and hysterical. Psychotic hallucinations are the result of a violent fragmentary projective process. They show no respect for the natural lines of demarcation between objects. Consequently, if you are with a patient in a florid psychotic state, trying to make any sense of a situation is liable to leave you with a headache, the aftermath of feeling that your head is being pulled apart while you try to keep your bearings.

Bion contrasts this violent hallucinatory process that arises through the operation of the psychotic part of the personality, with a more benign process that creates hallucinations that are understandable, which he called hysterical hallucinations. Hysterical hallucinations arise through dissociation, a process that does respect the natural lines of demarcation between objects. Hysterical hallucinations relate to whole organs or the body in general and are linked to the work of the non-psychotic part of the personality. Understanding the content of hysterical hallucinations can help treatment to progress.

As Bion's patient progressed in treatment, his fragmentary psychotic hallucinations began to give way to more hysterical hallucinations. Bion thought that this was because the patient's capacity to tolerate depression had increased. He observed that the onset of depressive feelings is particularly intense in schizophrenia and when such feelings emerge the danger arises of either suicide or of a secondary fragmentation of such severity that it could reach a point where recovery of the ego is no longer possible (Bion 1958, p. 80).

Bion summarises: 'The hysterical hallucination contains whole objects and is associated with depression; the psychotic hallucination contains elements analogous to part-objects. Both types are to be found in the psychotic patient' (Bion 1958, p. 82).

## Dreams in the context of psychosis

Bion observed that 'much work is needed before a psychotic patient reported a dream at all, and that when he did so he seemed to feel that he had said all that was necessary in reporting the fact that he had dreamt' (Bion 1958, pp. 77–78). Bion viewed dreams at night as sharing many characteristics of hallucinations occurring in the day in the consulting room: to the psychotic 'a dream is an evacuation from the mind strictly analogous to an evacuation from his bowels' (Bion 1958, p. 78).

The patient described in 'On hallucination' said that he had had a 'peculiar dream', and added 'you were in it'. For Bion, the 'peculiarity' of the dream to the psychotic is not its fragmentation, but the appearance of whole objects in it, resulting in powerful feelings of guilt and depression, associated with the onset of the depressive position.

In summary, the psychotic part fragments and projects sense impressions into objects in the outer world, creating bizarre objects that obey the laws of natural science rather than emotions, and the patient moves 'not in a world of dreams, but in a world of objects which are ordinarily the furniture of dreams' (Bion 1957a, p. 51). As he progresses he may start to report dreams, as he begins to introject meaning from the analytic encounter, but early on in treatment his dreams serve a purely evacuatory purpose of discharging fragmented part-objects, as in psychotic hallucinations when awake. Later, the patient's report of 'peculiar dreams' indicates the presence of whole objects that matter to him, as he approaches the threshold of the depressive position. Such dreams are similar to hysterical hallucinations.

Bion's patient was afraid that he had taken in, attacked and evacuated a real person when he produced his hallucination of the man in the corner of the room. This led to his subsequent report of a linked dream as 'peculiar' as it contained a whole person, namely Bion, in it.

Freud suggested that delusions may be the 'equivalents of the constructions that we build up in the course of an analytic treatment – attempts at explanation and cure', though he pointed out that under the conditions of a psychosis they are bound to be ineffectual (Freud 1937, p. 268). Bion thought that during the period of work with his patient described in 'On hallucination', 'some of his delusions were attempts to employ bizarre objects in the service of therapeutic intuition' (Bion 1958, p. 82). The patient could be seen as attempting to use his delusions for constructive purposes.

## *Hallucinations as evacuations*

Psychotic projective hallucinatory activity (as distinct from hysterical hallucinations) should not be seen as an attempt to test out the environment or alter it to understand its way of functioning better. Rather, Bion views such hallucinations as a muscular activity aimed at unburdening the psychic apparatus of accretions of mental stimuli linked to an inability to tolerate frustration.

The expulsion of fragments of the mind into the external world can result in a state of megalomania, where the patient feels that as he has created the world surrounding him and that he is the only one who understands it.

Any patient coming into a ward review conveying an 'all-knowing' affect, like 'the cat that has got the cream', should alert one to the possibility that they are living in an internal megalomaniac world of their own creation.

## *Frequency of hallucinations*

Bion writes of 'the analyst's need to appreciate that the presence of hallucinations is much more frequent than is realised' (Bion 1958, p. 85).

Certainly in general psychiatry the genesis of hallucinations at interviews is far more frequent than realised. One can see hallucinations being generated whenever one asks a recently admitted patient in an acute psychotic state an emotional question. If patients are asked factual questions they may reply appropriately, but when one turns to emotional issues, patients are liable to roll their eyes around the room or stare out of the window. Like Bion's patient, they may be evacuating the emotional sense that one has put into them and generating hallucinations. The patient might then turn to the person sitting next to them with a look that seems to say, 'Who is that funny person asking the silly questions?'

Psychiatrists in training are used to asking patients if they hear voices, but they are not used to thinking in terms of voices arising as a projective process from the patient. Neither are psychiatrists accustomed to try to understand the genesis of their patients' visual hallucinations. Bion's insights into hallucinations open the door for further detailed observational studies of this whole area.

## A theory of thinking

In this very original theoretical chapter, Bion (1962) suggests that thinking depends on the successful outcome of two main developments. The first is the development of thoughts and the second is the development of an apparatus for 'thinking'. Bion contends that we do not develop thoughts through the operation of a thinking apparatus, but rather have to develop a thinking apparatus to cope if we have thoughts (Bion 1962).

Psychopathology can arise in the developments of thoughts or in the thinking apparatus brought into play to deal with thoughts, or in both. I will briefly consider the contribution of Bion's original ideas in this area to our understanding of psychotic processes.

## Development of thoughts

'Thoughts' can be classified according to their developmental history as preconceptions, conceptions or thoughts, and finally concepts, which are named and therefore fixed conceptions or thoughts. As an example, Bion suggests that the infant is born with a preconception (inborn expectation) of a breast. If the preconception meets with a realisation, then it develops into a conception of the breast, with an attendant sense of emotional satisfaction.

## Intolerance of frustration

Bion then considers what happens if a preconception meets with a frustration, the 'no-breast' or absent breast. The outcome of this inevitable experience will depend on the infant's capacity to tolerate frustration.

> If the capacity for toleration of frustration is sufficient the 'no-breast' inside becomes a thought and an apparatus for thinking it develops. This initiates the state, described by Freud in his 'Formulations on the Two Principles of Mental Functioning' (S. Freud 1911b), in which dominance by the reality principle is synchronous with the development of an ability to think and so bridge the gulf between the moment when a want is felt and the moment when an action appropriate to satisfying the want culminates in its satisfaction. A capacity for tolerating frustration thus enables the psyche to develop thoughts as a means by which the frustration that is tolerated is itself made more tolerable.
>
> (Bion 1962, p. 112)

If the infant's capacity to tolerate frustration is inadequate, then the development of an apparatus for thinking is disturbed and 'instead there is a hypertrophic development of the apparatus for projective identification' where 'evacuation of the bad breast is [felt to be] synonymous with obtaining sustenance from the good breast' (Bion 1962, p. 112).

The end result in psychosis is that rather than developing an apparatus for thinking, the individual develops an apparatus for ridding the psyche of bad internal objects. Anything indicative of the existence of an object separate from the subject is also to be obliterated. In this context space and time are perceived by the psychotic part of the personality as identical to a bad object, to be repeatedly annihilated. Bion graphically illustrated this with the description in *Alice's Adventures in Wonderland* of the Hatter's mad tea party, where it is always four o'clock. In a more familiar setting we can appreciate this dynamic in the case of patients whose aim seems to be to destroy time by wasting it; such as in patients with severe chronic schizophrenia where intrinsically powerful forces keep them in a state of inertia.

## Learning from experience

If frustration can be tolerated then one can learn from experience. If, as in the case of the operation of the psychotic part, frustration cannot be tolerated then no learning from experience can occur, only projection and paranoia.

If intolerance of frustration is not so great to activate mechanisms of evasion through projection, and yet is too great for the dominance of the reality principle to be bearable, then Bion points out that a sense of omniscience may develop, an all-knowing state based on morality, as a substitute to thinking and learning from experience. Being able to distinguish between true and false lies within the capacity and structure of the non-psychotic part, and 'omniscience substitutes for the discrimination between true and false a dictatorial assumption that one thing is morally right and the other wrong' (Bion 1962, p. 114).

## The role of maternal reverie: alpha-function, alpha- and beta-elements

So far, Bion has focused his theories on the working of the patient's mind. He now turns to the effect of the environment, in the first place the mother's mind. The infant projects out whatever feels unbearable, like his fears of dying, into the mother. Bion calls these unbearable states of mind beta-elements. It is like projecting bits of undigested food. A well-balanced mother can accept these fears and make them more tolerable. By entering into a reverie state she converts the baby's intolerable beta-elements into a tolerable sense of himself, which Bion calls alpha-elements. The mother's alpha-function thus enables the infant to become conscious of himself.

If the mother cannot tolerate the infant's projections, for example of his fears that he is dying, the infant must resort to continued projective identification carried out with increasing force to denude his projections of their penumbra of meaning. In the consulting room the patient will convey an internal object that has the characteristics of 'a greedy vagina-like breast' that strips away all goodness and starves the infant of a development of understanding. The development of a capacity for thinking is then seriously impaired with a precocious development of consciousness (Bion 1962, p. 115).

## Nameless dread

Normal development follows if the relationship between infant and breast permits the infant to project a feeling, say, that it is dying into the mother and to reintroject it after its sojourn in the breast has made it tolerable to the infant psyche. If the projection is not accepted by the mother the infant feels that its feeling that it is dying is stripped of such meaning as it has. It therefore reintrojects, not a fear of dying made tolerable, but a nameless dread.

(Bion 1962, p. 116)

The object's failure to contain projections is key to understanding borderline states and will be described in Chapter 10, where it is linked to another of Bion's papers, 'On arrogance' (Bion 1957b). However, to my mind, Bion's concept of nameless dread can also be linked to the agitation that is the overriding symptom in psychotic depression: persistent insecurity in relation to an internal object that is not supportive to the subject's feelings. I will return to expand on this area in the chapters addressing depression.

## *Communication*

Bion thought that a sense of truth is experienced 'if the view of an object that is hated can be conjoined to a view of the same object when it is loved and the conjunction confirms that the object experienced by different emotions is the same object' (Bion 1962, p. 119). A commonsense view can then be established for sharing with others.

A sense of truth is crucial to any shared communication. As it is acquired, it builds up the strength of the non-psychotic part, reducing its need to employ splitting and dissociation. Our task with all our patients is to work towards achieving such moments of shared communication through honest and meaningful interactions.

## Summary

In this chapter I have attempted to review some of the key concepts relating to psychosis described by Bion in his three seminal papers. I had two supervisions with Bion late in his life. When I told him how helpful I had found his ideas, he replied that the fun starts when you go and do your own thing! I feel a deep gratitude that his ideas have helped this to happen. I hope to show in later chapters how the ideas presented here can be further developed and usefully applied within the general psychiatric setting.

# 7

# A contemporary Freudian perspective
# on psychosis

This chapter briefly reviews the contemporary Freudian perspective on psychosis presented in the work of Tom Freeman (e.g. Freeman 1988, 1998). Freeman had a long and distinguished career as both a psychoanalyst and general psychiatrist, first in Glasgow and later in Northern Ireland. He also worked closely with Anna Freud at the Hampstead Child Therapy Clinic in London. He wrote many books and over a hundred papers related to the study of psychosis. The purpose of this selective review is to clarify and discuss some differences between the perspective on psychosis represented by Freeman's work and the one presented in this book.[3]

## Introduction

Freeman was concerned at the widening divide in approach to neurosis and psychosis within general psychiatry. While a psychotherapeutic approach of talking to the patient was regarded as appropriate for neurosis, it was seen as unsuitable for the treatment of psychosis where increasingly the prescribing of medication was becoming predominant.

Freeman held that psychotherapy was an integral part of psychiatric practice, as a means of participating in, as well as observing the patient's subjective experience. He was concerned that psychotherapy was being gradually divorced from general psychiatry, resulting in the loss of a clinical tradition in psychiatry that would equip psychiatrists in training with the ability to relate to their patients. In his book, *The*

*Psychoanalyst in Psychiatry* (Freeman 1988), he provided a detailed exposition of his individual approach based on thirty-five years of experience in psychiatry and psychoanalysis.

Freeman viewed psychosis from a developmental perspective. He worked closely with Anna Freud, sharing her developmental theoretical approach, and constructed a psychoanalytic schema for examination of psychotic patients which was adapted from the one she developed for use with neurotic patients. He understood schizophrenia and organic psychoses in terms of a dissolution of the personality and consequent regression to earlier stages of development in which the mind works in less sophisticated ways. He drew attention to the similarities between psychotic children and certain adult cases of schizophrenia. In children there was a failure to reach the libidinal cathexes of objects, while in the schizophrenic there was a failure to maintain them. The loss of developmental achievements, as a result of the illness, account for the negative symptoms in schizophrenia. With the dissolution of the adult personality, less developed forms of mental life come to the fore, and these account for the positive symptoms of schizophrenia. Freeman emphasised the importance of sharing in the patient's experience while they were going through it and relating to them according to their state of mind.

The dissolution of the personality led to the emergence of symptoms reflecting the loss of the capacity to discriminate between mental representations of the self and others. Freeman adopted terms used by Bleuler (1911) and Wernicke (1906) – transivitism, parts of the self externalised on to the external object, and appersonation, features of the object remaining in the self, to describe this state. He regarded the phenomena of transivitism and appersonation as at the heart of differing psychoanalytic theories of psychoses.

Freeman's account of the origins of psychosis is very different from Bion's understanding in terms of a never-ending conflict between the life and death instincts with a psychotic part of the personality developing separately from the non-psychotic part (Bion 1967). To make sense of these differences, we must consider some of Freeman's basic analytic beliefs in more detail.

## Freeman's basic analytic beliefs

Freeman saw Freud's pleasure principle as the key to understanding the clinical material of both neurotic and psychotic patients. He noted similarities in the contents of dreams and in the thought disorder of non-remitting schizophrenias, for both contained a plethora of substitutions with the aim of satisfying a wish fulfilment.

In schizophrenia, as a result of the dissolution of the cognitive organisation that underwrites logical thought, the patient expresses his psychically fulfilled wishes in the manner available to the healthy dreamer. Freeman gave the example of a patient with the delusion that he was Christ thrice martyred and restored, and brought back to life and reunited with his girlfriend.

The partial or complete dissolution of the secondary process, with a backward course (topographical regression) leads to the character-istics of the presentation in schizophrenia. Freeman describes a 35-year-old woman with non-remitting schizophrenia, whose hus-band had left her, who said 'They are all dirty, Persian Oil and Glas-gow Royal. Oil is mental'. Her statement was a condensation of memories of an unhappy life in Persia with her husband, when he had worked in an oil company. He had been unfaithful to her and now she was a prisoner in a mental hospital. 'Oil is mental' gave expression to her conviction that it was her husband who was ill and not herself.

In Bion's terms, I would understand this patient's resistance to accepting her illness, by attributing it to her husband, as an instance of the power of denial of the psychotic part of the personality, fuelled by the death instinct.

Freeman felt that Freud's topographical model and his concept of the pleasure principle was the theoretical framework that enabled him to be most in touch with his patients' clinical material. To quote, 'The theory of the pleasure principle demonstrates that Freud judged the value of his theoretical formulations in accordance with their proxim-ity to clinical observations'. Freeman felt that Freud's reformulation of his theory of the mind, starting with *Beyond the Pleasure Principle*, took one further away from the clinical material.

In Freud's (1920) reformulation, a new principle emerged, the Nirvana Principle, whose action was to convert 'The restlessness of Life . . . into the stability of the inorganic state'. The Nirvana Principle was put on the same footing as the pleasure principle. By attributing the movement to reduce unpleasure to the death instinct,

103

wish-fulfilment, real and psychical, were now seen as being under the governance of the Nirvana Principle.

Freeman proposed an alternative to acceptance of Freud's concept of the death instinct. Prior to introducing the death instinct, Freud had envisaged hatred as a reaction of the self-preservative aspects of the ego-instincts to unpleasure. He reasoned that in schizophrenia, hatred and physical attacks on others are the result of ego instincts striving to reduce the unpleasure stimulated by contact with real persons. Destructive attacks on the body are, paradoxically, a desperate attempt by the ego instincts to preserve the mental self. Only by destroying the body can the unpleasure caused by bodily needs (sexuality), affects, and violent urges be removed.

Freeman's reluctance to accept the notion of the death instinct was not only because it seemed to be based on theoretical speculation rather than on a clinical foundation, but also because he felt that it undermined Freud's earlier analytic thinking, and the beauty of its application in his case histories, which all preceded the introduction of the structural model.

However, I would argue that there might be a need to use different theoretical frameworks of understanding depending on the presenting clinical case. For example, young adolescents may attack their body by cutting or taking overdoses. This could be appreciated in terms of an attempt to preserve the mental self while undergoing an adolescent crisis, along the lines Freeman describes.

> A different framework of understanding may be required to comprehend the action of a patient with a depressive illness who killed himself by cutting his throat, body, arms and legs with a kitchen knife, for his brother to find on returning from work. His family had continually offered this man their loving support and after his suicide they asked for help to understand the event; they did not wish to blame anybody. I saw his behaviour in terms of a destructive independent narcissistic part that had never allowed the patient to develop in life, keeping him dependent on his relatives' support. When approaching mid-life, and confronted by his negative behaviour, the narcissistic part of the patient's personality silenced the healthy part. His relatives needed to know that the tragedy was no one's fault and that the love they had given him was for another, non-murderous, part so that they were not left feeling that all they had given had been without meaning.

Here one might say that the line I have taken, derived from another part of Freud's thinking, originates from his 1914 paper 'On narcissism'. In this paper Freud described two modes of functioning, the anaclitic and narcissistic. In the anaclitic mode the individual was able to develop by taking in nourishment from parents and teachers. In the narcissistic mode the individual took himself as the object and no development was possible, like the chronic hospitalised schizophrenic who had renounced real life for his own world. Freud's distinction between the anaclitic and narcisstic modes of functioning foreshadows Bion's theory of the separate psychotic and non-psychotic parts of the personality. Freud's introduction of the concept of the death instinct, with Klein's addition of envy as its external manifestation, underlines the powerfulness of the innate destructive forces linked to the narcissistic mode. While the pleasure/unpleasure principle was central to Freudian theory, one might say that relatively early on in his writings Freud was also beginning to elaborate his thoughts in other directions.

Because of his strong adherence to the topographical model, and his theory of the dissolution of the personality in schizophrenia, Freeman does not see the superego as capable of becoming a pathological entity in its own right. He views it as arising from the ego and then experienced outside it, in terms of the ego ideal, but vulnerable again to dissolution. He was critical of Fairbairn and Klein's contributions on splitting, seeing them as a reinterpretation of clinical facts, with splitting replacing dissolution. He also did not see Klein's concept of the manic defence as a universal unconscious dynamic, but rather saw it as applying only to the small group of patients where a manic attack follows real object loss.

He shares Katan's view that a change to pathological (secondary) narcissism takes place when there is extensive psychical dissolution. This results in the exposing of an 'undifferentiated state' (Katan 1979). This raises the question of whether neurosis and psychosis can be thought of as differing only in terms of the degree of psychic dissolution. Freeman recognised this dilemma in commenting, 'The theories described here to account for narcissistic object relations reflect a long-standing controversy on the nature of non-psychotic and psychotic illness. Are they or are they not quantitatively different clinical entities?' (Freeman 1998, p. 113). This is the most crucial and controversial question of all the psychoanalytic debates on schizophrenia. The reluctance of analysts to recognise the special nature of chronic schizophrenia is manifest in the belief that, like neurosis, it can be cured, either by physical or psychological approaches.

Belief in the possibility of an analytic cure exposes us to inevitable disillusionment. Tom Freeman and I came to share the view that our priority as psychiatrists is to listen to and live with our patients rather than be concerned about cure. As I've already mentioned, I will always remember Dr Freeman once saying to me that the difference between us and the organically based psychiatrists was that they knew what was going on. We hadn't the faintest idea, so we had to listen to our patients to see if they could help us!

Those who approached patients with schizophrenia in the hope that their presence, their sympathetic understanding and their interest would strengthen what remained of healthy life did so because they adhered to the decathexis-recathexis theory. In other words, many non-analytically trained people may be understood as operating within an approach advocated by Freeman.

Freeman summarised the aim of psychoanalytic treatment in schizophrenia as to enable the patient to recover their lost independence.

> This aim will best be furthered if the analyst's contributions are limited to sweeping away the obstacles (transference, ego and superego resistances) that prevent the patient from giving expression to his wishes, fears, phantasies and memories. This restores the continuity between the patient's present and past mental life – continuity that has been lost.
>
> (Freeman 1998, p. 148)

Freeman ended his last published book with a trenchant restatement of his beliefs:

> The purpose of the book has been to show that Freud's introduction of the theory of the death instinct and the 'structural' formulations laid the foundations for the theories of contemporary psycho-analysis. The concept of the death instinct marked a change in Freud's thinking. He no longer found it necessary to anchor this concept in clinical observations, as had been his practice in the past. He used the new concept to reinterpret clinical facts. The effect was to cause his original ideas to slip into the background.
>
> (Freeman 1998, p. 149)

# 8

# The psychoanalytic treatment
# of schizophrenia
# Lessons from Chestnut Lodge

## Introduction

This chapter considers the important lessons to be drawn from the history of Chestnut Lodge, a famous psychiatric sanatorium in Rockville, Maryland, near Washington DC. Chestnut Lodge was opened by its first director Ernest Bullard in 1910 and closed in 2001. For a full summary of its history, contributions and references, the reader is referred to the writings of Ann-Louise Silver (1997). The purpose of this chapter is to highlight some lessons to be drawn from a unique establishment that focused on the management of severe and chronic psychotic disorders, particularly schizophrenia, as well as affective and borderline states, and which for a long time used an exclusively analytic approach. While important contributions to psychoanalytic thinking about psychosis were made by the eminent analysts working at Chestnut Lodge, the story illustrates the need to introduce a more flexible attitude, including incorporation of medication where indicated, when approaching psychosis.

## Background history

The initial aim of Chestnut Lodge was to provide a rest cure and work therapy. Ernest Bullard is reported to have said that it was better for people to grow real roses than to make artificial ones, foreshadowing

Joanne Greenberg's (1964) autobiographical novel based on her experiences at the Lodge, *I Never Promised You a Rose Garden*.

In 1931, Ernest Bullard died and his son Dexter Bullard took over. He was in psychoanalytic training and noticed the similarities between dreams and psychosis. This led him to look for an analyst to run the sanatorium. Frieda Fromm-Reichmann, a training analyst with the Berlin Psychoanalytic Institute, came over to the United States in 1935, looking for work. She had previously run her own sanatorium in Heidelberg, and was appointed to give Chestnut Lodge a uniquely analytic focus. Her approach was described in her book *Principles of Intensive Psychotherapy*, which was widely read by psychiatrists (Fromm-Reichmann 1950).

Fromm-Reichmann had a classical analytical training and a very strong personality. In line with Freud's view that no transference occurred in psychosis, she held that the classical analytic technique could not be applied to schizophrenia. Nevertheless, all the patients at Chestnut Lodge received individual fifty-minute sessions, termed 'intensive psychotherapy' in order to maintain the sense of a distinction from psychoanalysis. These sessions took place only four times a week, and incorporated a long-term dedicated supportive element.

Harry Stack Sullivan was never formally on the staff of Chestnut Lodge, but strongly influenced Lodge styles and attitudes (Sullivan 1962). In contrast, Harold Searles, an eminent psychoanalyst, was on the staff and his own analytic contributions on schizophrenia were based on his work within that setting (Searles 1963a).

Fromm-Reichmann died in 1957, but the power of her personality influenced the approach at the Lodge long after her death. I visited in 1988, and was told the following story.

> A junior analyst in training was on night duty. He was required to visit all the wards at night at a stipulated time with the matron. He asked if they could do their rounds slightly earlier, so that he would be in time to watch an important sporting event. He was told that Dr Fromm-Reichmann would not have liked it. She had in fact died fifteen years previously!

At the same time I met a young analyst working at the Lodge, who took great exception to using the word psychoanalysis to describe his work with patients, whom he was seeing four times a week. Despite this inflexible adherence to Fromm-Reichmann's definitions, he described a problem that was preoccupying him, namely that a patient who had just been allocated to him for intensive individual therapy had assaulted his previous therapist. He was uncomfortable with the prevailing institutional attitude, which seemed to be that he should continue seeing the patient regardless.

## Chestnut Lodge's theoretical framework

Following on from Fromm-Reichmann, Ping-Nie Pao, who was then Director of Psychotherapy at Chestnut Lodge and a graduate of the Washington Psychoanalytic Institute, wrote a book describing Chestnut Lodge's development of an integrated theory and approach to schizophrenia by incorporating analytic contributions from Freud onwards (Pao 1979). The theoretical premise underpinning the approach was that a certain combination of nature and nurture in the first weeks of life results in a deficient capacity for adaptation, which becomes increasingly impaired resulting in schizophrenic illness. The birth of psychoanalysis at the beginning of the twentieth century was held to have revolutionised our conception of schizophrenia, enabling a shift from the previous view of a hereditary-constitutional-degenerative disease of the brain to considering it in terms of human development.

While each person with schizophrenia was held to be unique, such individuals were thought to have early traumatic interpersonal experiences in common. The degree of difficulty in early relationships determined the severity of the illness. Sullivan's interpersonal theory is mentioned within this context, with its assumption that the mother of the future schizophrenic is more anxiety-ridden than the average mother (Sullivan 1962).

Pao (1979) divided schizophrenia into four categories depending on the severity of the early trauma, and also distinguished acute, sub-acute and chronic phases. He held that 'intensive psychotherapy' was a must in the sub-acute phase in order to head off a self-perpetuating regression, with a move into a chronic state.

Delusions were seen as extensions of pre-existing fantasies. For the patient they contributed immensely to the re-establishment of a badly needed sense of self-continuity. In the chronic phase a resolution or correction of delusions in patients was not expected; rather, the aim was to increase the patient's capacity to tolerate instinct-affect

109

tensions to enable them to arrive at the best solutions without resorting to extremely distorted views about the object world.

Hallucinations were seen as the patient's attempts to ward off painful affects, as illustrated by an example of a woman with schizophrenia who developed breast cancer. She came from a background of social isolation and for her the voice she heard was a comfort. Fromm-Reichmann was said to have often told her patients that 'you may keep your voice as long as you feel you need it' or 'you will give it up when you are ready' (Pao 1979, p. 264). For Pao, the background dynamic was that, while acknowledging patients' desire to rid themselves of something unpleasant, one was also reassuring them that an end to the unwanted experience was conceivable.

Pao (1979) wrote that his aim in treating schizophrenic patients was to improve their self- and object-representational world. A decision would be needed as to whether the patient could be treated in his office or would require admission. While antipsychotic medication removed florid symptoms (e.g. terror, confusion, hallucinations), this would only result in a temporary remission. Without provision of adequate intensive psychotherapy the symptoms would come back, accounting for the development of the 'revolving door' phenomenon.

Fromm-Reichmann introduced the term 'psychoanalytically orientated intensive psychotherapy' for the treatment at Chestnut Lodge (Fromm-Reichmann 1950). Intensive psychotherapy was to be distinguished from psychoanalysis by allowing patients not to use the couch and not requiring them to free associate, and refraining from transference interpretations in the early stages. The aim was to enable patients to study and resolve their conflicts within a developmental perspective and subsequently change their self- and/or object-representational world. It was a 'modified psychoanalytic treatment', which also gave support but was more than just supportive therapy. Pao remained very cautious about prescribing psychotropic drugs, despite the efficacy of some of them in removing symptoms. He felt:

> Prescribing antipsychotic drugs to such a patient whenever symptoms arise may temporarily give him some relief but may inadvertently distract him from the goal of resolving his conflicts and make subsequent modification of his personality that much more difficult.
>
> (Pao 1979, p. 319)

## The lawsuit

In 1982, a patient initiated a lawsuit against Chestnut Lodge. He was regarded as having a depressive illness with psychotic features. He claimed that as a result of staff negligence in not administering medication, which would have quickly restored him to normal functioning, in the course of a year he had lost a lucrative medical practice, his standing in the community, and custody of two of his children. An arbitration panel found for the plaintiff, in that the psychiatrist has a responsibility to provide information on alternative treatments, such as efficacy of medication or behavioural approaches (Klerman 1990).

In summing up, Klerman wrote:

> In the current situation in psychiatric practice, where there are large areas of ignorance, it behoves individual practitioners and institutions to avoid relying on single treatment approaches or theoretical paradigms. Thus, in modern psychiatry, treatment programmes based only on psychotherapy or only on drugs are subject to criticism. Professionalism requires balancing available knowledge against clinical experience and promoting the advancement of scientific knowledge. In the case of treatment practices, such knowledge best comes from controlled trials.
>
> (Klerman 1990, p. 417)

## Outcome research

Following the lawsuit, other treatment modalities became available beyond a purely analytic approach. However, prior to the change, Chestnut Lodge provided a unique cohort of patients with diagnoses of affective disorders, borderline patients, and patients with chronic schizophrenia, who had been treated solely with intensive analytic psychotherapy and could be studied for outcome research purposes. McGlashan (1984a, 1984b) instigated a follow-up study whereby 446 patients (72 per cent of the total) treated at Chestnut Lodge between 1950 and 1975 were followed up an average of fifteen years later. They were typically chronic psychotic and borderline patients who had been in long-term specialist residential treatment for severe illness.

McGlashan found that roughly two-thirds of the schizophrenic patients were only marginally functional or worse at follow up, compared to one third of the unipolar affective disorders (McGlashan 1984a, 1984b). Borderline patients were comparable with unipolar affective patients and scored significantly better than schizophrenic patients on most outcome indexes. Outcome also varied over time, with borderline patients functioning best in the second decade after discharge (McGlashan 1986a, 1986b). Better global outcome for chronic schizophrenia was predicted by less family history of schizophrenia, better premorbid instrumental functioning (interests and skills), more affective signs and symptoms (especially depression) in the manifest psychopathology and absence of psychotic assaultiveness (McGlashan 1986a, 1986b).

## Learning the lessons of history

There are lessons to be learned from Chestnut Lodge that should be noted by all workers who become involved in the field of psychosis, especially with chronic schizophrenia, whether they are psychoanalytic or organic in orientation.

Schizophrenia is a condition that demands to be studied in its own right, from both a psychological and organic perspective. In the fullness of time many differing aetiologies may emerge, some more clearly genetically based and some in which environmental factors may play an important contributory role. Our problem is that, in our ignorance, instead of accepting the complexity of the condition and the limitations of our knowledge about it, we are tempted to impose a solution, a cure. This applies equally to one-sided attempts to impose either a talking cure or an organic cure.

On the organic side, we have seen the harmful effects of insulin coma and leucotomies. We have seen the drive to cure through medication, creating the revolving door syndrome. More recently we have seen again the drive to cure in the attribution of the cause of schizophrenia to institutionalisation, resulting in the closure of the asylums with community care held to be the cure. R. D. Laing also attributed the cause of schizophrenia to both society and the medical profession's intolerance of eccentricity, and advocated the solution of a laissez-faire attitude. None of these approaches cured the psychoses.

Chestnut Lodge is another example of an attempt to treat psychosis by a single method, intensive analytic therapy, which again was not supported by the follow-up outcome figures. Similarly in the UK, a Kleinian approach to psychosis, after much initial enthusiasm, also failed to produce dramatic outcome results for patients with schizophrenia.

This raises the question of whether all the psychoanalytic input has been a waste of time and effort. I think that the answer to this question is a definite no. The mind of the psychotic patient demands to be studied and understood in its own right if we are to improve our ways of relating to patients and handling crises. The lifetime involvements and insights of those working at Chestnut Lodge, including eminent analysts such as Searles, were not in vain.

We need to keep in mind Ron Britton's warning not to get too caught up in our favourite beliefs and see them as the only way forward, treating our own overvalued ideas as selected facts (Britton 1998). We may not be able to synthesise the organic and psychological approaches into a single theory, but neither should we try to aggrandise one at the expense of the other. The different approaches to schizophrenia each have something to contribute, even if we can never be absolute, so that we need to remain open to consider all aspects. As Britton emphasised, there is nothing so dangerous as a half-truth, and we can see this clearly in the history of schizophrenia, where attempts have been made to impose half-truths as the whole truth, whether from the organic or analytic perspective, with disappointing results (Britton 2009).

While we cannot merge the organic and psychological approaches into one, from a psychoanalytic perspective we should be facing towards our organic colleagues and taking an interest in their discoveries, rather than turning our backs on them while pursuing our own interest. A flexible approach to schizophrenia is required where different perspectives are considered while making use of psychoanalytic insights to provide an integrative framework (Alanen 1997).

The lesson from Chestnut Lodge is that no single approach to schizophrenia can provide the answer. This does not mean that people should not dedicate themselves to a lifelong study of their area of expertise and interest, but in such studies it is important to keep in mind that only one aspect of the overall picture is being examined. Given our current state of knowledge about schizophrenia, we must strive to remember that our object cannot be to bring about a cure of a condition that has remained stubbornly resistant to treatment, but to avoid harmful treatments, while learning all the time about how to help the patient and their relatives to live as comfortably as possible with the condition.

## Summary

Chestnut Lodge is a unique institution where for decades patients with schizophrenia received only an analytic approach. Follow-up studies revealed that while patients with more borderline pathology produced positive outcome figures, those with a diagnosis of chronic schizophrenia did not. While both the expertise and dedicated care given over many decades by the staff at Chestnut Lodge and the insights gained from individual work must be acknowledged, there is a lesson to be learned. When we are dealing with severe psychotic disorders, we need an integrated approach that is open to differing modalities of treatment, including medication.

# 9

# The divided self
# Evaluating R. D. Laing's contribution to thinking about psychosis

## Introduction

R. D. Laing's most famous work, *The Divided Self*, was first published in September 1960. Only 1,600 copies were sold in the first four years but by the time of Laing's death in 1989, over 700,000 copies had been sold in the UK alone. This chapter will consider whether the issues Laing raised in this seminal work are as pertinent today as when the book was first published in 1960.

## Laing's background

After qualifying as a doctor in 1951, Laing began his medical career at Killearn hospital neurosurgical unit, where he was taken under the wing of Joe Schorstein. Schorstein, a neurosurgeon, had an extensive knowledge of philosophy, and Jaspers, Nietzsche, Kierkegaard and Kant were common ground between them. Schorstein, who acted as a surrogate father to Laing, was a strong opponent of leucotomies, electroconvulsive therapy (ECT) and the 'mechanisation of medicine'.

Laing had his first experiences in psychiatry during his national service from 1951 to 1953, when he was stationed at the British Army psychiatric unit at Netley. In *Wisdom, Madness and Folly*, Laing (1985) wrote movingly of the nightmare of administering insulin coma, where he would work in total darkness, apart from a torch strapped to his head. He had difficulty telling on intubation if the tube went into the stomach rather than the lungs.

From the beginning of his psychiatric work Laing made efforts to enter into his patients' experiences. He recalled joining one patient, John, in a padded cell, and feeling strangely at home. He took another patient home for the weekend from the insulin ward. This patient became the case of Peter in *The Divided Self*.

After he was demobbed in 1953, Laing returned to complete his general psychiatric training at Gartnavel Hospital in Glasgow. With two psychiatric colleagues, Drs Cameron and McGhie, he participated in a year-long experiment, where patients from a refractory ward were provided with a room with nurses. The room was pleasantly equipped with material for knitting, drawing, playing records and so on. The patients responded to the more stimulating environment. It was called the 'Rumpus Room', and was later written up in the *Lancet* (Cameron et al. 1955). For Laing, the experiment acted as a prototype for Kingsley Hall. In January 1956, Laing completed his Diploma in Psychological Medicine (DPM) and was registered as a psychiatrist. In the latter half of that year, he moved to the Tavistock Clinic in London.

From adolescence, Laing had studied the German philosophers, but Adrian Laing (1977) records that between October 1951 and July 1954 his father ploughed through the works of Kafka, Camus, Sartre, Wittgenstein, Simone Weil, Coleridge, J. S. Mill, Bleuler, Rex Warner, Schoenberg, T. S. Eliot, Tolstoy, Freud, Schweitzer, Rousseau, Husserl, Tillich, Dylan Thomas, Jaspers, Kierkegaard, Heidegger, Martin Buber, Marx and Minkowski.

Out of all this reading arose an overriding ambition to write something in the tradition of existentialism and phenomenology. He also wanted to publish his first book before the age of 30. By 1957, Laing had completed the manuscript of *The Divided Self*.

## The Divided Self

Drawing on his experiences in psychiatry, in *The Divided Self* Laing sought to address his fellow professionals, trying to persuade them to think about their psychotic patients in a different way. He argued that it is possible for the psychiatrist 'to know in fact, just about everything that he can know about the psychopathology of schizophrenia or of schizophrenia as a disease without being able to understand one single schizophrenic' (R. D. Laing 1960, p. 33). Laing criticised Kraepelin for his preoccupation with classification (Kraepelin 1905), and argued, for example, that his demonstration of catatonia in a patient could have been the result of the patient being placed in a tormented and untenable position in front of students. Laing wrote, 'in his eagerness to find signs and symptoms, the psychiatrist has not time to simply try and understand the patient' (R. D. Laing 1960, pp. 29–31).

In *The Divided Self* the key to understanding the schizophrenic patient lies in Laing's differentiation between physical birth and existential birth. The physical birth of infants is fairly closely followed by their existential birth, that is, their sense of themselves as an entity with continuity in time and a location in space. Existential birth is a development which is usually taken for granted. However, whereas most people develop a sense of being an entity in infancy, Laing argued that in schizophrenia this firm core of 'ontological security' is not established. He acknowledged that this could partly be due to genetic predisposition but argued that an individual's family also play a vital role in facilitating or impeding the establishment of ontological security.

Laing thought that the psychotic patient is beset by fears of engulfment, implosion (fear of the world crashing in on you at any moment) and petrifaction (turning to stone). He argued that dividing the self defended against these threats. To preserve the 'true self', a 'false self' was offered as an ambassador and hostage to the world. Real contact was avoided through secrecy and over-compliance. Laing claimed that the schizophrenic's apparently mystifying behaviour and language could be understood by imaginatively entering into their strange and alien world.

The clinical material for *The Divided Self* was derived largely from Laing's time in the army and at Gartnavel, and written mostly from memory. The patient called Julie in the book was a chronic schizophrenic at Gartnavel. Her mother would not let her live and she was trying to become a real person. She was taken as a prime example of 'ontological insecurity'.

Laing held that no one has schizophrenia; rather, someone is schizophrenic if, for example, 'he says he is Napoleon, whereas I say he is not, or if he says I am Napoleon whereas I say I am not . . . etc.' He suggested that 'sanity or psychosis is tested by the degree of conjunction or disjunction between two persons where the one is sane by common consent' (R. D. Laing 1960, p. 36).

## Existentialism and psychoanalysis

At the time of writing *The Divided Self*, Laing was a member of a group of intellectuals in Glasgow with a marked existentialist orientation, which included Joe Schorstein, Karl Abenheimer, a Jungian psychotherapist, John Macquarrie, Jack Rillie and Ronald Gregor Smith. Rillie, who has written on existential theology, noted that Smith, a theologian, was a guiding member of the group and had little time for psychoanalysis. He also shared with Laing a strict religious upbringing. It was with this group that Laing discussed *The Divided Self* in its formative phase (Beveridge and Turnbull 1989).

Adrian Laing (1977) has traced the existential origins of some of the terminology used in the book. The title of *The Divided Self* came from the eighth chapter of *The Varieties of Religious Experience* by William James (1902). The concept of the false self came from Kierkegaard's *Sickness unto Death* (1849). The state of mind Laing deemed 'ontological insecurity' was based on *The Opposing Self* by Lionel Trilling (1955). However, while the connection that Laing made between the disciplines of existentialism and phenomenology and psychosis was not entirely novel, the intense and persuasive manner in which the ideas were expressed were Laing's, and his alone (A. Laing 1977, p. 68).

Laing's psychoanalytic training did not begin until the latter half of 1956, when he came to London. Jock Sutherland, then medical director of the Tavistock Clinic, had introduced a scheme for promising young psychiatrists outside London to train as analysts. His hope was that they would then return to the provinces. Sutherland decided on Charles Rycroft as Laing's analyst, and had him appointed part-time consultant psychotherapist in the NHS, at the Tavistock, for this specific purpose. Marion Milner and Donald Winnicott were appointed his supervisors.

Rycroft's and Laing's backgrounds contrasted sharply. Rycroft was upper-middle-class English and Laing lower-middle-class Glaswegian. They had an amicable relationship, but Laing's primary aim was to qualify as an analyst and he saw analysis as a place to relax and put his feet up after a long day. Rycroft acknowledged that Laing came to analysis primarily to qualify. He also accepted that there was a deep underlying depression that was never reached. He saw Laing's psyche as 'an extremely effective schizoid defence mechanism against exhibiting signs of depression' (Clay 1997, p. 66).

Laing's qualification was controversial because of his irregular attendance at seminars and because of the training committee's concern that he was quite disturbed and ill. Nevertheless, by the age of 33, Laing was a qualified psychoanalyst.

However, in his book, *Self and Others* (1961), Laing began to distance himself from the psychoanalytic approach with his critique of Susan Isaacs's classical paper on 'The nature and function of phantasy' (Isaacs 1952) in which he regarded 'The unconscious' simply as 'what we do not communicate to ourselves and one another' (R. D. Laing 1961, p. 32).

Although Laing acknowledged Freud for his courage in descending into 'the underworld' and describing the 'stark terrors' he met there, he criticised psychoanalysis, with its emphasis on object relations, for its tendency to treat people as 'things'. Zbigniew Kotowicz (1997), in his book *R. D. Laing and the Paths of Anti-Psychiatry*, observed that while Laing's relation to existential philosophy was quite simple – he agreed with its basic tenets and then freely borrowed from it for his purposes, which are not philosophical but clinical – in contrast, his relation to psychoanalysis was more complex. Laing's commitment to existentialism did not allow him to accept the metapsychology of psychoanalysis. He rejected the centrality of unconscious processes and unconscious guilt. He denied the importance of pre-oedipal disturbances or Klein's paranoid–schizoid position in understanding psychosis (Kotowicz 1997, p. 23). In Laing's view, his concept of ontological insecurity was the key to understanding psychosis. He had no difficulty with accepting Winnicott's view of a facilitating environment and his emphasis on interpersonal relations converged with the American school of Frieda Fromm-Reichmann, Harry Stack Sullivan, Paul Federn and Harold Searles.

Juliet Mitchell (1974) in *Psychoanalysis and Feminism* has commented on how, for Laing, the unconscious could be understood or rendered intelligible in exactly the same way as consciousness. In analytic terms, psychosis can be seen as having its origins in the narcissistic pre-oedipal stage, while neurosis has its nucleus in the Oedipus complex. In contrast, Laing's approach to psychosis attempted to dissolve the differences between 'normal', psychotic and neurotic behaviour and Mitchell argued that this was unhelpful, although she did feel that his work enhanced understanding of the nuclear family.

Laing's rejection of the operation of the unconscious may clarify why many psychoanalysts do not read Laing. One exception was Nina Coltart, an analyst who was deeply involved with the Arbours Crisis Centre. Coltart (1995) expressed appreciation of Laing's careful and human efforts to make sense of what was happening to a mad patient.

## After *The Divided Self*

In 1962, Laing met Gregory Bateson, whose 'double bind theory' (Bateson 1972) profoundly influenced Laing's thinking on the functioning of families of schizophrenics. *Sanity, Madness, and the Family* (Laing and Esterson 1964), based on Laing and Aaron Esterson's recorded interviews with families of patients with a diagnosis of schizophrenia, was seen as implying that families were responsible for causing the problems in the patient.

In 1958, Laing first met David Cooper, with his anti-psychiatry stance and his 'Villa 21' experiment at Shenley, akin to Laing's own 'Rumpus Room' experiment. They obtained the lease of a property in the East End of London, Kingsley Hall, from 1965 to 1970, to continue to implement their ideas. They aimed to provide a regressive therapeutic experience for those who otherwise might have been admitted to a mental hospital for physical treatment. Their most famous resident, Mary Barnes, wrote a joint book with her therapist Dr Joseph Berke (Barnes and Berke 1991) and also became the subject of a play by David Edgar.

At its height, Kingsley Hall attracted much interest and visitors from all over the world. However, the laissez-faire attitude prevailing there led to incidents such as someone climbing on to the roof and making noises late at night, disturbing the neighbours, and at times the atmosphere grew ugly. Laing eventually tired of the project and moved out of Kingsley Hall, and the lease was not renewed.

## Laing's legacy

Laing was clearly right to condemn the damaging and dangerous practices of insulin coma and leucotomies, which were widespread in the 1940s and 1950s before the introduction of antipsychotic medication. He was right to challenge the reductionistic view in psychiatry that fails to comprehend patients as total human beings rather than as an illness.

He was also right in drawing attention, with others, to the negative effects of institutionalisation, prior to the introduction of the therapeutic community approach, and the excessively restrictive powers held over patients in the days preceding the Mental Health Act 1959, and its further amendments.

However, he was wrong on a number of fundamental issues, and the biographies by Adrian Laing (1977), Clay (1997) and Kotowicz (1997) allow one to appreciate the reasons for this. Laing was determined to make an impact early in his life, through his writing. However, in his chosen field of psychosis, he was still a very young and inexperienced psychiatrist when he wrote *The Divided Self* (1960). Accumulating psychoanalytic experience, clinically speaking, is inevitably a slow, difficult, lifelong learning process. One cannot possibly grasp transference and countertransference experiences in an immediate manner, other than in a superficial intellectual way.

Laing must have known this. Therefore, to support the notion of his making an original contribution to the theory of psychosis, he had to be dismissive of psychoanalytic theories.

Having read existential and phenomenological literature widely, he had no problems in utilising their concepts to write in his own compelling style. However, the theory he brought to bear on psychosis came primarily not from existing existential theory, but from his own tangled childhood experiences with a difficult mother. It centred on the role of the parents, in particular the mother, with her double-bind messages, resulting in the recipient being unable to express himself openly in interpersonal communications.

While Laing was accepting of any analytic literature supporting a general facilitating attitude, such as Winnicott or Fromm-Reichmann's approach to psychosis, he later showed no interest in Bion's seminal work on schizophrenia (Bion 1967). In marked contrast to Laing's view of psychosis as an expression of a healthy real self, Bion described the psychotic part as fuelled by an envious hatred

121

of psychic reality and attacking the mental apparatus for thinking. Once I had the opportunity to raise this contrast with Laing for debate, but his response was a maddening silence.

Material presented by a psychotic patient invites the clinician to ignore the psychosis and accept a rationalised explanation. In his critique of Kraepelin's patient with catatonia, Laing made the mistake of assuming a plausible reason for the catatonia. He assumed that the patient was disturbed by being exhibited before students, thereby inviting one to ignore the patient's psychosis.

While appealing widely to a general audience, Laing's work never influenced mainstream psychiatry, perhaps because his theory did not relate to the problems posed in daily management of psychotic patients. Unlike Bion's theory, it did not provide a framework adaptable for utilisation in everyday psychiatry (Lucas 1993).

Nevertheless, Laing's refreshing criticism of the reductionist attitude in mainstream establishment psychiatry, with its overemphasis on the mental state examination, remains as pertinent today as when *The Divided Self* was first published. Laing's invitation to question any assumptions held too rigidly in the management of psychosis is perhaps his greatest legacy to those left working in this difficult area.

## PART THREE

# Tuning into the Psychotic Wavelength

# 10

## Differentiating psychotic processes from psychotic disorders

### Introduction

The aim of this chapter is to discriminate the central psychopathology of borderline states from that found in schizophrenia and affective disorders.

In recent times, within the NHS, there has been increasing recognition of the fact that patients with borderline personality disorders, who have difficulty in processing their feelings and a vulnerability to act out through self-harm, are in need of specialist, analytically informed services. Such services include specialist psychotherapy day hospitals that provide a combination of individual and group therapies. This finding is the result of research work by Anthony Bateman and Peter Fonagy, based on the application of attachment theory and particularly Fonagy's theory of mentalisation (Fonagy and Bateman 2006). Staff are trained to be especially sensitive to the patient's difficulties in mentalisation, and progress can be made and admissions prevented through this approach.

At the level of international classification, analytic concepts have predominated in the diagnostic classification of narcissistic and borderline states (Kernberg 1984). In contrast to psychosis, psychoanalytic thinking is widely accepted as having a key role to play in both diagnostic categorisation and treatment approaches to borderline personality disorders.

Psychoanalysts rarely encounter cases of the major psychotic disorders, schizophrenia and manic depression, in their daily practice. However, they often encounter psychotic *processes*, particularly in patients with borderline states. In contrast, psychiatrists often have to determine whether they are dealing with a patient with a borderline personality disorder who is having a transient psychotic episode, possibly drug induced, or a major psychotic disorder. This distinction is not always easy to make.

In the treatment of borderline states the primary emphasis is on individual analytic therapy, even if in some cases groups and day hospitals can provide valuable ancillary back-up, and patients are typically committed to their therapy. In contrast, in cases of major psychotic disorders, where admissions are more likely, working psychoanalytically requires the clinician to work closely with the patient's family, GP and psychiatric services for treatment to be a viable proposition. Thus, the discrimination of borderline states from major psychotic disorders has both theoretical and practical importance.

## Borderline states

### *Clinical aspects*

Before considering the theoretical aspects underpinning the diagnosis of borderline personality disorder, the following would serve as a typical clinical example encountered in an analytic psychotherapist's practice.

> A somewhat reclusive young woman is referred with problems in sustaining meaningful relationships, feeling an overall sense of despair rather than depression. She describes a relationship with a difficult mother with whom she could never somehow have a satisfying emotional relationship, while her account of her father portrays him as an ineffective background figure.
>
> At the beginning, just as he would with any patient, the therapist makes a relatively innocuous interpretation in order to open up a joint exploration of material that the patient seemingly presented for this purpose. However, the patient's response to this is 'You can talk to other patients like that but not to me!' There is no way that therapists can be forewarned that they will be receiving a person with borderline characteristics. In time one appreciates with such patients that their transference is directly to the clinician, who is perceived as the source of all their problems, as a concrete representation of the originally perceived unhelpful mother.

Initially, the patient says that she could be more helpful if she wanted to, but since she seems to experience the therapist as the unhelpful mother, her responses often seem to be attempts to get her own back for the insensitive way that she feels that she was treated.

Inevitably, at first the atmosphere is electric, as if the therapist is surviving on a knife-edge. If he says the wrong thing, there is an explosion. If he is lulled into feeling that it is safe enough to make an interpretation that he feels is presented sensitively, nevertheless the patient seems to feel it to be the very opposite, as a premature rejection of what she has said, leading to another crisis in her confidence in the therapist. If the therapist feels strongly that what he is saying has a point and persists with his interpretation, this only exacerbates the patient's distressed state of feeling rejected.

Sooner or later the therapist will realise that he needs to stop and listen from the patient's perspective. He needs to contain the patient's projections and her criticisms of the therapist, and appreciate them as communications to an object that she feels has rejected her feelings prematurely and failed to stay with them for long enough. The therapist then needs to interpret to her that this was the problem and that she wanted him to stop and listen to her.

This sort of interpretation, which is analyst centred rather than patient centred, initially leads the patient to feel a rush of warm feelings towards the therapist for showing understanding, leading to talk of feeling prematurely ejected from the mother's womb and needing the analyst to act as a marsupial pouch.

The patient's rush of feelings of warm appreciation, which come from the experience of having been understood, rapidly turn into a feeling of being at one with the therapist. The problem then becomes that the inevitable separations of the fused couple are experienced as disastrous ejections that enrage her.

In some sessions the therapist may be aware of the fantasy of fusion and the inevitability of its collapse when his next response to the patient's material highlights their separateness. At other times the warm atmosphere is disturbed only by the end of the session, with the inevitable change in atmosphere occurring during a break such as at the weekend, after which the patient returns feeling furiously critical of the analyst.

Occasionally, when the explosion occurs in a session, the patient storms out in an angry state. When she returns, she accuses the therapist of being 'stupid' for subjecting her to disintegrative states without even real-ising the effect that he was producing. Sometimes she talks about finding another more competent analyst, but then says that she has no choice but to persist with her analyst, as there is no one else. This feeling of having no choice is due to the fact that the analyst is being experienced concretely as the problematic mother; the patient feels that she has no choice but to come back and try to work with the analyst/mother, to try to improve the analyst's capacity to become a properly functioning containing person.

With borderline patients the transference can be so intense in terms of the concreteness of the projections that early on in treatment the analyst may be confused about whether the patient's critical observa-tions are correct. For example, the patient may complain that the therapist is restless in his chair and he may find himself wondering whether this is an indication of his negative response to the patient's intense projections.

One might think of experiences with borderline patients such as the one described above as delusional countertransference experi-ences. One is not sure if one was being restless for the reason given, or whether the patient's longing for a total fusion at that moment is so intense that any movement at all is felt to indicate separation and disinterest. Only over a period of time can one start to feel more able to breathe, and separate oneself from the patient's projections. This shift may go hand in hand with the patient gradually beginning to experience the analyst's involvement as committed, and feeling that he is genuinely trying to provide an understanding container, rather than triumphing over her.

At times patients in borderline states may appear to have crossed the border into psychosis. For example, they may become convinced for a while that their sessions are being recorded or that the neigh-bours are persecuting them. However, such states of mind are short-lived, in contrast to patients with schizophrenia.

Moreover, despite all the intensity of criticism of the therapist, patients with borderline states remain committed to the therapy and place great emphasis on intellectual understanding.

The difficulty for the therapist throughout the analysis of such patients is the requirement to accept unbearable projections until the patient feels able to explore them. This can produce a feeling that one may be colluding with their perversity by not analysing, but such acceptance of unbearable projections may be required for long periods when working with patients with borderline states.

With borderline patients the therapist must act as the reflective part of the patient until they have the capacity to do this for themselves. This is inevitably a long-drawn-out affair. Gradually, a reflective part of the patient is strengthened, so that therapy no longer feels like walking a tightrope, but as if a broader base has developed, becoming for the therapist and patient more like walking a wider-based gymnastic beam.

I have given this clinical illustration first to help the reader make sense of the theoretical aspects.

## Theoretical aspects

Patients with borderline states provide valuable learning experiences for the clinician. I had the privilege of being initiated by Henri Rey when training at the Maudsley Hospital. At that time, organically orientated psychiatrists would prescribe chlorpromazine for psychosis and diazepam for neurosis. However, when they encountered patients who complained of despair rather than depression, and whose symptoms did not fit a category for medication, they were referred to Henri Rey in the psychotherapy department. These patients suffered from borderline disorders and provided rich material for Rey to develop his insights into the working of their minds.

Working in the psychotherapy department as a junior doctor, I saw ten patients individually, all in borderline states, over a nine-month period. I learnt a lot about psychotic mechanisms from these patients.

> For example, one patient started his first session by asking if I had a tape recorder in my drawer to record the session for his father, and yet this patient proved not to have schizophrenia. Without any psychoanalytic knowledge, he seemed to use strikingly concrete symbolism quite naturally. For example, he went to stay with a female pen-pal in Paris. It turned out that she had a boyfriend who came round with them while they visited the sites. The patient felt like a gooseberry, unwanted. He had a dream that featured the Eiffel Tower. He said to me, without my having said anything, 'to you the tower was a penis, but to me a breast as I was homesick, missing my mother'.

This concrete thinking was also illustrated by another patient, who had dropped out of university and led an isolated existence as a lorry driver. Again one might think of typical symptoms of onset of schizophrenia with social withdrawal, but he did not progress into a full-blown psychosis. He showed himself to be at ease with concrete symbolic thinking by describing his lorry as a womb.

Rey had a particular facility for getting in touch with the internal worlds of borderline and schizoid personalities. Being with him while he engaged with new patients was like having the curtain of the unconscious opened before you for the first time. In his paper, 'The schizoid mode of being and the space–time continuum (beyond metaphor)', he summarises the characteristics of the borderline patient (Rey 1994b).

When first seen by psychiatrists, schizoid and/or borderline patients are usually in their early twenties. They complain of an inability to make any warm or steady relationships. If they do engage in relationships, these rapidly become intense or dependent. They quickly begin to feel that they are fused with the object and experience a loss of identity.

They oscillate in object choice in their minds between homosexuality and heterosexuality. They tend not to be homosexual, but often have fears that they may be. They can easily feel that they are being persecuted by society, they often have grandiose ideas and are preoccupied with phantasies of being big or small.

They characteristically have a feeling of deadness rather than feeling the pain associated with true depression. They search for stimulants to deal with this feeling of deadness, including alcohol, drugs, hashish, cutting, perversions and promiscuity. If they are working when they come for treatment, it is often the case that they have given up their work or studies in favour of manual work, although they can do well in a structured environment.

Women tend to present with a hysterical overlay, while men are schizoid. However, Rey described a claustrophobic-agoraphobic dilemma which is basic to both sexes in both borderline states and schizophrenia. When such patients project out their unbearable feelings, they then feel surrounded by them and feel obliged to physically get away from them. However, once they move on to another place the same phenomenon recurs.

Patients with borderline states function at a part-object level with concrete symbolisation. They use splitting into good and bad objects.

Splitting causes formation of concrete or 'bizarre objects' in Bion's terms (Bion 1957a). They can experience great fear of separation, as if separation means taking parts of them away.

> After working for a while in the psychotherapy department I was on duty one night when a patient came into the emergency clinic after taking an overdose. He told me his life history and then became alarmed when I moved to leave the room. I could appreciate that he felt that he had concretely projected something of himself into me and was concerned about where I was now going with it. He was relieved when I appreciated his anxiety.

For Rey, the difference between borderline states and schizophrenia is that, in the latter case, the container for their projections has been destroyed so that schizophrenics are living entirely in a delusional world of their own making. Schizophrenics do not concern themselves with external reality but declare and delusionally believe whatever they wish. In contrast, borderline patients remain very concerned over the functioning of the container, as seen in the clinical illustration given above.

In borderline states, the individual's feelings of guilt about having damaged their internal objects result in wishes to make concrete, omnipotent repairs to the damaged objects rather than true reparation which would entail acknowledgement of the damage done. In this context, Rey highlights the operation of manic reparation. In manic reparation, concrete repair to the breast and the babies inside mother that have been attacked in phantasy is made through the phantasy of a magical penis that can restore milk to the breast and the attacked babies. However, this phantasy of an immeasurably grand penis serves not to make reparation but rather to deny the reality of the individual's destructiveness. This was vividly illustrated by a reported dream of a man in a borderline state of balancing a baby on the tip of his erect penis and saying to himself in the dream 'this thing is too fucking big to be of use to anyone' (Rey 1994b, p. 18) In the absence of any capacity for forgiveness or reparation the patient operates in an Old Testament world of an eye for an eye, the law of the talion. With time in therapy, the dominance of the law of the talion can decrease.

With reference to Piaget's work on the development of the sense of space, time and objects, Rey elaborates a theory of the infant's development of a sense of self out of his experiences of space both inside the mother before birth and in what he calls the marsupial space created after birth by her care of the infant. The persistence of the concrete character of these early experiences is characteristic of borderline states. Borderline patients feel a desperate need for a maternal container or space, but they conceive the object of their longings in concrete terms. They want a marsupial pouch, part of the analyst's mind kept just for them, in fulfillment of a phantasy of returning to the womb. In a concrete way, they may even follow the analyst in search of this space by following them home and watching their house.

With regard to treatment, Rey points out that kindness and support alone are not enough. A thorough knowledge of the mental processes, dominating phantasies, and underlying structures is required, as well as an affective understanding. One needs to know about part-objects and their language. Rey was fond of saying that the whole of a psychotherapeutic exchange could be summarised by answering the question of what part of the subject, situated where in time and space, is doing what to the object situated where in time and space, with what consequences for the subject and object (Rey 1994a, p. 7).

The question arises, why use the term borderline to describe these patients? Rey's answer is that the only safe position for such patients is the border between the depressive and paranoid-schizoid positions. If the demand for perfection experienced in the depressive position becomes too much, the pain is split off and projected, and the patient reverts to a paranoid-schizoid mode of functioning. Rey points out that the border is the only safe position where both depressive pain and persecution from the paranoid-schizoid position can be avoided. In this context, Rey described a dream recalled by a borderline patient. He was in a football match where the coin was tossed to decide who started the match and the coin landed exactly upright in the mud!

In borderline patients there is a hypertrophy of intellectual functioning, as this is felt to be the only safe area of their own and the analyst's mind, and thus there is a real commitment to analysis (Steiner 1979). Although such patients may prove very challenging to engage, their psychopathology has stimulated much creative analytic thinking in addition to Rey's seminal work in this area.

To my mind, Bion's (1957b) paper 'On arrogance' refers to the primary problem in borderline states, though he does not refer by name to borderline states in his description of a particular group of patients. While Freud used the analogy of the archaeological uncovering of a primitive civilisation to describe a central aim of analytic work, in the case of the patients that Bion discusses what seems to be uncovered by analysis is a primitive catastrophe, that is, an early failure of maternal containment. The situation is complicated by the fact that the analyst's work of interpretation is also felt by the patient to have potentially catastrophic consequences: his interpretations are experienced as mutilating attacks on the patient's methods of communication through projective identification, destroying the patient's link with the analyst (Bion 1957b).

Bion concludes:

In some patients the denial to the patient of a normal employment of projective identification precipitates a disaster through the destruction of an important link. Inherent in this disaster is the establishment of a primitive superego which denies the use of projective identification. The clue to this disaster is provided by the emergence of widely separated references to curiosity, arrogance, and stupidity.

(Bion 1957b, p. 86)

One can relate Bion's observations to the clinical material presented at the beginning of this chapter.

Steiner (1993b) addressed the technical problem of how to speak to such patients by differentiating between what he referred to as patient-centred and analyst-centred interpretations. In classical patient-centred interpretations one might say something to patients about what they are doing, thinking or wishing, often together with the motive and the anxiety associated with it. Analyst-centred interpretations recognise that patients are more concerned about what is going on in the analyst's mind rather than their own. The analyst might then say, 'You experience me as', or 'You are afraid that I', or 'You were relaxed when I'. Sometimes, and this is the essence of deep analytic work, it is possible to link the two together: 'You are afraid that I am upset because of the fact that you did such and such' (Steiner 1993b, p. 134).

Britton (1989) takes our thinking further in describing the primary relationship problem in the borderline as occurring within the overall setting of the Oedipus complex. He writes:

The idea of a good maternal object can only be regained by splitting off her impermeability so that a hostile force is felt to exist, which attacks his good link with the mother. Mother's goodness is now precarious and depends on him restricting his knowledge of her.

(Britton 1989, p. 89)

Hence, linking to Bion's observations, curiosity is felt to spell disaster, as the mother's relationship with father is felt as a disastrous exclusion.

For the patient to develop a reflective part, the oedipal triangle has to be formed as a space in which the patient can reside, allowing the parental couple to be internalised as a separate reflective part.

In the borderline patient, initially this reflective part is absent. This is why an interpretation may not be received as a containing reflection but rather as a rejection. Britton graphically described the case of a patient for whom his reflecting was experienced as a form of intercourse, corresponding to the parental intercourse, which she felt threatened her existence, leading her to exclaim 'Stop that fucking thinking!' (Britton 1989, p. 88). The only way Britton was able to find a place to think was to articulate his experience to himself, while communicating to her his understanding of her point of view. In this way the parental intercourse could take place without being felt as too intrusive to the child's mind, and without being felt to annihilate the child's link with the mother both externally and internally.

While there are similarities, there are also fundamental differences in the underlying psychopathology of patients with borderline states and those with major psychotic disorders, and these will require differing understandings and interpretive approaches. Like Rey, Steiner characterised the central defensive structure of the borderline as a 'pathological organisation' of a 'sitting on the fence' state that enabled the neutralisation of both the unbearable envy of the paranoid schizoid position and the unbearable guilt of the depressive position (Steiner 1987).

In contrast, the central psychopathology in psychotic disorders is the conflict between the psychotic and non-psychotic parts of the personality (Bion 1957a). Bion invites us to ask, in relation to our countertransference feelings, from which part of the personality (psychotic or non-psychotic) is the message coming, and with what purpose in mind (Bion 1977). I will come back to these issues, but first I would like to give an example to illustrate the differences in approach depending on whether the material comes from a patient with a psychotic disorder or a patient in a borderline state.

## Borderline state or psychotic disorder: differing approaches

I am grateful to John Steiner for permission to use material from his seminal paper on analyst and patient-centred interpretations. The material arose from a supervisory session.

> The patient had recently recovered from a major breakdown and had just left hospital. He complained about his employers, who had been unfair to him, and his analyst, who had done nothing to rectify this unfairness. He then described how his mother had had a breast infection when he was a baby and moved on to speak triumphantly about his ability to hurt the analyst. He then announced that he intended to change his job, which would mean moving to another city and ending his analysis.
>
> The analyst felt sad at the idea of losing his patient and interpreted that the patient wanted to get rid of his own sadness and wanted the analyst to feel the pain of separation and loss. The patient said, 'Yes, I can do to you what you do to me. You are in my hands. There is an equalisation.' A moment later he started to complain about being poisoned and began to discuss government policies of nuclear deterrence. He argued that these were stupid because they involved total annihilation but that policies of nuclear disarmament were no better because you could not neutralise existing armaments. He then complained of gastric troubles and diarrhoea, and said he had been going to the toilet after each session recently. He explained that he had to shit out each interpretation the analyst gave him in order not to be contaminated by infected milk.

Steiner wrote: 'It seems to me that the patient found the patient-centred interpretation to be threatening because it exposed him to experiences such as grief, anxiety and guilt'. He experienced the interpretation as his feelings being forced back into him concretely, like poison, and he tried to evacuate them in his faeces. His talk of nuclear disaster indicated the catastrophic nature of his anxiety. He needed the analyst to recognise and hold the experiences associated with the loss of his mind and to refrain from trying to return them to him prematurely. Steiner makes the point that although the analyst's interpretation was correct, it made the patient feel that the analyst disapproved of his wish for the analyst to feel the pain of their separation. This led the patient to withdraw once more to the protection of a psychotic organisation, wherein he felt that disturbing insight was poison (Steiner 1993b, p. 134–135).

One can appreciate this material as a clear example of the dangers of prematurely made patient-centred interpretations when working with a severe borderline patient who was prone to returning to marked psychotic states of mind. However, the material can also be used to consider a different perspective.

Let us suppose that this patient has just left hospital after a psychotic breakdown related to an underlying major psychotic disorder. If a psychotic disorder is the primary diagnosis then, in Bion's terms, by definition the patient must be dominated by a more powerful psychotic part that tries to deal with feelings by projection and annihilation, overriding the sane non-psychotic part.

On leaving the hospital, the psychotic part of the patient attempts to solve the problem of his awareness of his need for further analysis by attacking the analyst and his own thinking mind. The nuclear explosion and equalisation with the analyst is the solution. Of course, this results in persecutory feelings that he is about to be poisoned, that is attacked in return. He then attempts to disown and distance his action by talking of nuclear weapons being a governmental problem. However, his statement that he does not believe that it will ever be possible to get rid of armaments, that is aggressive and paranoid feelings, indicates that he is not able to fully rid himself of the sane part of his personality.

The next strategy for the psychotic part is to project his attacked needy feelings into his own body as a physical problem: if the governmental disownment does not work, then perhaps the bodily one will. He also projects concretely into the analyst, so that he feels his problem to be the analyst's words, which, like the infected milk, can be shitted out.

The patient's worry about his own state of mind is indicated by his reference to the diarrhoea. In Bion's terms, the weaker non-psychotic part is frightened of being taken over by a mad part. This part of the patient feels regret that the consequence of this would be that he would be excluded from further analysis, for as well as envy, he also has warm feelings towards his analyst, which are manifest in projected form in the analyst's sadness at the thought of the patient moving to another town.

The patient is asking the analyst to spell this out, in order to support him at a time when he has temporarily been overwhelmed by the psychotic part of his personality. In such a case, where the analyst is dealing with a person suffering from a major psychotic disorder rather than a severe borderline state, the analyst's support for the weaker non–psychotic part would be crucial to restoring the balance of forces in the patient's mind.

## Contrasting countertransferences

I want for a minute to consider the difference in the countertransference experience between a borderline and a psychotic patient. It seems that while one cannot tell before referral whether one will encounter a borderline patient, once in treatment the therapist will immediately recognise the borderline patient's sensitivity to interpretations and the intensity of the transference. As already described, in borderline patients paranoid states of mind only briefly reach delusional intensity. More persistent psychotic states of mind should lead to a questioning of the borderline diagnosis, especially in the absence of the characteristic intense personalised transference to the therapist. The following example serves as an illustration.

## A psychotic disorder masquerading as a borderline state

A patient was referred for analysis from a psychoanalytically informed psychiatric unit. She had had a breakdown while her husband was working in another country. She saw a psychologist for therapy while they were abroad and fell in (unrequited) love with him to such an extent that she stayed behind and allowed her husband to bring their newborn baby to England on his own. She was initially admitted to a local hospital abroad before being transferred and detained, initially under Section 2 of the Mental Health Act 1983, in an eminent psychiatric unit in London for further assessment.

It was noted that the patient was hearing voices but that she reported them as coming from inside her head. Using a phenomenological approach, she was regarded as experiencing pseudo-hallucinations, which were therefore not regarded as of pathological significance. She was keen to leave hospital and claimed to be sincerely committed to the opportunity of gaining an analytic understanding of her state of mind. A diagnosis was made of a borderline disorder.

She came to analysis for only a short time. She began to talk about her mother-in-law, who was elderly and ill and living abroad. The patient felt an increasing urge to leave the analysis and go to her, for no good reason, as the mother-in-law already had close family attending to her. She became more and more insistent on leaving the analysis and her husband also did not seem keen to provide financial support for the continuation of the analysis. Before her final abrupt departure, she reported a dream. In the dream there were a hundred friends. Ninety-nine of them said that she was fine and needed no help. Only one friend, a psychologist, said that she was in a bad state and really needed analysis.

Here we have a patient who presented as apparently very keen and dedicated to having analysis, who is described as being borderline in pathology, and yet who leaves her analysis very quickly. How do we explain this?

To my mind the answer is that she has a major psychotic disorder. First, she must have been in a severely disturbed state while abroad to stay behind when her husband went home with their baby, showing more interest in the psychologist who did not reciprocate her feelings for him than in her own baby. Second, she required hospitalisations. However reasonably a patient may present afterwards, a history of hospitalisation should always alert one to consider the possibility of an underlying major psychotic disorder. This would make her sudden termination of the analysis less surprising.

In psychotic disorders, the psychotic part of the personality is the stronger. It is against understanding and dominates the weaker non–psychotic part. The balance of power in this patient's internal world was made very evident in the dream she reported. In order to maintain an analytic treatment in the face of such powerfully negating forces, it is crucially important to have unequivocal support from the nearest relative.

Finally, it is interesting to note how this patient managed to convince the professionals that she was committed to an analytic approach.

The commonest symptom of psychosis is not hearing voices or experiencing paranoid delusions, but denial and rationalisation. The commonest countertransference response is therefore an attack on one's sanity, pressure to ignore the patient's psychosis and a pull to regard their presentation in more understandable terms, as neurotic or borderline, and to overlook the underlying psychosis. I would imagine that the psychotic part of this patient wanted to hide her state of mind from the professionals in order to have the section rescinded so that she could leave hospital. To achieve this she presented herself as a patient who was dedicated to understanding herself and initially succeeded in convincing the professionals that her commitment was genuine.

## Differing treatment parameters for borderline states and major psychotic disorders

Embarking on analytic therapy with a borderline patient is very different from working with a patient with a major psychotic disorder. In the former case, despite the intensity of the transference to the analyst, and the fear of experiencing catastrophic states of mind accompanied by the feeling of living on a knife-edge, the patient remains committed to her treatment, and does not need outside support. The analyst of course may feel in need of supportive supervision with such personally demanding cases, but that is another matter.

A therapist who is thinking about seeing a patient with a major psychotic disorder for individual therapy needs to consider the following issues.

### Being mindful of the underlying condition

If one is thinking of embarking on treatment of a patient with a major psychotic disorder, one should never forget the presence of the underlying condition. Any patient referred with a history of hospital admission, especially if he or she plays down the significance of these admissions, should alert the therapist to the possibility of an underlying psychosis. We all have strong wishes to play down psychosis and give reassuring dynamic explanations to enable us to feel in control, rather than having to face the presence of an underlying out of control state of affairs. We like to feel that through our familiar analytic approach we can work with any patient who is referred to us and seems prepared to commit themselves to treatment.

139

## Accepting the risk of relapses

An underlying major psychotic disorder such as bipolar affective disorder has an inbuilt autonomy, like recurrent volcanic eruptions. The therapist has to accept that however dedicated and committed they may be to the analytic cause, further relapses and admissions are likely to occur. It is therefore essential that some understanding and support for the venture is established with the local psychiatric service, before embarking on an analytic treatment.

## The position of the nearest relative, and issues of confidentiality

Since a patient with a psychotic disorder is vulnerable to outbursts of unpredictable behaviour, which may include self-harm and/or violence to others, the therapist has to be prepared to engage in discussions with the nearest relative. Also, as the example above illustrates, it is impossible to conduct the analysis without their unequivocal support.

In the earlier days of the British Psychoanalytical Society's ethical code, while respect for confidentiality was given central importance, exceptions were made in work with patients with psychosis. In fact, tragedies are more likely to occur if anxieties are not shared. Where necessary relatives should feel free to update the therapist on disturbing incidents and the therapist should also feel free to contact the consultant psychiatrist or GP.

## Differentiation from depression

Nowadays it has become fashionable to think of anyone who has a history of acting out with taking overdoses or cutting themselves as having a borderline personality disorder. However, this may not always prove to be the case. The clue lies in the countertransference. As I will show in a later chapter, in contrast to the intensity of the transference in borderline states, the experience with the depressive is quite different. They may repeatedly evacuate material in the sessions but then show no interest in committing to any work within the sessions. The therapist may feel disheartened until they are able to tune into the underlying psychopathology and try to turn the depressive monologue into a dialogue (see Chapter 19).

## Summary

In this chapter I have contrasted borderline states with major psych–otic disorders. Borderline states are primarily approached through individual analytic psychotherapy and provide the clinician with rich learning experiences about psychotic processes. The knowledge gained from such experiences can be applied to understand similar processes occurring in major psychotic disorders. However, there are important differences in psychopathology and management. These differences are not always obvious. They are explored further in Chapter 11.

# 11

## The psychotic wavelength

### Introduction

In Chapter 10 I discussed the need to recognise the specific problems posed by patients with major psychotic disorders, in contrast to those (such as borderline patients) who show psychotic processes without an underlying psychotic disorder. I argued that the ability to make these distinctions is essential for clinical practice.

Some have argued that schizophrenia is a term that is too stigmatising and has outlasted its usefulness. From this perspective general psychiatrists have been criticised for their apparent lack of empathy with patients as fellow human beings and their over-reliance on medication. However, such criticisms overlook the special nature of major psychotic disorders, and the particular demands that they make on all those involved.

While many professional staff may work very sensitively with psychotic patients without having formulated a theoretical framework, it is a matter of concern that some approved social workers and members of hospital manager's hearings do not have any theoretical framework by means of which they can orientate themselves to the special problems posed by psychotic disorders, especially the ability of the psychotic part of the personality to cover up its murderousness with denial and rationalisation.

### Tuning into the psychotic wavelength

Following years of experience of intensive psychotherapy with schizophrenic patients at Chestnut Lodge in the United States (see Chapter 8), Frieda Fromm-Reichmann wrote:

It is my belief that the problems and emotional difficulties of mental patients, neurotics or psychotics, are in principle rather similar to one another and also the emotional difficulties of living from which we all suffer at times.

(Fromm–Reichmann 1950, p. xi)

Another leading American, Peter Giovacchini, shared Fromm–Reichmann's view. He argued that difficulties in the treatment of psychotic patients do not derive so much from the contents of the patients' psychopathology as from the analyst's sensitivities. He added that being aware of our sensitivities, that is, the countertransference, broadens the range of patients we can treat (Giovacchini 1979).

These statements are representative of a widely held view that the difficulties presented by psychotic patients are not dissimilar to those presented by non-psychotic patients, and the chief problem is the analyst's or general psychiatrist's sensitivities. A critical examination of this widespread assumption is necessary.

While it is obviously necessary to be sensitive in our attitude to all patients, we also need to understand the underlying psychopathology; in other words, what is meant by psychosis. Our 'normal' or 'neurotic' sensitivities can be likened to being on wavelength 1, while the psychotic patient may be operating on an entirely different radio frequency, wavelength 1,000! Tuning into this frequency cannot be achieved solely through a sensitive, caring attitude.

In my experience of supervising staff engaged in the overall management of patients with psychotic disorders, I have come to appreciate the need for all staff, as well as patients, to be correctly attuned. In clinical practice I have frequently come across situations in which the psychotic patient's wavelength is not appreciated.

In order to illustrate what I mean by tuning into the psychotic wavelength, I will present five case examples from everyday psychiatric practice. They are not analytic cases, but psychoanalytic concepts are central to their understanding.

## Case 1: Planning for reprovision

My first example, Mr A, is an illustration of what can happen if one relies solely on humane feelings in planning for a psychotic patient's care. This example is taken from around the time when the large mental hospitals were being closed in the UK in the mid 1990s. At the time I was working at one of these hospitals. It was sited in North London and in its heyday before the Second World War had accommodated 2,500 patients. In the 1950s, it was one of the pioneers of the therapeutic community approach. Single-sex and locked wards were broken down and temporary flatlets were built in the hospital grounds, to serve as a stepping stone, where possible, for patients' reintegration into the community (Martin 1968).

When I arrived as a consultant in 1978, Claybury Hospital had approximately 900 inpatients. At the time of its closure in 1996, it had 400. At this time, the management were keen to move all the patients back into the community, to become as self-sufficient as possible. The problem was that the most easily rehabilitated patients had already left. Psychological measurement confirmed that most of the patients still left at Claybury would require a structured environment in the community equivalent to the one provided in the hospital (Carson et al. 1989).

However, the management remained keen to move patients on, and started to find community homes for them. The following material was presented at a fortnightly seminar held by Dr Anthony Garelick, consultant psychotherapist, and myself at Claybury Hospital as a forum for discussion of the psychodynamics operating in psychosis.

A new group home was being planned to accommodate patients with chronic schizophrenia who had previously been on long-stay wards. At first, it was decided that the responsible nurse should have a separate office. However, the management then felt that it was wrong to have a room from which the residents might be excluded since this would make it feel too much like a psychiatric ward, rather than a home. So the room was filled with another reprovision patient.

Into this setting was placed Mr A, a 51-year-old patient with a long history of chronic schizophrenia. Yellowing case-notes from thirty years previously recorded the interview when he was first admitted to hospital. He had sat in the doctor's chair and said, 'I'm the boss.' This statement could be regarded as a summary of his whole psychopathology. Over the years he had been nursed with some difficulty, mainly on the open ward. Periodically, if he did not get his own way, he would become aggressive, claiming that he was the Messiah, or Jesus Christ, and would then need a period on the locked ward to settle down again.

He had been an only child, with a disturbed early history. His mother had reported that when she left him, at a year old, to visit his father who was in hospital, he was crying; when she returned from the visit he was still crying. Throughout his school life he was reported to be disturbed in behaviour, and

144

by his early twenties he was already spending long periods of time in hospital.

Many years later, after his mother had died, his elderly father visited him in hospital. He seemed calm, but when father and son went for a walk outside the hospital, the father was badly shaken when his son suddenly pushed him in front of the traffic. This showed how unpredictable feelings could suddenly erupt, despite a superficially calm appearance.

Initially, staff helped to run the group home, but the aim was gradually to turn it into a self-sufficient private home. The patients would then be expected to do everything for themselves. When the staff moved into the group home, they had no private room in which to discuss the patients. They had to resort to holding their meetings on the landing upstairs. In response, Mr A became increasingly difficult in his manner. He could not tolerate the staff talking about him. So they had to resort to whispering on the landing.

Finally, one day, during the staff meeting, Mr A became furious, shouted that he was the Messiah, and assaulted a member of the nursing staff. He had to be readmitted to hospital.

There are several interesting points to be made about this case. First, decisions about reprovision of care for chronic psychotic patients cannot be guided solely by ordinary sensitivities. There is specific psychopathology that it is risky to ignore. As Freud said, the unconscious is timeless. The envious feelings aroused in Mr A by exclusion and separateness remained as rife now as they had been at that first interview when he had sat in the doctor's chair and said 'I'm the boss'. The managers had ignored his history.

Second, the managers had succumbed to psychotic rationalisation. They had fallen into the trap of thinking that removing the office would remove the cause of frustration – namely, exclusion by the parental figures. It is like the story of the schizophrenic who was paranoid about the last carriage on a railway-train, so had it removed. Of course the next one then became the last one! The source of frustration moved from the office to the landing. The truth is that, like parents who need the privacy of their own bedroom, the staff needed their own room in order to be able to function; and like the children, the patients needed to be protected from scenes that aroused unbearable envy.

Third, of course, one must ask whether it is reasonable to expect a patient like Mr A, with a history of chronic schizophrenia, to continue to function if he is gradually left to cope on his own.

145

Mr A's rehospitalisation was the inevitable consequence of the failure to consider these issues. The management had failed to distinguish between the psychotic and non-psychotic parts of the personality. In a patient with a history like Mr A's, the mind will be dominated by the psychotic part, which reacts to any frustration with paranoia and omnipotence. In other words, the management failed to appreciate the need to tune into the psychotic wavelength when they were thinking about setting up the group home.

## Case 2: A tale of a wig

Whenever we encounter a patient with a major psychotic disorder, in our interactions with them we should be constantly asking ourselves whether we are dealing with a straightforward communication from a non-psychotic part or a rationalisation from the psychotic part masquerading as normal. We have to ask ourselves this question all the time in reference to every communication from the patient.

The case of Mr B illustrates the need to keep this question constantly in mind. The case shows how we can be misled and accept rationalisations. I was asked to see Mr B when he was on remand in prison. The only information I was given was that he had knocked off a woman's wig. I went with my senior nursing staff to see him. He appeared a bit vague and said he had knocked off the wig for a lark. There was a past history, from which I gathered that a year previously he had been hospitalised for a few months after complaining of being persecuted by electricity coming from the television. The hospitalisation had followed the break-up of a relationship with a woman. He had been treated with trifluoperazine and his mental state had settled. This information made the diagnosis easier. After all, here was objective evidence of a past florid psychotic state. Given Freud's view of the timelessness of the unconscious, the propensity to psychotic states must still exist in Mr B. Tuning into the psychotic wavelength in this way made me suspect that the psychotic part of Mr B was masquerading as normal, presenting a picture of vagueness and having done it all for a lark.

The process of assessment raises the issue of the countertransference feelings aroused by contact with a patient in a psychotic state. One can doubt one's sanity and feel one is being unfair, prematurely judging the patient adversely and assuming the attitude that the patient is guilty till

146

proved innocent. However, awareness of such uncomfortable feelings can alert one to the fact that one may indeed be dealing with a patient in a psychotic state.

I filled in the necessary part of the Mental Health Act 1983, Section 37, as did the prison medical officer, and awaited the patient's expected transfer from the court to our hospital.

The next I heard of the case was several months later, when I was summoned to appear at the Crown Court. All I knew was that a serious offence must have been committed, or it would have been resolved at the Magistrates' Court. When I appeared, the judge supplied me with the facts of Mr B's case. An Orthodox Jewish woman, wearing a traditional wig, was walking down the street with her 9-year-old daughter. Mr B came up to her and punched her in the face, fracturing her nose. While she lay on the ground screaming, he tried to pull the child away from her. Passers-by heard the woman's screams and came to the rescue. Mr B was arrested.

Mr B's story had changed only slightly in detail. He said that it was Boxing Day and he had had a few drinks with a friend and had assaulted the woman for a dare. He insisted that there was nothing mentally wrong with him and said that he was prepared to accept punishment. The defence psychiatrist could find no evidence of psychosis and agreed with the patient that the offence was simply bad behaviour. The judge said that if the defence case was accepted, she would have to give Mr B a severe ten-year prison sentence, in view of the fact that the charge was attempted kidnapping. The defence psychiatrist's view was that labelling Mr B as mentally ill, sending him to a psychiatric hospital and giving him medication, when he was without symptoms, would be equivalent to the Russians giving neuroleptic medication to political prisoners.

If approached from an ordinary wavelength, the defence case of bad behaviour is easy to follow. Mr B had had a few drinks and had behaved badly. There was no evidence of first-rank symptoms of schizophrenia and there was no evidence of psychiatric disorder that required treatment, especially with drugs.

The other way of understanding the episode is that Mr B was functioning on a psychotic wavelength. He had projected and disowned his emotional problems and covered them up with a rationalisation.

Mr B's background history was that he had been sent as a child of 10 to a boarding school in the Lebanon, while his younger sister had stayed at home in Iraq with his parents. It seems a likely hypothesis that unbearable feelings of isolation, especially over the Christmas period, had led to his

147

acting-out behaviour. The girl he tried to drag away from her mother may have represented his envied sister.

The judge accepted the view that Mr B was mentally ill, especially in view of his past history of hospitalisation and response to medication. She directed that he should be placed in hospital under Section 37 of the Mental Health Act 1983, which meant he could be discharged whenever we felt he was ready. The defence persisted with the view that as there was no evidence of mental illness, this decision was inappropriate.

Interestingly, as soon as the judge pronounced that Mr B was psychiatrically unwell and in need of treatment, Mr B, who had previously stood silently in the dock throughout the proceedings, turned to the prison officer next to him and thumped him. The bewildered guard asked me afterwards, 'Why did he do that, Doc?'

I have encountered similar incidents on several occasions. The psychotic part of the personality hates to be confronted with the fact that he is going about things in a mad way (i.e. that he is mentally ill), but does not mind a prison sentence. This contrasts with the psychopath, who typically tries to disown responsibility for his antisocial behaviour on the grounds that he is suffering from mental illness.

When Mr B came into hospital he became acutely paranoid and antipsychotic medication was represcribed. His uncle visited and we discussed Mr B's socially isolated position. It was arranged that when Mr B was ready for discharge, he would go and live with his uncle's family and work in his uncle's factory.

In summary, this case illustrates the need to consider whether a patient is functioning on a psychotic wavelength, to be wary of accepting rationalisations, and to stay with and carefully examine the related countertransference feelings of doubt about one's judgement.

## Case 3: A patient for the day hospital

The third case illustrates how keeping the concept of the psychotic wavelength in mind can help staff in their management of patients.

Miss C was a 19-year-old girl who I saw for the first time in my outpatient clinic. She was brought by her older sister. She showed florid features of

148

schizophrenia. She presented with a childlike smile and a vague manner. She was totally preoccupied with voices in her head from the Devil telling her not to worship Jehovah. She felt that the Devil was putting poison in her coffee and linked this with a person bringing pictures of Jesus to her mother when she was three. She was laughing while she was saying all this, presenting a picture that closely resembled the classical description of the hebephrenic schizophrenic. My attempts to make sense of it all left me with a headache (the result of trying to listen to a schizophrenic who is tearing one's mind to pieces). I felt despairing and at a loss to know where to start with a patient like this, who seemed to have so few resources of her own to draw on.

Four weeks previously, Miss C had set fire to the flat where she lived with her father. She had the delusion that her aunt from Africa had come round, at her grandmother's instigation, and was telling her to flick lighted matches into the bin in the kitchen. She did this and then went to have a bath, not realising that a fire might result. She subsequently had to escape from the fire via the balcony. As she was flicking the matches, she saw the bin as her father's head.

After the fire, her father moved temporarily into a one-bedroom flat until the fire-damaged flat was renovated, while Miss C stayed with her sister. She continued to behave irrationally while she was there, for example hitting her three-year-old niece for no apparent reason.

Miss C's family came from Ghana, where her mother now lived. When Miss C was 3 years old, her mother had a schizophrenic breakdown. Miss C and her sister were sent back by their father, with their mother, to live with their grandmother in Ghana. Six years later they returned to England to live with their father, after Miss C's sister had written threatening suicide if he did not bring them back. The mother reportedly remained in a chronic psychotic state with persistent paranoid delusions.

After returning to England, Miss C relied totally on her older sister for thinking and guidance. Her father ignored them emotionally. Two years before her breakdown, her sister had left home to live with her boyfriend. She was concerned for Miss C, but soon had her hands full with her own baby. Miss C spent the next two years at home studying for two subjects for the general certificate examination. She attended a college sporadically and did not succeed in taking her exams. She had persistently presented a desire to study as her main concern.

It is not uncommon for a patient with schizophrenia who comes from North Africa, where there is a great cultural emphasis on the importance of study, to think of study as the answer to all life's problems in an unrealistic way. It is also not unusual for young people with schizophrenia to keep themselves together, throughout childhood, by relying on a sibling, through a process of massive projective identification, when the parents are not available for their emotional needs. When they separate from the sibling in adolescence, the breakdown occurs.

We admitted Miss C to hospital to assess the situation further. She was under pressure to come in because her sister could no longer cope with her. If she had refused voluntary admission, I would not have hesitated to complete a formal section order. It is necessary to be firm in standing up to the psychotic part of the patient's personality both for their own and others' safety.

Again, the patient may engender in the countertransference the feeling that one is acting unfairly or in an arbitrary manner. In fact, if the police had been involved at the time of the fire, Miss C could well have been detained in custody and then come to hospital via prison.

Miss C's father confirmed her sister's picture of lack of involvement. He said that he had just left Miss C to get on with her studies over the last two years and had noticed nothing untoward. He seemed to fill his own time with work or drink.

In hospital, with time and medication, Miss C's delusional experiences receded. However, her manner remained smilingly vacant and child-like, and she continued to talk unrealistically of returning to her studies. She intended to return to live with her father once the flat was ready. The ward staff did not feel optimistic about making any progress with her.

My view was that here was a young woman with schizophrenia, at the start of her life, seemingly with few internal resources. All that she seemed able to do was to project everything out and then live in a dream-world (the vacant smile). She needed a long period in the right environment, involved with caring professionals, not unrealistically trying to pursue her studies in isolation. My plan was for her to attend our psychiatric day hospital, which had active groups and therapeutic input from the nursing staff, occupational therapists, social workers and others, as well as my own supervisory involvement.

I firmly told Miss C that what she needed, at this point, was time spent mixing with others in a helpful environment to develop more of a sense of herself, not studies. Her college had contacted me and I told her that they were in full agreement. Again this illustrates the need to be firm in standing up to the psychotic part of the patient. My only straw of comfort in thinking about Miss C's case was the fire, which I felt was the only evidence I had of life in her. It symbolised her attempt to draw her unresponsive father's attention to her needs.

When she started at the day hospital, Miss C's vacant manner remained the same. Like the inpatient staff, the day hospital staff felt unable to make a meaningful contact with her. A few days later, on leaving the day hospital, Miss C met a man when his car stopped at the traffic lights. She got into his car and spent the night with him. The next morning she was tearful and upset when she told the day hospital staff about it. However, she then reverted to her vacant smiling state. The staff felt at a loss to know how to understand Miss C, so her case was presented at our weekly seminar.

The issue raised was that Miss C appeared so vacant and inaccessible, with nothing to get hold of, that her case seemed hopeless. However, if one remembers the need to be attuned to the psychotic wavelength, her case looks quite different. This is a young woman who uses projective processes to empty her mind of problems. Having emptied her mind of her problems, she is then free to produce any phantasy she likes. Here the man in the car has the idealised penis, which she imagines can look after her totally. Later, she starts to feel uncomfortable about the events.

I felt that a rapport with Miss C could be established only through our understanding involvement with the acting-out and major life events that had impinged on her. As her only available response to these events was to evacuate and go vacant, we needed to do the initial thinking for her about her projections. In Bion's terms this would be the work of converting unusable beta-elements into alpha-elements, through alpha function or maternal reverie; in Winnicott's terms, our aim would be to provide a state of primary maternal preoccupation, through her key worker (Bion 1967; Winnicott 1960). Miss C's mother had previously been unable to fulfil these functions for her, due to her own psychosis.

Looked at from this perspective there are many issues that can be taken up with her:

- the unavailable ill mother
- the sister she had relied on, who had left
- the need to resort to massive projective identification by hallucinating her aunt, to try to make contact with her father's mind
- the issue of trying to use education and study to solve her emotional problems
- the proneness to evacuate and look for quick ideal solutions, the idealised penis, in preference to real involvement in the day hospital.

Looked at from the angle of attunement to the psychotic wavelength, a case that may appear arid from an ordinary viewpoint is full of life events with which to be involved. It is possible to help staff to orientate themselves to this. They also need help to realise that the patient will keep resorting to projection and escapism, and will continually need to to be brought back to face reality. For example, a few weeks later, Miss C was talking about going to see her mother in Ghana and had formed other unsuitable relationships.

After the seminar, one of the nursing staff felt sufficiently encouraged to take Miss C on for individual sessions. With the support of her sister, arrangements were made for Miss C to move to a specialised community placement, from where she would continue to attend the day hospital.

In ordinary analytic practice, analysts are wary of referring to separate parts of the personality. Speaking to the patient in terms of a part of themselves that behaves in a certain way is felt to reinforce defensive structures, unless they have a sufficient degree of integration to recognise internal painful conflicts (Feldman 2007).

Analysts are more accustomed to think in terms of split–off parts or autistic islands that require reintegration during analysis to form a more whole person. They may therefore be quite resistant to thinking about a separate psychotic part that operates in major psychotic disorders, among which I include affective disorders as well as schizophrenia. For the moment I will concentrate on schizophrenia, as depression will be considered in detail later in the book (see Part Four).

Within everyday general psychiatric practice it is crucial to be always thinking in terms of the two separate parts, psychotic and non-psychotic, in order to relate to the patient effectively. The following serves as a telling example.

## Case 4: Making contact with an apparently inaccessible state of mind

Miss D, a late adolescent girl with a diagnosis of schizophrenia, was admitted to hospital in a vague and confused state. Her father had died two years ago and she and her mother had moved into our catchment area. Recently, Miss D had become so confused and disjointed in her thinking and behaviour that her mother found her too much of a handful, and she was admitted.

In hospital, her mental state remained the same, despite antipsychotic medication and individual time spent with the staff. She remained vague and unforthcoming, requesting no help, and when she was questioned she denied having any depressive or suicidal feelings. This situation went on unchanged for several months.

I was on leave when a decision was made to allow her out of hospital to spend a weekend at her mother's place. That weekend, with no prior warning, she jumped out of an upstairs window, fracturing a leg. She was initially treated in an orthopaedic ward in the general hospital, where I also ran my outpatient clinic. While she was recovering on the orthopaedic ward, she came on crutches, with her leg in plaster, to see me in my outpatient clinic.

She was in a frightened state and asked if she could be readmitted to our psychiatric hospital ward as soon as she was ready for discharge from the orthopaedic ward. At the time I was struck both by her frightened state and her clear expression of a wish to be readmitted, in contrast to her usual vague state.

On readmission to the psychiatric ward, however, Miss D went back to her previous unforthcoming state, acting as if nothing had happened. We seemed to have reached an impasse; it felt as though Miss D would continue for ever in this state of mind.

It then occurred to me to look at the situation in terms of two divergent parts of the self. On reaching adolescence, one part felt quite unequipped emotionally to cope with life and felt frightened, bewildered and in need of constant support and help in a non-pressurised environment; while another part, which in Bion's terms would be called the psychotic part of her personality, was totally impatient, intolerant of frustration, and dealt with the needy part by trying to get rid of the patient.

Following this line of thought, one could look at the suicide attempt, not as an expression of depression and despair by a needy part of the self, which would be a more normal way of looking at things, but as a murderous assault by one part of the patient on another part. This explains Miss D's frightened state when she came to me from the orthopaedic ward requesting readmission; we can understand this as the frightened needy part of her seeking protection from the murderous part.

Following this insight, I put it to Miss D that she had not jumped out of the window, but that the needy part of her was actively pushed out of the window by an impatient part that hated her neediness. Saying this to her was like pressing a magic button. Seemingly from nowhere her mental state changed. Instead of continuing in her habitual slow, vague and confused state, she began to talk rapidly. She denied that what I had said was the case, started to stress the importance of religion, and in the next ward group, instead of her usual silence, advocated organised holiday trips.

Miss D's internal state had now been brought into the open. The murderous part was in full view, advocating going on holiday rather than being a patient, propounding adherence to religion and omniscience as a substitute for thinking. Through religion, which was not to be challenged, she propounded that she was a very moral person; anyone questioning her views was made to feel that they were the intolerant one. As Miss D's psychotic murderousness was no longer hidden it became possible to challenge her on whether this was the only way to go about dealing with her emotional needs and lack of confidence.

While account had to be taken of Miss D's severe disabilities, she then began to make progress. She moved to live in a group home, responded to help in socialising, accepted continued support from her mother and attended for outpatient monitoring.

This case shows how thinking in terms of Bion's concept of the two divergent parts of the personality helped to overcome an impasse. It also illustrates that not all situations with psychotic patients are amenable solely with drugs. It offers a good example of how a murderous part of the personality, dominated by the death instinct, tries to cover up its tracks and present as a more rational, reasonable person.

## Case 5: Evaluation of suicide risk in a woman with longstanding schizophrenia

This case illustrates the need for senior nursing staff to appreciate the functioning of the psychotic part of the personality. Mrs E was a woman in her fifties, with a long history of schizophrenia. Her husband had died a few years previously, and since then her admissions to hospital had become much more frequent. Her elderly mother, who lived some distance from her, was the main monitor of the patient's mental state, with some back-up from the community psychiatric nurse and social services.

Mrs E's latest hospital admission had followed her getting the flu. This precipitated a catatonic state, in which she took to her bed and did not eat, until her mother discovered her when her daughter failed to visit her as usual.

Mrs E had to be admitted to hospital on a compulsory order, as when she was seen at home she denied that there was anything wrong, saying that she was feeding and looking after herself satisfactorily. In fact, she was so dehydrated on admission that initially she required an intravenous drip and management on the medical ward.

She was soon transferred to the open psychiatric ward at the hospital. There she presented with a calm exterior, denying that anything was troubling her. She went for a walk with the nurses and managed to get away from them. It was getting late and it was a very cold winter's night. The ward sister was concerned, as it had been established that she had neither gone home nor gone to her mother's place.

Fairly near to the hospital was a large forest. The ward sister had wide clinical experience, and I had often discussed with her the splits in psychotic patients, and the presence of a murderous part of the personality. This dynamic was already in evidence within this patient, who had dealt with the ill-flu part of herself by starvation and dehydration, while claiming at the same time that she had been caring well for herself.

The ward sister was sufficiently worried that she managed to persuade the police to send a helicopter over the forest, quite a feat in itself, as she was worried that the patient might die of hypothermia. The police in fact found her there. The patient claimed that she had just lost her way and had decided to sleep in the forest.

The next morning, when seen in the ward review, she was terribly polite. There were several empty chairs and she asked which one she should sit on. She made no mention at all of the recent incident. I pointed out the murderous hypocrisy of the part of her that was now being so polite, and yet had tried to get rid of the needy part of herself that she had got in touch with through getting the flu. Of course, there had been no one else available at home, since her husband's death, to offer the alternative of a caring attitude.

In contrast to Miss D, Mrs E's internal mental structure was so ingrained that she continued to behave in similar ways, with further admissions, although at least the staff (inpatient and outpatient), as well as her mother, were now fully aware of the underlying dynamics that made repeated episodes of self-neglect likely.

## Summary

In this chapter, I have endeavoured to demonstrate through clinical examples the need for a theoretical framework in approaching major psychotic disorders that differs from the framework we use in thinking about neuroses or borderline states.

The issues that need to be considered include the following:

First, major psychotic disorders have to be related to in their own right. We cannot rely solely on understanding and empathy gained through experience with less disturbed patients. We have to develop a capacity to tune into the psychotic wavelength in order to understand our patients' conflicts and resulting states of mind and behaviour.

Second, when approaching major psychotic disorders, we have always to think in terms of two separate parts of the personality, the psychotic and the non-psychotic, and ask ourselves which part we are being confronted by at any particular moment in time.

Third, we need constantly to bear in mind that the commonest symptoms of psychosis are not hallucinations, delusions or first rank symptoms, but in over 95 per cent of cases, denial and rationalisation. We therefore must keep asking ourselves whether in listening to the patient we are hearing denial of problems and plausible rationalisations by a psychotic part covering up its murderous intolerance of frustration, rather than a reasoned argument or complaint emanating from the non-psychotic part. Keeping this framework in our minds can help us to stay attuned to the psychotic wavelength.

Once the psychotic part of the patient has been recognised as a separate entity to be studied in its own right in major psychotic disorders, one is in a position to give further consideration to the needs of patients presenting with severe and enduring mental illness. This includes the need to build up a supportive environment or exoskeleton around the patient, and this is the subject of Chapter 17.

# 12

# Dreams and delusions

## Introduction

Freud always considered *The Interpretation of Dreams* to be his most important work (Jones 1972). He famously described dreams as 'The royal road to the knowledge of the unconscious activities of the mind' (Freud 1900, p. 608). In psychosis, delusions replace dreams as the key to understanding the underlying conflicts. In order to understand these conflicts, we need to decipher the meaning behind the delusions.

I will briefly consider the role of dreams in current psychiatric practice before turning to delusions. Some organically orientated psychiatrists regard dreams as the meaningless residues of the day's work by the brain. Others of us might think differently. I will start with a case that vividly illustrates the importance of dreams as a guideline in psychiatric assessment.

## Case 1: The dream as a guideline

Mrs F presented as a new outpatient. She was in her forties, of Kurdish extraction, seen with a link worker. Her sole presenting problem was that she would wake up terrified every night after a nightmare in which the ceiling was coming down. She would then turn to her husband and say to him, 'I don't know who you are', and he would have to reassure her.

This had been going on for three years, but it had become worse over the last three months. Mrs F reiterated that she had no other problems.

She had been brought up on a farm and had had an arranged marriage when she was 17. She was grateful that her husband turned out not to be a bad man. She had three children who were all still living at home,

157

the youngest of whom was now 17. They had come to the UK ten years previously, because of the political problems in their country of origin.

I was unable to elicit anything abnormal until I asked about her husband's health. She said, 'Oh yes', and mentioned that he had had stomach cancer for the past three years and had undergone chemotherapy. He had told her not to mention his illness to the children, but she felt that they might suspect something anyway.

Freud thought that dreams represented our minds' attempts to deal with emotional conflicts at night through dissociation, repression and symbolism. We can see clearly here that the ceiling falling down in the dream is a symbolic representation of her husband's illness. We can see dissociation at work, as she tries to distance herself from her perception of her husband's illness and his dying. We can see repression and return of the repressed, her anxieties emerging at night in her nightmares.

Culturally Mrs F's role was as the housewife, she looked after the house and children, while her husband was the one in charge. She was emotionally isolated since she did not speak English and had no friends or family over here.

We decided to refer her to a Kurdish-speaking women's centre and to arrange to see her with her husband and a link worker. We were also aware that the whole family might need some help.

This example illustrates how reported dreams can play a role in everyday psychiatric clinics in alerting workers to the patient's internal concerns. Of course psychotherapists routinely recognise the importance of enquiring about dreams in their assessment interviews, but we might consider enquiring about them in general psychiatric assessments, as we search for understanding.

## Case 2: The importance of dreams as indicators of progress in therapy

In a review on the function of dreams, Segal points out that we have expanded our thinking beyond Freud's classical theory. Freud held that repressed wishes found their fulfilment in dreams by means of indirect representation, displacement, condensation and symbolisation. A compromise is reached between repressing agencies and return of the repressed. Dream-work is the work needed to achieve this compromise. Segal points out that Freud never altered his views on dreams, following his later formulation of the duality of libidinal and destructive forces (Segal 1981c).

Many aspects of dreams have received further consideration since Freud's seminal discoveries (Flanders 1993; Quinodoz 2002; Sharpe 1937). My aim here is simply to illustrate how dreams can act as indicators of progress in analytic psychotherapy, and as such could be appreciated by a trainee when seeing an individual psychotherapy case under supervision.

The following material, taken from a woman in her thirties in twice weekly analytic therapy, illustrates the important role that dreams can play in indicating a progressive strengthening of the ego.

Mrs G presented with a diagnosis of depression linked to chronic fatigue syndrome. She came from a strict religious sect. Her mother had a history of depression, but had never received treatment for it.

Mrs G was married with no children. She was not working due to episodes of severe fatigue, often feeling exhausted when she woke in the morning. She had had one lengthy hospital admission. She felt that antidepressants had not worked for her and did not want to stay on medication. A cognitive approach had been attempted as part of her treatment, but this had not helped either. She experienced the cognitive daily diary tasks as demands that exacerbated her symptoms of fatigue. Through contact with a friend she had been referred for analytic therapy.

She was afraid that the development of her own mind would have a catastrophic effect on her family, especially on her religious father, who would not be able to tolerate her having a separate mind.

In analytic terms, one could see Mrs G as having an ego-destructive superego, a part of her that was present from early on in development, that never changed, and that constantly criticised her for not being perfect. In severe depression, the ego-destructive superego holds the ego in a vice-like grip, refusing to allow it to breathe and develop. The task of therapy with a patient like this would be gradually to displace it by a more mature reflective superego. As Mrs G got more involved in her therapy her dreams provided indications of this gradual displacement.

Initially Mrs G's dreams were full of dismembered body parts or heads blown off. Gradually they changed into representations of conflicts between two parts of herself. One part, identified with an extreme restrictive religious attitude, was linked in her mind to a dream of being imprisoned in a barren concrete building. A crack was starting to appear in one of the walls, but she was still trapped inside.

159

Another dream featured a large black metal mechanical spider that had her in a vice-like grip. It was not hard to appreciate this in terms of her feeling of being in the grip of her depression.

Much later on in Mrs G's treatment, her husband was left some money, and for the first time the couple could put a deposit on a home for themselves. Despite her pleasure in this, her depression still maintained a grip on her, although she tried to underplay it. At night, she would be overtaken by a compulsion to clean all her pots and pans, and she would then wake exhausted and fit for nothing the next day.

When I referred to the grip that the depression still had on her, and related this to her spider dream, she recalled that that night she had had another dream of a black spider. She had awakened absolutely terrified. The spider was the size of the consulting room wall and she was entrapped in it. This time, though, it was made of bamboo. An acquaintance of her husband's, who was friendly towards her, managed to break off one of the legs.

The scene in the dream then shifted to her father driving the car. They were taking a day return trip to where she bought the flat. She didn't want to go, but agreed in the end. Her father was very angry while driving. She was crammed in the back with her siblings, like in childhood. However, she had a famous young actress with her. This woman stood in her mind for all her good wishes for herself: attractive, independent with a good mind.

In her associations she was able to consider the father in her dream as an internal object, part of her own make-up, rather than just an external father. She was able to talk of the two problems that she had to face, her religion and what she referred to as 'her madness', her crippling depression and tiredness, linked to identification with the demands of the controlling father in the driving seat.

In this example the patient's dreams develop in complexity and detail as she makes progress in coming to grips with her depression, and her dreams go from part–object representations to representations of whole objects.

## Dreams in the context of psychotic disorders

In patients with a major psychotic disorder, whether schizophrenia or recurrent manic depressive disorder, dreams can be deceptive in terms of raising one's hopes for change because of the insight apparently expressed in the dream.

Bion observed that in schizophrenia, as the patient progresses, he may start to report dreams, the consequence of his introjection of meaning from the analytic encounter. The dreams have arisen as a result of work done by the non-psychotic part of his personality. However, if the psychotic part is in the ascendance, the dreams may be the night-time equivalent of hallucinations during the day, representing material to be evacuated: 'to the psychotic a dream is an evacuation from the mind strictly analogous to an evacuation from his bowels' (Bion 1958, p. 78).

However, the psychotic part cannot stop the functioning of the non-psychotic part, with its capacity for observation; it can only evacuate the insights reached. Steiner (1993a) described the antagonistic quality to this complex relationship between the two parts of the personality.

Steiner noted: 'Both Freud and Bion describe the co-existence of psychotic and non-psychotic parts of the personality in the psychotic patient, and both speak as if a sane and psychotic person exist within the one individual' (Steiner 1993a, p. 67).

Freud wrote:

> The problem of psychosis would be simple and perspicuous if the ego's detachment from reality could be carried through completely. But this seems to happen only rarely, or perhaps never. Even in a state so far removed from the reality of the external world as one of hallucinatory confusion, one learns from the patient after their recovery that at the same time in some corner of their mind (as they put it), there was a sane person hidden who, like a detached spectator, watched the hubbub of illness go past him.
>
> (Freud 1940, p. 201)

Steiner also noted that for Bion,

> The non-psychotic part was concerned with a neurotic problem, that is to say a problem that centred on the resolution of a conflict of ideas and emotions to which the operation of the ego had given rise. But the psychotic personality was concerned with the problem of repair of the ego.
>
> (Bion 1957a, p. 56)

The problem with dreams in psychotic patients is that they may

161

well represent an evacuation of sanity in order to avoid disrupting the status quo and having to face the need for psychic change. This evacuation is the work of a psychotic part in envious rivalry with sanity, which is projected into the analyst.

I learned this lesson the hard way over many years of analytic involvement with a patient with recurrent manic depression (see Chapter 14). I learned that dreams reported by patients with recurrent psychotic disorders should always be considered as possible evacuations of insight rather than necessarily the signs of internal progress that they might be in the case of a patient with a more neurotic disorder.

> Just before a prolonged manic episode, my patient had a dream in which she was both the onlooker at a Roman orgy and a participant in it. She did not like what she saw but could do nothing to stop it. Schreber also reported disturbing dreams prior to his relapses. In both cases, the dreams seem to be predictors of relapse, illustrations of awareness arrived at through the work of the non-psychotic part which is about to be overwhelmed by the power of the momentum emanating from the psychotic process.
>
> After her fifth manic phase, my patient reported a dream which seemed to give hope. In the dream she was having another baby and saying to herself that this time she needed to look after it if she did not want to return to hospital. In fact despite my attempts to work on the dream with her, she developed another severe depressive episode, and when she recovered from this she had lost all recollection of having had the dream.

This alerted me to the fact that material that may appear terribly sensitive and full of meaning may prove to be an evacuation of insight by the psychotic part and that it will not necessarily be possible to utilise this material for therapeutic purposes. It is easy to get very enthusiastic about the expressed content in psychotic disorders, but time helps one to become more aware of the power of resistance to change.

Yet we still have to look after patients who are resistant to change. In such patients with schizophrenia, where delusions replace dreams, the challenge remains to decipher their meaning in order to find clues about the cause of a relapse. Case 3 illustrates such a situation.

## Case 3: Deciphering a delusion – what lies behind the smoke detector?

I was asked to visit Miss H, a patient in her late fifties. She had a diagnosis of chronic schizophrenia. She had never married and had lived all her life in her parents' house. Her parents had died a number of years ago. She had no other siblings or close family. She used to work in a factory but had been made redundant. She had been referred to our day hospital, but had recently stopped coming, refused all medication and become reclusive at home. Her care coordinator was worried about her increasing isolation and self-neglect leading to a need to consider formal admission.

Miss H lived in a gloomy, neglected terraced house that was in need of general attention. When I arrived the smoke detector in the hallway was bleeping, indicating the need to replace its battery.

Miss H remarked to me that the battery needed replacing. Then she switched her view and said that her neighbours were bugging her through the smoke detector. It was a bugging device. She was quite convinced that this was the case. She was in a withdrawn mental state, lacking insight into her delusional experiences.

She was subsequently admitted under the Mental Health Act 1983. In hospital she was prescribed medication but I also then had the opportunity to review her current life situation with her and other involved professionals.

When I initially saw Miss H at home, I had no associations to the bugging, merely experiencing it as a presenting symptom of a patient with a relapse of her psychosis. However, I was now able to think differently. The way the psychotic part of the mind works in psychosis is to project out and disown mental pain. It projects into objects in order to identify the object with what it is getting rid of, so as to distance itself from the problem.

Once she had been admitted and was being cared for by others in hospital, I think that Miss H felt less burdened and more supported. This led to a reduction of her need to project concretely into my mind that her smoke alarm was a bugging device so that I could start to feel freer to associate to the delusion and think about its meaning as a communication.

The question then became, 'What is it that has been bugging the patient?' What was it that she had needed to disown into her next-door neighbours and was now coming back at her through the smoke detector?

I then realised what was bugging her. She had lived all her life in the parental home. She was no longer working and in any case her pay would only have covered day-to-day living expenses. She had no money for the house, which was in need of urgent renovation including a new roof. The psychotic part disowned the worries that arose from thinking about all of this and projected the worry into the next-door neighbour. However, the worry would not go away and came back in the form of the neighbour bugging her through the smoke detector.

I put this to Miss H, who at that moment was able to see the problem and consider a possible solution, whereby the house would be sold by the council and arrangements made for her to move into a comfortable flat that would be financially manageable. Miss H appeared to be grateful for the understanding and response.

One might consider that Miss H's acceptance of this proposal arose out of the functioning of the non-psychotic part of the mind that is capable of thinking and reflection, the part that could realise that a new battery was required in the smoke detector and that the solution to her current difficulties lay in a new infusion of energy from outside helpers.

The psychotic part of the personality cannot metabolise and think; it can only project and disown what it cannot face. It may also enter into competitive envious rivalry with offered help, insisting that its way should prevail. A few days later, not wanting to face the need to move, Miss H's psychotic part projected her worries further. This time the bugging was experienced not as coming from the next-door neighbour but from a house twenty doors away and she even wrote from the ward to this house, whose owners were complete strangers to her, complaining of the bugging. A continued dialogue with Miss H became necessary to help her to face up to the problem.

Her case shows how delusions in psychosis, like dreams in neurosis, can be seen as important communications of the patient's concerns. However, in the psychoses, we also have to take account of the separate functioning of the psychotic and non-psychotic parts of the personality, and be mindful of the fact that the delusion is caused by the psychotic part disowning the work of the non-psychotic part. After the meaning of the delusion has been deciphered, the challenge is to find a way to create and maintain a constructive dialogue about it with the patient.

## Summary

Dreams may provide important clues in first assessments in general psychiatry. They may also offer indications of the patient's progress in psychotherapy. In supervised psychotherapy, trainees can learn first-hand about the depth of meaning that dreams can have.

Patients with major psychotic disorders may report dreams that seem very insightful, but it is always important to consider the possibility that they may be an evacuation of insight. We therefore need to be aware of the differences between dreams presented in neurotic disorders and those presented in psychotic disorders, and their potentially different clinical implications.

In schizophrenia, the challenge moves from understanding the hidden meaning in a dream to deciphering a delusion. Arriving at an understanding of the delusion may help us to understand the cause of a relapse. Typically, in contrast to dreams, the patient will be unable to provide associations to the delusion and one has to rely on information gathered from others as well as the workings of one's own mind to arrive at an understanding.

# 13

# Utilising the countertransference in psychosis

## Introduction

This chapter examines the importance of countertransference experiences in work with psychotic patients. In conjunction with a consideration of the content of delusions, countertransference experiences are of crucial importance when trying to understand the patient's communications. It takes time to gain confidence in examining and using one's feelings in this way. One is helped if one has had this experience in personal analysis, as well as the opportunity of exploring one's countertransference in supervision with less disturbed patients. However, junior doctors do not start psychiatry with the luxury of these experiences. They are thrown in at the deep end, finding themselves on the receiving end of psychotic patients' projections from their first day in psychiatry. This is not a subject that normally receives consideration in standard psychiatric textbooks.

I will begin by reviewing some theoretical psychoanalytic contributions on the transference and countertransference in psychosis. I will then use some clinical examples to illustrate the central importance of utilising the countertransference in clinical practice.

## Some theoretical considerations

In psychoanalytic terms the countertransference has been defined as 'The whole of the analyst's unconscious reactions to the individual analysand – especially to the analysand's own transference' (Laplanche and Pontalis 1973, p. 92). In terms of psychosis, this means our emotional reactions to what the patient projects into us. Since projection is predominantly an unconscious process, we become aware of it only through aspects that are more preconscious and accessible for examination, as the clinical examples will illustrate.

However, before considering countertransference in psychosis, we must first clarify that transference indeed occurs, and consider its intensity and effects.

In 1915, Freud expressed the view that no transference occurred in schizophrenia. He thought that these individuals' repudiation of the external world represented an attempt to return to a primitive object-less narcissistic state. Since the psychoanalytic method relied on the interpretation of the transference, there was no place for this approach in schizophrenia and ipso facto no countertransference experience to explore.

Herbert Rosenfeld (1952) revived interest in the analytic technique in psychosis, using Melanie Klein's seminal work with small children as inspiration. In Klein's work, through interpretation of the positive and negative transference from the beginning of the analysis, the fundamental principles of analysis were retained, and a transference neurosis developed. Rosenfeld writes:

> All the experience thus gained has been used as guiding principles in the analysis of psychotics, particularly acute schizophrenic patients. If we avoid attempts to produce a positive transference by direct reassurance or expressions of love, and simply interpret the positive and negative transference, the psychotic manifestations attach themselves to the transference, and, in the same way as a transference neurosis develops in the neurotic, so, in the analysis of psychotics, there develops what may be called a 'transference psychosis'. The success of the analysis depends on our understanding of the psychotic manifestations in the transference situation.
>
> (H. A. Rosenfeld 1952, p. 65)

Rosenfeld drew attention to Freud's (1924) statement that 'Transference neuroses correspond to a conflict between the ego and the id, narcissistic neuroses to a conflict between the ego and superego, and psychoses, to one between the ego and external world.' In Rosenfeld's view this implied that Freud did not think the superego could play a

167

significant role in schizophrenia (Freud 1924, p. 149; H. A. Rosenfeld 1952, p. 68).

Rosenfeld emphasised the usefulness of the classical Kleinian account of the early development of the ego and superego, linked to introjection of the good and bad breast, in understanding psychosis. The degree of harshness of this early superego could affect the individual's capacity to work through the depressive position. Persecutory delusions, such as experiencing critical voices or paranoid delusions of being observed or followed, could be explained as manifestations of a harsh superego. The analyst may be the recipient of projections of an idealised object in order to protect the good object and Rosenfeld emphasised the need to resist acting out in the countertransference through direct expressions of love rather than sticking to interpretation. If feelings are experienced as unbearable then the patient might regress from the depressive position to paranoid–schizoid states or become manic; either way Rosenfeld strongly advocated a close adherence to the analytic interpretive approach.

He regarded problems encountered in early object relationships as the primary issue to be addressed in schizophrenia, analysing on classical Kleinian lines, though he conceded that, 'One has to assume that a certain predisposition to the psychosis exists from birth' (H. A. Rosenfeld 1963, p. 168).

In part Rosenfeld's statement of his views evolved in response to the approach at Chestnut Lodge where the technique of strict adherence to classical transference interpretation, as opposed to the introduction of more non–analytic supportive responses, was not accorded the same central importance. However, Searles, who worked there, was also very aware of the intensity of transference phenomena and the need to avoid being drawn into any acting out of an erotic transference, which could be covering over underlying feelings of despair.

Searles' theoretical concepts of schizophrenia were based on Mahler's (1952) ideas on symbiosis. He writes:

The aetiological roots of schizophrenia are formed when the mother-infant symbiosis fails to resolve into the individuation of mother and infant – or, still more harmfully, fails even to become at all firmly established – because of deep ambivalence on the part of the mother which hinders the integration and differentiation of the infant's and young child's ego.

(Searles 1961, p. 524)

He developed his own formulation of progress through an 'out-of-contact' phase, a phase of 'ambivalent symbiosis', towards a 'full or preambivalent symbiosis' and finally the phase of 'resolution of the symbiosis'.

Searles summarises:

> I consider it valid to conceive of the patient's transference to the therapist as being in the nature, basically, of a relatedness to the therapist as a mother figure from whom the patient has never, as yet become deeply differentiated. Furthermore, I believe that this 'sickest' – least differentiated – aspect of the patient's ego functioning becomes called into play in any relationship which develops anything like the intensity that the therapeutic relationship develops.
>
> (Searles 1963b, p. 662)

Despite their differing theoretical frameworks, both Rosenfeld and Searles highlight the intensity of the transference in psychosis and therefore the stimulation to act out in the countertransference to seek some quick relief for the patient rather than stay more thoughtfully with the situation.

This points to the need to consider the place of countertransference feelings in thinking about patients with psychosis, a subject given relatively little specific mention in the literature. An exception to this was David Rosenfeld (1992), a psychoanalyst from Argentina who wrote:

> I feel that the study of the countertransference (and of psychotic transference) are the *via regia* to future investigations in the treatment of the psychoses, just as dreams were the royal road to the investigation of the neuroses. The patient makes the therapist experience intense and violent emotions, which he cannot express in words.
>
> (D. Rosenfeld 1992, p. 4)

In a general review of the countertransference, Hanna Segal points out that there is a difference from the transference.

> The analyst's capacity to contain feelings aroused in him by the patient can be seen as an equivalent to the function of a mother containing the infant's projections, to use Bion's model (1967). Where the patients act instinctively, however, the analyst subjects

his state of mind to an examination – a reflection, albeit, much of the time preconscious.

(Segal 1981b, p. 83)

Segal remains critical of aspects to the countertransference 'where analytic sins have been committed in its name. In particular, rationalisations are found for acting out under the pressure of countertransference, rather than using it as a guide for understanding' (Segal 1981b, p. 87).

She was referring to experiences with analytic supervisees in training, with non-psychotic patients, who say things like 'the patient projected into me' or 'made me angry' rather than realising that such feelings indicate a failure on their part to understand and use the countertransference constructively.

Segal's comments indicate the need for caution in our attempts to use the countertransference. Freud had warned that as a result of the patient's influence on the physician's unconscious feelings, 'no psycho-analyst goes further than his own complexes and internal resistances permit' and consequently emphasised the need for the analyst to submit to a personal analysis (Freud 1910, pp. 144–145; Laplanche and Pontalis 1973, pp. 92–93). Unfortunate incidents of acting out in the analytic setting, such as Jung's relationship with his patient Sabina Spielrein, help us to understand how the emphasis on the need to control and master countertransference feelings developed (Britton 2003).

It was many decades before Paula Heimann (1950) redressed the balance by stressing the fact that all analysts were having countertransference reactions and using them to increase their sensitivity towards their patients. Such reactions need to be recognised and thought about in order to minimise the risk that they may stimulate the analyst to act out. Joseph has also written about how the patient invariably nudges one to act out. This is the price of involvement, but it needs constant monitoring and thinking about within the total transference situation (Joseph 1985).

The experience of the countertransference in more neurotic patients contrasts markedly with the experience with psychotic patients in general psychiatry, where every day one is projected into by the patients in ways that threaten to overwhelm one's mind. Clinicians must not only be aware of the risk of mishandling the countertransference, as in neuroses, but also learn how to recognise it and survive with their own questioning faculties intact, even when subjected to the most powerful projections. Yet, if one can survive the experience and get support from others with one's thinking and associations, the countertransference indeed becomes the *via regia* to understanding psychosis.

## Clinical issues

When working with psychosis in everyday psychiatry, the clinician needs to develop the ability to understand the patient's presenting delusions as a form of communication. Understanding one's countertransference reactions as projective communications from the patient will help in making sense of the delusional material and will facilitate a movement from an initial psychotic monologue into a meaningful dialogue with the patient. The following vignettes illustrate the crucial importance of taking into account one's countertransference experience when dealing with psychotic states.

### *Monitoring one's changing countertransference experience*

A patient previously unknown to our service presented to the emergency clinic in an unpleasant and demanding mood. He was referred on to my outpatient clinic where he presented in a similar mood, indiscriminately angry and unsatisfied with any suggestions I offered to try to help. In the end he stormed out, somewhat to my relief as I did not fancy trying to instigate a section in the outpatient setting. At the time I felt that I was seeing someone with a difficult personality disorder with poor tolerance to stress who could become quite unpleasant if things were not the way he wanted them.

I was familiar with the countertransference feelings stirred up by a patient with a severe personality disorder who cannot face their own depressive states and deals with them by blaming others for neglecting their needs, making one feel very negative towards them. In the case of this patient there was no evidence of any delusions and at the time I did not consider that I might be the recipient of a powerful projection from a patient with schizophrenia, with a psychotic part that was angry about his currently being in a needy state.

The difference in his state the next time I saw him took me by surprise. He had been admitted to our hospital. At this point I learned that the background

171

history was that he had a diagnosis of paranoid schizophrenia, had lived in a group home, but had recently been moved on to independent accommodation which lay in our catchment area, without anyone being informed of the move.

His affect now was completely cold and flat. He said that he had a rat in his stomach. This came across as a very concrete delusion. I felt that I had no associations to it, and did not realise at the time that this in itself was a very marked countertransference reaction. I felt that all my analytic beliefs in psychosis were being challenged and found wanting, as I could not make any sense of the delusion. I felt that all the organically orientated psychiatrists who regarded analytic contributions to understanding psychosis as manufactured phantasies, based on no scientific evidence, were right, certainly in this case. I remembered an eminent organic psychiatrist, when I was training in psychiatry, saying in relation to the varying contents to delusions, that there was pathogenesis, the cause of the condition, and pathoplasty, the variations in the individual make-up that led to the varied forms that delusions took, but that delusions could be looked at entirely from an organic perspective.

We kept the patient in hospital and treated him with antipsychotic medication and supportive team involvement. Three weeks later, when seeing him for review, I found that my countertransference had completely changed. I was able to think and feel warmly towards the patient with sympathy for his current problems. Moreover, the delusion of the rat in his stomach had now become full of meaning.

I was no longer thinking of it as a rat in his stomach but as his rattiness that he could not stomach. The psychotic part of the mind cannot think; it can only seek relief through acting as a muscular organ to evacuate the thinking done by the non-psychotic part. It collects memories, Bion's ideographs, for the purpose of evacuating or communicating the problems it is encountering.

Here is a patient with chronic schizophrenia who is being moved into independent accommodation and expected to cope on his own. The non-psychotic part is troubled by this. The psychotic part deals with the rattiness that it cannot stomach by concretely projecting it in the delusion of the rat in his stomach. In Segal's terms this is a symbolic equation, or in Bion's terms the formation of a bizarre object, where what has been projected, and what has been projected into have become one and the same.

Since the patient's aim was to disown his rattiness in order to avoid having to think about it, it produced the countertransference response in me of being unable to have any creative associations at the time. This also accounts for the patient's flattened and cold affect when he described having

172

the rat in his stomach, as the aim of the delusion was to obliterate all associated emotional feelings. However, at the same time the psychotic part could be seen as aiming to communicate the patient's problem by expressing it in the form of a delusion, in order to seek help. Getting his state of mind into others led to his admission.

When the patient felt more relaxed and contained on the ward, from both medication and the team's involvement, his need to project so concretely receded. I then felt that I had the space to think in my own right and I could appreciate the symbolic meaning of the delusion of the rat in his stomach. Moreover, instead of being dominated by the projection of a cold affect that flattened my sensitivities, I was now able to experience warm, caring feelings. When I put it to the patient that he had been left on his own and that what he wanted from us was active support, he expressed appreciation for this understanding.

This case illustrates the central role that the countertransference plays when relating to a patient's delusional material. In an area where one might be tempted to think that one's own personal reactions are not relevant, namely in an encounter with a patient in a severe psychotic state, I hope that I have shown that paradoxically they are of the utmost importance, and that we need constantly to note our reactions and think about them, until we find an opportunity to use them in the service of the patient's needs.

## Paralysis in the countertransference

The case of a young man of 23 with a diagnosis of schizophrenia was presented for discussion at a fortnightly psychosis workshop I used to run jointly with Dr Garelick, consultant psychotherapist at Claybury Hospital, for professionals in training. The problem was that he remained in a persistently disturbed state.

This young man was the eldest of three children. As a child he was always seeking his mother's attention and from adolescence was openly aggressive to his father. On leaving school, he failed to settle into a job.

There was a strong psychosomatic theme to his childhood medical history. As a baby he had an operation for undescended testes and at age 11 he presented with tics and a squint. At 15 he had his ears pinned back and at 17 had one eyebrow raised, both operations undergone for no good reason, according to his mother.

He spent time in his teens in remand homes for petty crimes. Eventually, after setting his clothes on fire, he had his first psychiatric admission at 18. He had a series of short admissions in psychotic states, which at first were thought to be drug induced. Later he was diagnosed as schizophrenic and placed on depot antipsychotic medication.

He was persistently aggressive towards his father and disinhibited in his behaviour towards his mother; he wanted to kiss her and talked continuously of wanting sex with her. He was therefore sent to stay with his grandmother. Increasingly disturbed behaviour with paranoia towards her neighbours had led to the current admission.

After seven months on an acute ward he was transferred to a rehabilitation villa. Following an initial settled period, he again became increasingly disruptive. He was responding to voices, and kept absconding from the home and returning, complaining by turns of being persecuted by the staff and by his parents.

He had the delusion that he had a silver and silk lined scrotum that made him attractive, and that he had a three-year-old son by his girlfriend whom he wanted to give as a gift to his family. In reality, he had only a superficial relationship with a girl in the rehabilitation villa.

He developed a belief that if his girlfriend sneezed, he would get better. This later changed into a persistently held delusional belief that if one of the doctors sneezed in his presence, he would be cured. As his paranoia and thought disorder increased, his medication was changed to clozapine, the drug of choice for the most intransigent cases of schizophrenia.

At this point the presentation of his history concluded and the case was opened for discussion.

## The workshop discussion

The presenting junior doctor was asked how he understood the situation. He replied that it was a case of loss of ego boundaries in schizophrenia and the treatment was clozapine.

He added that the patient's mother colluded with him in referring to his illness as 'the sneeze', because she was frightened of his anger. He also reported that while the patient kept himself isolated, he worked very hard in the hospital factory making crackers. Prior to this he used to deliver the hospital post, but kept opening it to read! He also talked about joining the army.

I felt that the problem was how to make contact with this patient beyond just prescribing clozapine. It was necessary to stand up to his intimidating behaviour but also to become involved with him and attempt to understand the way his mind was working. His history showed that the patient had found ways to disown his emotions by projecting into his body and requesting repeated operations. When this failed he then turned to petty crime and drug taking. Finally he had resorted to projecting his desires and difficulties more directly into others, ending up by tormenting his family.

The staff's problem now was to find a way of thinking and helping the patient to think when they were at the receiving end of such concrete projections. However, as Dr Garelick pointed out, there seemed to be something more positive around now than previously with this patient. His hard work in the hospital cracker factory suggested a movement towards reparative attempts, in contrast to his earlier mindless destructiveness. Nevertheless, he seemed to centre all his hopes on a quick cure through the doctor's sneeze!

## The doctor's countertransference experience

Workshop members then asked the presenting junior doctor about his countertransference experience while he was with the patient. It emerged that he and his senior registrar shared the same experience, namely that they were both extremely worried about what might happen if they were to sneeze in a session with the patient, fearing that this would have a catastrophic effect. Both doctors had become immobilised by the power of the patient's projections. They needed to be freed to think, and to feel comfortable about blowing their noses or sneezing in front of the patient!

In the ensuing discussion about the power and concreteness of the patient's projections, the presenting junior doctor recalled how the patient had acquired a lock of his girlfriend's hair and swallowed it, expressing a wish for a magical merging with her through oral incorporation. This idealised incorporation led people to link this with his delusion of the special attractive silver and silk scrotal lining.

The workshop seemed now to be freeing itself from concreteness to ask further questions about the sneeze. It transpired that the patient's phantasy was that he would be enveloped by the sneeze which, through processes of splitting and projection, would contain minute fragments of the other person. Thus the patient would take in the other person, the doctor, and identify and merge with them in an idealised identification.

Now the workshop members were in a position to fully understand the doctors' countertransference experience. The doctors feared that, if they sneezed, they might lose their patient as potentially responsive by giving him a magical cure. The fear was that the patient would then remain

175

forever in an inaccessible, mad, unthinking state that they would have been responsible for producing.

Understanding their countertransference fears of sneezing helped to free the doctors to think, enabling them to address the patient about his conflicting wishes on the one hand to achieve an isolated omnipotent identification and on the other hand to find a way of being with others as separate supportive fellow human beings.

The case again illustrates the importance of paying careful attention to the countertransference experience in attempting to overcome an impasse, beyond relying solely on medication for the answer.

*Doubt in the countertransference*

Whenever we encounter a patient with delusions, we are likely to feel doubts about the fairness of our reactions in judging his experience as delusional. We oscillate in our minds between seeing the material as straightforward and as pathological. We are likely to feel a tremendous pressure to take the patient's story at face value as we can then avoid any uncomfortable feelings of chaos, madness and uncertainty. We all hate to feel that we have lost our bearings. We have to constantly ask ourselves whether we are hearing a straightforward communication from the non–psychotic part of the patient's personality or a rationalisation from the psychotic part in denial about its disturbed state.

In these situations the way to move forward is through a full, open discussion with the team and the carers to sort it out. Only when dealing with psychotic states will one have the countertransference experience of uncertainty about whether patients' statements are true or delusional, so this experience can be a clue to alert one to the possibility of an underlying psychosis. Since patients are likely to deny and rationalise their problems, one has to turn elsewhere to get information as to the true state of affairs, whether from the nearest relative or key worker. Problems occur when doctors are unable to understand or accept the conflict inside themselves, which may lead them to accept everything their patient says uncritically and discount any different view expressed by the close relatives or professionals as intolerant and prejudiced. This is particularly likely to occur at times when decisions are being made about compulsory admissions or in relation to tribunals making decisions about discharge.

A real danger can arise at hospital managers' hearings, where members are unable to accommodate the uncertainty engendered by the patient's communications because they lack the theoretical framework that would enable them to differentiate between the psychotic and non-psychotic parts, and rely on a solely logical legalistic approach.

> A patient was brought into hospital by the police because he had behaved aggressively and inappropriately to two total strangers, young women on a bus. The police were called and decided that he was mentally ill, so brought him straight to hospital and did not charge him. At first he was placed on the locked ward, where he assaulted another patient and was also threatening to the nursing staff. He had only recently been transferred to the open ward when he appealed against his detention. The staff felt that the assault was a serious one and that the patient needed more time in hospital for further careful assessment.
>
> The manager's hearing took the line that there was no legally demonstrated proof that the patient had ever committed an offence in the community, since the police had never charged him, and in the absence of such evidence his continued admission was not sustainable.

Occasionally, what might appear delusional may prove otherwise, so we always need to keep an open mind.

> A patient had been admitted the previous year in a florid and chaotic psychotic state in a state of self-neglect, after a friend had alerted the mental health team about her concerns. The patient was a woman from the Far East who was living an isolated life in the UK. A year later, she had a relapse that necessitated a further admission.
>
> While she was clearly again in a bewildered florid psychotic state, she reported that a tenant living in her place had been murdered. The junior doctor was sufficiently questioning about this to phone the local police. At first he received a negative response, but he was not convinced. When he persisted further, he found out that indeed a tenant had been murdered and his torso dismembered.
>
> When this was discussed with the patient, her response was dismissive. She showed a complete lack of interest in this extraordinary event. Apparently the tenant had occupied a downstairs room in her place. She showed no curiosity at all about when it had occurred, saying she was upstairs at the time praying in her temple. When asked how the murder had been discovered, apparently the next day through a broken window,

she again showed no interest, dismissively saying that she had been praying at an outside temple.

Even though the murder actually occurred and was not a delusion, the patient's total lack of interest in an event that anyone in a non-psychotic state of mind would have shown some curiosity about was quite extraordinary and indicative of the capacity of the psychotic part of the mind to annihilate curiosity.

### Humour, humanity and perseverance

Humour is an important means by which we can communicate a common interest and involvement, and links with humanity and caring. Other involved professionals may share in the humour, where a common sense of purpose is present. For humour to occur one needs to have been able to separate oneself out to think independently. Humour is impossible when one feels overwhelmed by psychotic projections that obliterate difference.

In a personal communication, Ronald Britton summarised the role of humour:

I seriously think 'Don't take yourself too seriously' implies a third position.

In other words, humour enables one to step aside from the intensity of involvement in the transference/countertransference situation, adopting the third position in a reflective parental role. The patient may move into the third position with you, for example when my patient on admission said that he was God's older brother, but smiled and joined me in the reflective position, when I said that he must have been really pissed off with his younger brother getting all the publicity!

The message to the patient is 'Don't take yourself too seriously', meaning do not become too dogmatic in your assertions. In fact, the patient who asserted he was God's older brother remained very controlling and pedantic in his way of talking when our paths crossed again many years later.

In severe psychotic states, where the patient persistently presents in an overwhelmingly concrete fashion, humour and reflectiveness can still have a place among the staff. When dealing on a daily basis with severe psychotic states, humour represents a countertransference response of interest, self-belief and survival. It is an implicit statement that one has preserved and supported one's own separate viewpoint. Humour is linked to an appreciation of the power and complexity of the underlying psychopathology and provides us with a means of sharing this appreciation with others, who are also involved in a situation where they are seemingly faced with overwhelming odds and yet surviving them.

The following serve as clinical illustrations.

*An 'intermittent explosive disorder'*

I was asked to go abroad to give a talk to an organisation that specialised in early intervention services in psychosis. They indicated that their priority was a presentation of the latest statistics around such services in the UK, rather than a dynamic understanding, so I had to amend my original presentation, and went to the meeting with some apprehension. However, when I arrived, somewhat contradictorily, they now said that they were much more interested in what I personally had to say. I was still concerned that the meaning of whatever I said might become lost in translation.

> I was made most welcome and well received at the conference. In the afternoon, a young doctor, a member of an early psychosis intervention team, presented a case that was giving him problems. The set-up of the service was similar to the UK, where patients are followed weekly by the team for two to three years.
>
> The patient was a man in his early thirties who had never left home. He developed paranoid beliefs that he was being followed and watched, for which he sought help. He had been placed on antipsychotic medication by the early onset service and delegated for supervised individual sessions to the young doctor. The doctor described how the patient was not forthcoming in the first year, but in the second didn't seem to stop talking.
>
> The patient had said to the therapist, 'I don't suffer from schizophrenia but an intermittent explosive disorder!' The history was that prior to becoming troubled by his paranoid state, he had for the first time in his life had a brief relationship with a woman. He described sex as boring. His sister was now trying to get him involved with a female friend of hers to encourage another relationship.
>
> The challenge was to find something to say to help the doctor out of an impasse in which he felt impotent. The shared humour was to realise that the

179

patient was quite right in what he was saying about having 'an intermittent explosiveness disorder', even if his insight was very limited.

He was right that he did not suffer from schizophrenia; rather, he had an affective disorder dominated by a severe ego-destructive superego that had prevented him from separating from the parental home and developing a mind and life of his own. Only in his thirties was he beginning to show some signs of change, which were noted and encouraged by his sister.

Of course any sign of movement stimulated an envious backlash from his superego, leading to his experiences of being watched and followed. For the first time, recently, he reported that he had had two very minor temper tantrums. While most of us may have emotional outbursts as every-day occurrences, for him these felt very unusual, and led to his self-diagnosis as having an intermittent explosive disorder.

This discussion helped to free the doctor from regarding the patient as having a paranoid schizophrenic disorder, which had made him feel that he could only be a passive listener unsure of what to say, and enabled him to consider adopting the role of an auxiliary superego supporting the patient's developmental growth. In this context, one would agree with the patient about the correctness of his self-diagnosis, while pointing out that the explosiveness is in fact a manifestation of health to be encouraged, not stifled.

Having survived the initial pressures around the presentation, the doctor, the involved audience and I had arrived at an understanding that enabled us to experience a shared humour over the interesting way the patient presented his problems through his self-diagnosis.

### The broken alarm clock

A penalty of involvement with psychosis is that one is constantly liable to be misunderstood. The doctor may be tuning into the psychotic wavelength as the priority, while others who do not appreciate the need for this may complain that the way he is talking to the patient shows a lack of sensitivity to their feelings.

Many years ago I was asked to attend another event abroad in which as well as giving a talk, I would be involved in a case discussion. The case history was to be presented by the psychologist who saw the patient to be discussed. Apparently the patient, who was seen in his group home, had disrobed in a recent session, upsetting the psychologist, who then did not attend the event as he was reported to be unwell.

180

The plan was changed for the patient alone to come, with the group home manager to attend and provide the background history, and for me then to interview the patient. I learned from the group home manager that the patient suffered from a recurrent schizo-affective disorder and if he stopped his medication, he would become increasingly disturbed and very difficult to contain in the group home setting. However, there were very few hospital beds available, as the government policy was that most patients with psychotic disorders were to be managed in group homes.

Recently the patient not only had stopped his antipsychotic medication, but also was diabetic and was being inconsistent about taking his insulin. When I saw the patient he presented in a quite relaxed state. He said that he spent his days going to the library. He had been up all last night preparing what he would be saying to me. He talked at some length about how in his adolescence he had spent some time in Australia with his mother, and waxed lyrical about the particular texture of the leaves of the eucalyptus tree. His group home manager had warned me that this was what he tended to do. The patient then said that he did not have any problems apart from the fact that his alarm clock had broken, so that he needed someone to wake him in the morning.

I saw the situation as a crisis in which the group home manager needed to be listened to and given support. The psychotic part of the patient had gained the upper hand, so that he was disruptive of his sessions with the psychologist, unreliable with his insulin injections and failing to take his antipsychotic medication. The psychotic part had been up all night acting as a lawyer preparing for his appearance in court the next day to present his case to me. There was only one glimmer of hope in the patient's disowning of the insight arrived at by the non-psychotic part, that he was in an alarming state which he was trying to ignore. The presence of this insight was indicated by his referral to the broken alarm clock, by means of which he suggested that others would need to awaken him to the true state of affairs and stand up to the psychotic part of his personality to prevent him losing his place in the group home. He had been there for a few years and valued it.

I put all this to him, and emphasised the importance of his cooperation with the group home manager, if he wasn't to relapse and lose his placement. This was a situation where it was necessary to confront the psychotic part when it was getting out of hand. The group home manager was very grateful for my intervention and support, and could appreciate the humour and symbolic meaning in the patient's statement that he was perfectly fine apart from his alarm clock being broken.

181

Unfortunately, the people who had invited me to the day event and to interview the patient did not see the situation from this perspective. They were especially doubtful about the need to confront the patient and regarded the patient as too cognitively impaired to understand the symbolic meaning to the alarm clock. They had expected me to be non-challenging, and more uncritically accepting of the material that the patient chose to bring and to become involved in an exploration of his references to the eucalyptus leaves and their association to his feelings about his mother. They were unhappy with my view that there was something that felt quite perverse, slippery and triumphant about the way the patient brought this well-worn story, which to me seemed to cover up the danger of an imminent relapse.

While establishing an empathic understanding of the reality of suffering from schizophrenia is important in building up a relationship with a patient, and at times it is important to accept that psychopathological symptoms can be protective against the threat of disintegration (Thorgaard and Rosenbaum 2006), at other times, as this case illustrates, one has to stand up to the psychotic part to try to forestall a more serious relapse.

## Summary

Historically speaking psychoanalysts have remained wary about making use of their countertransference. While exploring the countertransference can facilitate increased sensitivity and empathy, if not first carefully thought through it can lead to inappropriate acting out by the analyst or to blaming the patient for one's own lack of understanding.

However, paradoxically, in psychosis where one initially can feel quite bewildered by the presented material, countertransference experience remains one of the most important and essential tools in reaching an understanding of delusional content. This is because the main defence against the awareness of psychic pain is projection of this by the psychotic part. The awareness is disowned into objects to create delusions and into caring people to create their countertransference feelings. With delusions, unlike with dreams, we cannot ask the patient for associations but have to undertake the reconstruction work ourselves on their behalf.

The clinician's countertransference feelings will mirror the patient's state of mind. If they have projected feelings that they have experienced as totally unbearable and have murderously attacked, then the clinician's mind will be affected so that he or she feels deskilled, unable to think or have constructive associations. If the projection becomes less intense and the aspect of the patient that wants help has more room to emerge, then one may start to develop constructive associations.

As we are always dealing with two parts of the personality, a common countertransference feeling is doubt about whether to believe that a communication is a statement of fact or the attempted rationalisation of a delusion. Feeling that we are faced with this conundrum can sometimes be a useful sign alerting us that we are in the presence of a major psychotic disorder, since such countertransference feelings are not typically encountered in the same way in borderline states or neurotic disorders.

Finally humour, linked with the interest aroused through sharing of countertransference experiences with involved staff, is important in maintaining interest and combating burnout when working in very demanding situations.

## PART FOUR

# The Psychotic Wavelength in Affective Disorders

# 14

# Why the cycle in a clinical psychosis?
# A psychoanalytic perspective on recurrent manic depressive psychosis

## Introduction

The opportunities for psychoanalytic study of manic depressive psychosis have become more limited since the closure of the specialist analytically orientated inpatient units in the NHS and the changes at Chestnut Lodge in the United States.[4] In this chapter, I discuss the case of a patient with recurrent manic depressive psychosis, who was followed in the NHS over a fifteen-year period. Both past and more recent contributions from the analytic literature are reviewed for the light they shed on this clinical material and the condition in general. Based on the case study, an explanation for the repetitive nature of the psychosis is suggested.

At the beginning of the twentieth century, Kraepelin divided major psychotic disorders into the organic and the functional. In the latter category he included dementia praecox (schizophrenia) and manic depressive psychosis. Kraepelin viewed manic depressive psychosis as a biological derangement, though he thought that in some cases psychological factors might act as precipitants. Kraepelin wrote, 'The real cause for the malady must be sought in permanent changes which are very often, perhaps always innate' (Kraepelin 1921, p. 180).

The psychopathology of manic depressive psychosis can seem to have 'a life of its own'. Recurrent manic depressive psychosis can produce unpredictable violent and destructive behaviour, especially during the manic phases, requiring extensive periods of hospitalisation.

There are very few case reports in the literature of analytic follow-up of recurrent manic depressive states over an extended period of time.

Perhaps this can be explained, not only by the difficulty posed by the patient's psychopathology, but also the need for institutional back-up facilities. Indeed Fenichel (1946, p. 414) wrote: 'the most extensive planned psychoanalytical study of the manic–depressive disorders, needed for the benefit of the patient and for the benefit of science, must be undertaken within the institutions'. The situation has not been helped over the years by the closure of the specialist analytically orientated inpatient units in the UK, at the Maudsley and Shenley hospitals (Freeman 1988; Jackson and Williams 1994), and the pressure for change at Chestnut Lodge in the United States (Silver 1997).

When I started work as a general psychiatrist, I decided that I wanted to see a patient analytically in the health service, with a disorder that I would not expect to see in my private practice. I was curious to learn more about the disorder through analysis, and wanted to apply any general understanding I gained to the non-analytic patients, as well as sharing any insights with my nursing and medical staff.

One might have expected that singling out one patient for analytic treatment would lead to resentment among the staff, as creating a special situation. However, because my analytic involvement was seen as part of a regular commitment to the unit, tensions did not arise. Murray Jackson (1989) reported a similar experience when giving analytic psychotherapy to a manic depressive patient.

I chose this particular patient because, at the time, her husband was supportive of an analytic approach, rather than a continued physical one. I had been impressed that during a period when she had been in hospital in a severely withdrawn state, her husband did not want her to have ECT, but to stay with the depression. When he expressed this view, she started to improve.

From my contact with her, I came to appreciate many features particular to recurrent manic depressive states. I will present the clinical material before considering the overall psychopathology in the context of the background psychoanalytic literature.

## Background history

Mrs J, now in her late forties, was brought up in the East End of London, part of an extended working-class family group. Her mother suffered from severe depression and was agoraphobic, but was never hospitalised. As a child, her mother was reported to have been very busy, with little time for her, and Mrs J was said to have sat silently for hours on her own, described as 'a miserable kid but mother's favourite'. Her father thought that children should be seen and not heard. Mrs J had a brother three years older than her, who was said to be mildly delinquent as a child, and was admired for this by his mother. Her mother had a stillbirth when Mrs J was 11. Throughout her adolescence her mother remained very controlling and was not to be contradicted.

Mrs J married a man from a similar working-class background, whose father had left home when Mr J was very young. Mrs J has two children, who have now grown up and left home.

Two years after the birth of her daughter, Mrs J moved from the East End to North London. At times Mrs J complained of feeling isolated from her background, though her new neighbours provided some support and did not ostracise her because of her illness. At times she has attended our psychiatric day hospital, which is adjacent to the outpatients' department where I saw her for sessions. The staff and day patients over the years have become somewhat like an extended family for her.

## Psychiatric history

Mrs J had her first breakdown in 1970 aged 23. She was admitted to hospital in an agitated state several weeks after the birth of her first child. During the analysis, she described what had gone through her mind at the time. She had developed the delusion that her daughter, who reminded her of her mother's stillbirth, was too beautiful to live. She had to fight an impulse to kill her daughter, finally cutting her own wrists. When Mrs J did not die, she went to the neighbours, was admitted to hospital and given ECT.

From my experience with this patient, as well as other cases of puerperal psychosis, I think that the baby daughter represented her individuality, whose separateness could not be tolerated by another part of herself, which was identified with an extremely narcissistic mother figure (see Chapter 15). In real life she was always supportive of her children's needs, in contrast to a markedly self-depriving attitude.

Five years later, she was again admitted with depression and treated with ECT. This admission took place a year after the birth of her son. The precipitant was a police inquiry at her husband's place of work. Since marrying, she had become totally reliant on her husband and was terrified that he would be taken away. From that time on she became dominated by an obsession with keeping the house tidy.

In 1980, 1981 and 1982 she had further hospital admissions for depression, and was treated each time with antidepressant medication.

In December 1982, arrangements were made for her to start analysis in January 1983. In January she had her first admission in a hypomanic state. Since then, she has had yearly admissions, always in a hypomanic state, lasting from three to five months, until the last three years.

During her admissions, she was given major tranquillisers as necessary, the prescribing responsibility left to the ward doctor. Since 1992, she has been on lithium, taken in therapeutic doses, but this did not have any immediate impact on her admissions pattern.

It was striking that all her admissions prior to analysis were for depression, and since for hypomania. She had had periods of hypomania prior to analysis, but they had not been severe enough to require hospitalisation.

The daily analytic support given during early protracted depressive phases meant that these could now be contained in the outpatient setting, but analytic intervention seemed to increase the length and severity of the manic phases of Mrs J's illness.

## Analysis

### Onset

The analysis began in a dramatic and unexpected way. The day she was due to start analysis, Mrs J presented in a hypomanic state requiring immediate hospitalisation. The day before admission, her husband had been quarrelling with his mother. Mrs J then heard a man's voice over her husband's CB radio calling her a whore, a prostitute and a Greek lover (it did not strike me at the time that Lucas is a common Greek name). She replied to the man's voice, saying that he should not talk like that in front of the children, and that she would meet him the next day at the local shopping green.

When she went next day to the green, she felt she was being followed and that she was going to be robbed. She then found herself going to the bank and opening a new account in her name. During the day she grew more and more hysterical and in the evening her husband took her into hospital. On arrival, she was convinced that he was the upset one who was going to be admitted, as he had fallen out with his mother. She thought that he had said to her, 'It's all right for you, you've got Dr Lucas'.

190

Looking back on this, I feel that she was reacting excitedly to the opening of a new account which the analysis provided, while her fear that it might expose her problematic relationship with her mother was disowned and located in her husband.

This initially hypomanic period lasted three months. She was far too restless ever to sit still in sessions. She spent a lot of time watering plants, and relating excitedly to other patients, often unable to control herself sexually. Towards the end, she expressed anxiety about lapsing back into depression if she could not keep up the mania, like Cinderella returning from the ball. Despite many different types of interpretation, her manic state seemed to have a life of its own. Eventually she returned to a depressive state, and became an outpatient.

## Depressive phases

In the ensuing sessions, in the first depressive phase, she sat in a chair, hardly moving and deathly pale, as if drained of all vitality. She stared ahead blankly. At times she would stare out of the window as if she was evacuating her aliveness through her eyes, and I would feel as though there was no one left in the room to talk to.

Anything I said felt like trying to conjure something out of nothing, and I thought to myself that other analysts would not put themselves in this situation, as it seemed so hopeless. To get any response, I had to ask her what was on her mind. Her replies were very pertinent, but the way she spoke had a deadening and distancing quality. For example, one comment she made was that she sat in a similar state at home, staring blankly at the television screen, and her husband was irritated by his inability to make contact with her. My attempt to interest her in what she had just said was greeted by silence. I felt that she only spoke because I asked her questions, as though she was still obeying her father's principle that children should only speak when spoken to. At one point she wondered why I put up with her, describing herself as a stuffed dummy. I felt that we were re-enacting a deadly feeding situation in which she was tremendously passive and could not criticise anything that I gave her. When I pointed this out to her, she said that friends had commented that she said nothing and kept herself hidden. This reply may sound misleadingly responsive; my dominating feeling was that I was having no impact on her.

Mrs J remained silent in sessions for months on end, unless I asked her what was on her mind. In the midst of this aridity, I was surprised when she reported an isolated dream, which seemed like an unexpected ray of hope. In her dream, it was my birthday, and I was being given the bumps; she had a larger house and both old and new acquaintances were present. I hoped that the dream indicated a celebration of my presence offering a larger place for her feelings. She rarely brought dreams, so it was interesting that a few years later, again in the midst of an arid depressive phase, she reported a similar dream, except that now it was her birthday. I hoped that this indicated a shift of an alive focus into herself, though objectively I had no external evidence for this movement.

The pattern of sessions in the depressive phases remained the same over the years. Sessions started with a few quick sentences, very hard to catch, followed by silence. This pattern mirrored her behaviour at home, when every morning she would get up at 6 a.m. to clear everything away in a panic, and then sit still.

I had drawn attention many times to the quick way she started sessions, followed by silence, yet the pattern persisted. She then often would not say anything else unless I asked her what was on her mind. Then she would say something directly related to her state, for example, describing how her daughter was frightened of visiting her grandmother (Mrs J's mother) as she was such a jealous and possessive person.

I formed the impression that as a result of the analysis, Mrs J was becoming conscious of what went on in the depressive phase, commenting, for instance, that she seemed to drain away her own aliveness. Yet the pattern persisted in which I would try to catch, rescue and enliven whatever she had said in her deadly dismissive way. When she then once asked me if she would ever change, I felt I could not find any evidence within myself at the time for an optimistic reply.

I felt that Mrs J was clinging on to an identification with an all-powerful mother figure, resistant to change out of both fear and obstinacy. She had become the all-powerful mother and I the helpless child. At times she became tight-lipped when I addressed her, as if she was actively refusing to take in food. This tight-lipped mannerism is something I have often since noticed with psychotically depressed patients in hospital, who refuse to acknowledge their needy state.

In the depressive phases of her illness, Mrs J had nothing good whatsoever to say about herself. She became socially crippled with agoraphobia and imagined that other people were unremittingly critical of her appearance and behaviour. Sometimes her obsessional preoccupations with tidying the house increased prior to her manic eruptions, although the suddenness of the change to hypomania always took me unawares.

At times, in the depressive phase, Mrs J talked more openly, but I still felt that what I would call, in shorthand, 'the deadening dynamic' was ever present. It was this self-suppressing quality that seemed to make an eruption into another manic episode inevitable.

## Manic phases

The first feature I would like to emphasise was the feeling of helplessness engendered by the autonomy and strength of the manic process. By the time of the third manic episode, Mrs J likened its start to an out-of-control period and said, 'This time my mania needs to be faced and worked at'. My ward registrar noticed how desperately she tried to stop it progressing.

At the onset of the fourth manic episode, she had a dream of a Roman orgy in which she was both a participator and an onlooker, not liking what she was seeing but helpless to stop it. I also felt like a helpless onlooker.

In the first four manic episodes, I felt that the dominating purpose was to triumph over me and anything that I said. Towards the end of the second manic episode, she said in a triumphant voice, 'Isn't it about time that you gave up?' I felt a dreadful despair, akin to the feelings I have already described, when Mrs J deadened and distanced herself in the depressive phase. These triumphantly deadening forces came across as a powerful, highly organised structure in her personality, along the lines described by Leslie Sohn in his paper on the narcissistic identificate (Sohn 1985b; see also Chapter 15). However, by the time of Mrs J's fifth manic episode, I was hoping that some change might have occurred. Although she was still extremely overactive, for the first time she was able to stay in her chair during sessions, and started to talk in a more concerned way.

At the onset of this manic episode, she recounted a dream in which the hospital was closing (it was in fact scheduled for closure) and I was leaving, and she said to me, 'What about myself?' She thought that the dream showed evidence of self-concern, and she contrasted it with what she called 'her usual sadistic dreams' when hypomanic. By this, she explained she meant dreams she had experienced in which she was being stabbed in the chest or penetrated anally by a hot poker.

She also started to express gratitude openly for the analysis, saying, 'I know you may not think it, but I do take in what you say. You must think I am worthwhile and are trying to help me see this'. She also thanked me for persevering with her, saying 'I am not an easy person, you know', and added that she felt 'more worthwhile now as a person'.

193

On the ward, she made an interesting statement to the nursing staff. She said that on previous admissions, when high, she felt as though she was behaving like a call-girl and so should have been paid for it. She now saw that this was not the way forward and said, 'I may as well work as a pimp for Dr Lucas – be Dick's angel'. She said that she would leave her husband and marry Dr Lucas, but then checked herself, and said that her husband was OK, and that she would marry Dr Lucas when her husband died.

I felt that she might be giving some recognition to the analysis, and her husband's supportiveness, as well as more openly expressing her hatred of this dependency, 'being a pimp for Dr Lucas'. However, when she started to talk of her analysis in idealised terms at home, her daughter's reported response was, 'Well, if Dr Lucas is so fucking good, why do you keep going back into hospital?'

I think that Mrs J's daughter's view was more realistic than my hope that change was beginning to materialise, although for a short while after the fifth manic episode abated, things did look more hopeful.

### A brief more accessible period

Following the fifth manic phase, there was a short period of about a week in which Mrs J appeared more open to considering her state. She reported a dream in which she had had another baby and found herself saying, 'This time I am going to have to support the baby if I'm not to go back to hospital'.

I felt that the dream represented the central problem of her need to look after herself as represented by the baby, rather than flatten her own individuality and resubmit herself to an internal tyrannical mother figure. I pointed this out to her.

Her response was that she was afraid that her husband and son were going to be mugged. They had recently objected to spending time at her mother's, as she was so domineering. She then recalled a recurrent child-hood fear when she went to school, that not only her parents but also the house would have vanished when she returned home. I felt all this indicated her dire fear of deviating from total submission to the internal mother figure for fear of losing everything.

For a few days she continued to be responsive to what I said, making me feel more hopeful, but this did not last long. She then reverted, in a more determined way than ever, to obliterating herself. This was evidenced by heightened obsessionality in the house, washing and ironing excessively, as if she was trying to wash herself away. One night this process reached a crescendo when she entertained active suicidal thoughts of going to drown herself, there and then, in a nearby canal, because she was unable to iron all the creases out of her sheets.

By this time, Mrs J was talking in an alarmingly cold and deadly manner about the possibility of committing suicide. Somehow we seemed to survive this phase and her manner became warmer again. However, it was interesting that by this point she had no recollection of her dream about the need to look after the baby. This episode seemed to illustrate how anything positive that seemed to be struggling to get itself established could be swept away by the presence of well-organised negating forces, bringing us back to the manic depressive cycle repeating itself.

## *Later manic episodes*

Instead of lessening in intensity, Mrs J's last two manic episodes increased in severity. She became quite aggressive and defiant, setting off fire alarms, and finally, in her last major admission she had to be sectioned for the first time. Her husband became quite disheartened, saying that he thought he would stick by her but nothing he did made any difference. I felt the same way. The last session before a summer break was typical of her state then. She came in and pulled up her dress to reveal shorts. She talked in a manic, very fast, controlling way.

I pointed out how dismissive she had been in the previous session about those who cared about her, her husband, me, the ward staff, etc. She then turned on me saying, 'I've got VD, AIDS. I'm going to fuck you with it!' I said that she wanted to attack and fuck my mind and her memory in me, so that she could keep a manic mindless state going which allowed no room for caring for herself.

She opened her bag and threw the contents on the floor. She picked out her lipstick and brush and said this is Ann (the caring ward domestic) and this is Joan (the caring ward sister), naming them. I pointed out her conflicting states of mind, on the one hand dismissing those that cared about her and on the other hand recognising them. She said, 'Quite right!' She then walked around the room in an intimidatory manner, telling me to shut up.

I reminded her that before I had sectioned her she had said that I did not have the balls to do it. I said that it was important she felt that I had the balls to stand up to her mania and not be intimidated. I felt both her contempt and my impotence. In the countertransference, while talking, I felt as if I was mad

195

to be trying to create some understanding in the face of a hurricane. Yet I also felt unimpressed with her mania and her attempts to fault me and make me feel guilty.

She then looked sidelong at me in a would-be flirtatious manner and said, 'I only did it for you'. I pointed out that having got rid of her memory and sanity by projecting them into me, and fucking my mind with mental VD and AIDS, she could then recreate a relationship with me in any way she chose.

At the end of the session, I helped pick up her bits and pieces from the floor. It felt as though we were trying to put her mind back together by picking up the scattered contents of her bag. As she left she said, 'I only did it for you, as it's not yours'. I was left to speculate on the meaning of the abortion that she seemed to be implying.

Another version of abortion was in evidence later in that admission, when at the height of her manic disturbance, for the first time, she required nursing on the locked ward. She was in a terrible state. Openly defiant, she said that 'her friends', a known group of psychopathic hospital patients, would get her out. I pointed out, with feeling, that she appeared to have lost all contact with those that really cared about her such as myself and her husband. I told her that her wishes for a better life seemed to be in danger of being swept aside by her mania if no one spoke up for them.

She appeared visibly moved by this intervention, which I made at the end of the session. She said 'thank you' as she left, and it felt genuine. However, after leaving the room, she stuck her head round the door and said, 'but no thanks!' At the onset of the last, severest and most protracted of her manic episodes, she had said, 'I'll go on like this forever and there is nothing that you or anyone else can do about it'. This statement felt real and convincing. The outlook then seemed very bleak indeed.

### The last few years

Paradoxically, Mrs J's state improved significantly after that last hypomanic episode. For three years there were no further hospital admissions, and then only a brief admission lasting one week, following a summer break when she had exhausted herself helping her daughter with her new baby.

She was aware of her exhaustion and that it followed being of help to her daughter. It seemed that the build-up of resentment that preceded the past protracted manic episodes was missing this time.

One can only speculate on the reasons for the seeming improvement.

196

Some might say that lithium was a factor, yet she had been taking it consistently for six years.

After the last major admission, her mother died. She was herself surprised by the absence of a bereavement reaction. It was striking that her elderly father, now freed from looking after the mother, would come around to Mrs J's house and constantly criticise her housework. His behaviour seemed to mirror Mrs J's primitive superego, whose commands she would obey, when in the past she had been driven obsessively to clean the house.

She is now no longer obsessional about cleaning and is, in her own words, 'deriving much contentment' from how well her children have developed despite all her own problems.

We can now enjoy reflective work together in her sessions. She no longer seems to need to evacuate her feelings as soon as she becomes aware of them. Perhaps, after all this time, analysis has helped in the growth of good object relationships. However, it was not so very long ago that I felt no hope that such a state of affairs would ever materialise. This may illustrate that with major psychotic disorders, one has to be prepared to persist, over many years, with a very uncertain outcome and accept the possibility that there may be no tangible reward for the effort. However, the experience of working with a patient like Mrs J may stimulate many reflections that can be applied to understanding in one's everyday psychiatric practice.

## Discussion

In 'Mourning and melancholia', Freud (1917) understood mania as a state where the emotional energy that had been bound in the painful suffering of melancholia became available once the ego had got over the object loss. The excess energy liberated caused the manic patient to act 'like a ravenously hungry man seeking new object cathexes'.

In 'Group psychology and the analysis of the ego' (Freud 1921), mania was seen as a temporary escape from the ego ideal. This was reflected in society by our need for organised festivals such as the Romans' Saturnalia (illustrated in my patient by her Roman orgy dream).

Abraham (1924) viewed mania as the ego throwing off the yoke of the superego by merging with it. Like Freud, he emphasised the oral roots of the psychopathology. Later writers, such as Rado (1928) and Lewin (1951), also emphasised that the aim of mania was a narcissistic fusion with the feeding breast.

In an earlier paper Abraham (1911) suggested that mania occurred when an individual's depression was no longer able to withstand the assault of repressed instincts. Like Freud and later Klein, Abraham stressed the dominance of obsessional mechanisms, and emphasised that the mania occurred when these failed.

Abraham thought that a 'free period' between the manic and depressive states was the most propitious time to start analysis. He wrote:

> in those patients who have prolonged free intervals between their manic or depressive attacks, psychoanalysis should be begun during that free period. The advantage is obvious, for analysis cannot be carried out in severely inhibited melancholic patients or inattentive manic ones.
>
> (Abraham 1911, p. 156)

The validity of this concept needs questioning. With my patient, there were no free periods. In the depressive phase, at times, superficial contact with the patient could deceive one into believing that the underlying pathological state of affairs was not in operation. In other cases, a patient may be so identified or fused with an omniscient internal mother that they appear calm and settled. A general psychiatric mental state examination may mislead the clinician into regarding them as 'normal' and 'free from pathology'. Clinically it proves extremely difficult to make analytic contact with a manic depressive patient at any time. They are never 'free' from their underlying psychopathology and, in that sense, there can be no 'free period'.

Klein drew attention to the clinging to pathological object relationships that occurs in manic depressive states. The early superego, due to splitting processes, is extremely moral and exciting. The individual clings to this superego because 'the idea of perfection is so compelling as it disproves the idea of disintegration. The problem of dependence and identification is too profound to be renounced' (M. Klein 1935, p. 271).

In her 1940 paper, Klein contrasted manic depressive states with mourning, noting that individuals who suffered from the former had been unable to establish their good objects and so felt insecure in their inner world (my patient had a recurrent childhood fear that the house would have gone when she returned from school).

Segal described in detail two central Kleinian concepts, that of the manic defence and manic reparation. The manic defence was based on the omnipotent denial of psychic reality, in order to defend against underlying persecutory and depressive feelings. It is characterised by triumph, control and contempt.

Manic reparation is to be distinguished from reparation proper. It is based on omnipotent control of the object and is paramount when love and concern, the hallmarks of genuine reparation, are weak (Segal 1973b, 1981d).

Rey added a new dimension to our understanding of manic states. In depression, the maternal breast, as part-object, represented the destroyed mother, and through identification, the subject felt depressed. In contrast, in manic states, the identification was with the penis as the object of reparation, with a magical ability to recreate the mother's attacked babies and breasts; that is through a phantasy of making her pregnant and refilling her empty breasts with milk (Rey 1994a).

However in the manic state, Rey argued that this identification is with a pseudo-penis that repairs nothing. It denies the reality of the destroyed objects, presenting itself as the universal substitute, while the aggressive impulses continue to destroy the object. As no reparation proper took place in the manic phase, the subject inevitably returned to his depression at the level of maturation previously reached, and so the cycle would repeat itself.

Rey saw the breast and penis as part-object prototypes representative of mother and father. The role of the penis was to integrate and repair. Manic reactions were seen as a pathological deviation, where there was identification with an immeasurably grandiose aspect of the erect penis. One might also add that the primary relationship was to a grandiose aspect of the breast, linked with the mother's underlying narcissistic personality structure. So manic mechanisms can be seen to predominate, whether the patient is in the depressive or manic phase.

Other authors have stressed the presence also of the 'life instinct' in mania. H. S. Klein from his analytic experience with a young manic patient commented, 'technically it is extremely important to realise that what may appear to be aggressive behaviour on the part of the patient is due in fact to the very intensity of his life instincts' (H. S. Klein 1974, p. 267).

In the depressive phase, H. S. Klein noted that his patient was projecting his aliveness into his analyst, which could have been for a variety of reasons. The wish to be alone with the severe omnipotent superego meant a need to distance oneself from a thinking part and the associated container–analyst. He also felt that the aliveness might have been projected into the analyst for safekeeping under the threat of retaliation from the murderously severe superego.

Patients may vary in their degree of resistance to change and some authors have written positively of the effects of analysis in manic depressive states (Jackson 1989; Rey 1994a). However, the resistance to change in a psychotic patient has a particularly organised quality, related to the functioning of the psychotic part of the personality (Bion 1957a). The psychotic part of the personality functions quite differently from the non–psychotic part. It is intolerant of frustration, and uses projective mechanisms as a substitute for thinking. The resulting emptiness is replaced by identification with an omnipotent and omniscient internal mother figure.

Bion wrote: 'I do not think real progress with psychotic patients is likely to take place until due weight is given to the nature of the divergence between the psychotic and non–psychotic personalities'. In their work at the Willesden Centre, Sinason (1993) and Richards (1993) have formulated this in terms of an internal cohabitee. In a truly major psychotic disorder, one would expect the psychotic part of the personality to predominate.

If, as a result of analytic intervention, the non–psychotic personality gets stronger and becomes increasingly able to think and resist the psychotic part's attempt to evacuate its thoughts, then a conflict may result. The psychotic part finds itself in envious rivalry with this development and may try to prevent the patient receiving help, resulting for example in my patient's husband becoming disheartened that no intervention by him helped and my experience of 'thank you but no thanks!'

Mrs J's deadly moods of dismissal could be regarded as illustrative of what many analysts mean by evidence of the death instinct. Certainly the problem of engagement remained a central issue. In a collective study in the United States of twelve cases of manic depressive psychoses using intensive psychoanalytic psychotherapy, it was interesting that the research group highlighted the main problem in therapy as 'a lack of interpersonal sensitivity' (Cohen et al. 1954).

Britton (1995) has described a situation that can arise in analysis, where through projective identification, the part of the patient that is capable of love and desirous of communication, and the patient's knowledge of this experience through previous analysis, resides entirely in the analyst's mind. He discussed the implications for analytic technique in such situations, which primarily arise in working with borderline patients:

> If this knowledge of the existence of a person capable of love and desirous of communication now apparently only exists in the analyst's mind, his own loneliness and frustration may prompt him to demand the patient admits it, or he may be tempted to try to sell it to the patient.
>
> (Britton 1995)

Reviewing my experience with Mrs J, I realised that this was what I had been doing with her most of the time. I was constantly trying to sell analysis to her, as an alternative way of functioning. However, involvement with a major psychotic disorder is different from involvement with a psychotic process. Major psychotic disorders have dominating characteristic psychopathologies of their own and perhaps it was inevitable that I was placed in this position by my patient.

## Why the repetitive cycle to the psychosis?

The manic phase of a recurrent manic depressive illness has often, analytically speaking, been understood in terms of a defence against underlying depression (Segal 1973b). Cohen et al. (1954) from their studies regarded mania as an escape from an unbearable depression to a more tolerable state. Indeed, I was struck by the dread that my patient expressed about returning to a depressive state at the end of her first manic episode in hospital.

However, my experience with Mrs J suggested the need for a different emphasis if the recurrent nature of her psychosis was to be explained.

The manic phase can be viewed as the uncoiling of a clockwork spring that has been progressively tightened during the depressive phase. The depressive phase is dominated by dependence on a tyrannical object, which demands total obedience and suppression of individuality. This was vividly illustrated in my patient by her obsessive drive to clear everything out of sight at home and then sit still in a catatonic state, a pattern that she would repeat day after day for months on end.

During the depressive phase, hidden resentment about this state of affairs builds up gradually and silently. It is like the patient saying, 'Why should I be the one staying at home doing all the housework, while you (the internal mother) are the one always out having a ball?'

These feelings of resentment gradually tighten the spring until eventually it unwinds explosively in the manic phase. I have learned from my patient that, once started, the explosive unwinding process continues with a momentum of its own, until all the previously suppressed anger has been spent.

It is impossible to halt this process once it has begun. Through the reflectiveness of the analytic situation, my patient became aware of this internal state of affairs. She likened it to an out of control period. She was even able at the start of one manic episode to encapsulate her awareness in her dream of watching a Roman orgy that was about to take place, in which she was going to be a participant, and in which she had the feeling that there was nothing she could do to stop it happening.

Major external life events are not necessarily required to trigger off another cycle as, once the anger has been spent, the pull to merge with the tyrannical superego can again reassert itself.

Any past or present experience of good object relationships is important in supporting the growth of reflectiveness and providing strength for a more productive type of object relationship.

Working with Mrs J gave me the opportunity to acquire increased awareness and understanding of the dynamics underlying a recurrent psychosis. It made me realise that the dynamics maintaining a recurrent psychosis can remain hidden from view in many cases managed in everyday psychiatric work.

As a general psychiatrist, one has to go on supporting staff, patients and their relatives in living with difficult circumstances. The experience gained through analytic case studies can help us to cope with seemingly intractable states of mind.

# 15

## Puerperal psychosis
## Vulnerability and aftermath

### Introduction

The puerperium is a particularly vulnerable time for a depressive psychotic breakdown, with important consequences for both mother and child. Hospital admission rates somewhat misleadingly suggest that puerperal psychosis is a rare condition (1 in 500 deliveries). In this chapter, evidence is given to suggest that puerperal psychosis may occur as frequently as 3 in 100 deliveries, and that many less severe cases remain undetected and untreated in the community.

While general psychiatric experience helps in the overall management of such cases, psychoanalytic insights can enable us to understand the central psychopathology. Understanding interventions in these cases can be therapeutic for the mother, as well as having major implications for the baby's development.

### The puerperal psychoses

In the nineteenth century, puerperal psychoses were thought of as specific entities, different from other mental illnesses. Later psychiatrists, including Kraepelin and Bleuler, regarded puerperal psychoses as no different from other mental illnesses (i.e. depression and schizophrenia) – they just happened to occur in the puerperium.

This is the current view and is reflected in the latest classification of mental disorders, the International Classification of Diseases (ICD-10: WHO 1994). The ICD discourages the diagnosis of puerperal psychosis, favouring depressive illness or, more rarely, schizophrenia. It defines mental disorders associated with the puerperium as those commencing within six weeks of delivery.

The incidence of puerperal psychosis based on hospital admission rates is about 1 in 500 deliveries. This is substantially higher than the incidence for psychosis in non-puerperal women of the same age. It occurs most frequently in first-time mothers with a past history and a family history of mental illness. It most commonly starts in the first two weeks post-partum, but rarely in the first two days. No differing hormonal pattern has been found in women who develop puerperal psychoses compared to others.

The risk of recurrence is 15–20 per cent in a subsequent pregnancy. Of those with puerperal psychotic depression, at least half will suffer a subsequent depressive illness that is not puerperal (Gelder et al. 1990).

Puerperal psychoses need to be distinguished from other, more common causes of mood disturbance post-partum. Up to 50 per cent of women experience 'maternity blues'. This is an emotionally labile state on the third to fourth day, which then resolves itself. Its cause remains unknown, but it is without pathological significance.

Postnatal neurotic depression occurs in 10 per cent of women post-partum. These women tend to be socially isolated and emotionally unsupported. In other words, they may come from a broken home, and have an absent or unsupportive partner. The child may be unwanted, or the mothers may find it hard to tolerate their babies' demands. Medication does not help, and extreme cases may result in the battered-baby syndrome.

Murray et al. (1991) have shown that emotionally unresponsive, depressed mothers can have an adverse effect on their infants' emotional and cognitive development. This highlights the need for involved health professionals, such as general practitioners, midwives and health visitors, to be aware of the emotional aspects of pregnancy, childbirth and early infant care, so that they can provide ongoing support.

A patient with puerperal psychosis may present in a confused state (see Case 1 below). In the past, this confusion might have been attributable to an organic cause, puerperal sepsis. However, with antibiotics and sterile procedures at delivery, sepsis is now a thing of the past. Thus, a confused state post-partum is indicative of the onset of a puerperal psychosis.

Because of the typically mixed symptomatology at initial presentation, it used to be hard to decide whether the psychosis was due to an affective (manic depressive) or a schizophrenic illness, and some psychiatrists would sit on the fence and use the term 'spectrum psychosis'. However, research has convincingly shown that virtually all puerperal psychoses are affective in origin (Kendell et al. 1987).

Kendell et al. (1987) demonstrated that of 120 patients admitted with puerperal psychoses, only 4 met the criteria for schizophrenia, and only 1 started *de novo* in the puerperium. Kendell noted that women with a history of manic depressive illness had a much higher incidence of admission in the puerperium than those with a history of schizophrenia or depressive neuroses.

Kendell et al. (1987) concluded that the high risk for psychosis in the first thirty days after childbirth in first-time mothers suggested that metabolic factors are involved in the genesis of puerperal psychoses. However, as unmarried motherhood, first-baby births, caesarean sections and perinatal deaths result in increased admissions or contacts, psychological stresses also contribute to the high morbidity (Kendell et al. 1987).

The general psychiatric treatment for puerperal psychosis is as for all depressive illnesses: drugs (antidepressants and major tranquillisers) and ECT. Early use of ECT is advocated to help the mother recover more quickly, so that she can start looking after her baby sooner.

Two special issues arise concerning the general management of psychosis in the puerperium. The first consideration is the need for mother-and-baby facilities. It is often advocated that each psychiatric ward should have separate side rooms available for this purpose. The nurses involved should be experienced in managing babies as well as trained in general psychiatry. The alternatives are specialist mother-and-baby units, such as those at the Maudsley, Shenley and Cassel Hospitals, in England (Zachary 1985).

The second issue that must be kept in mind is the risk of infanticide (and suicide). Severely depressed patients may have delusional ideas that their baby is malformed or otherwise imperfect, and try to kill the baby in order to save him or her from further suffering.

While general psychiatrists acknowledge the contribution of emotional and physical stresses to depression in the puerperium, their primary concern is to identify a biochemical change that can account for the high incidence of psychotic depression in the puerperium.

Psychodynamic understandings, based on psychoanalytic concepts, are absent from general psychiatric formulations. Psychoanalytic contributions in the literature tend to address general issues of mothering, rather than to focus specifically on puerperal psychosis (Raphael-Leff 1983). Using case material I hope to show how analytic insights can help us to understand why the puerperium is such a vulnerable time for a depressive psychotic breakdown, and the aftermath for both mother and child. Finally I wish to emphasise that the underlying psychodynamics are far commoner than is generally realised.

I will now briefly present three case studies, each of which highlights different issues relating to the dynamics underlying puerperal psychosis. I will conclude with a further discussion of some of the issues raised.

## Case 1: Some general psychiatric perspectives

Mrs K was a 30-year-old woman who was admitted to my acute ward in a psychotic state, eleven days after the birth of her first child, a boy. Her case raises many clinical issues to do with the attitude towards puerperal psychosis and its management in general psychiatry.

Mrs K had been married for four years. She worked as an artist. She had been apprehensive about having a baby, but responded to pressure from her husband. She had no previous knowledge of analytic theory, but interestingly brought drawings of babies at the breast with her, in which the breast had teeth.

For five days after delivery Mrs K was well. Then she started to have disturbed sleep, and became overactive and over-talkative. At times, she appeared incoherent and confused. She was discharged from the maternity unit on the eighth day. Her condition worsened at home. She was confused and forgetful, unable to finish a task she had begun. A deputising general practitioner was called, who gave her a tranquilliser injection. She slept for a few hours but, as soon as the injection wore off, her disturbed behaviour returned.

The day before her admission, Mrs K's behaviour became increasingly bizarre and unmanageable. She kicked her husband, called him a robot, and started to break things. She was seen by her GP and the duty social worker, and admitted to our psychiatric unit on a supervision order. On admission she was over-talkative and restless, with grandiose delusions that

'My mother is the Queen' and 'I am a millionaire'. She was emotionally labile, elated and jovial one moment, and weepy and tearful the next. She was disorientated in place and time, but recognised her husband, the nursing staff and doctors. Formal memory function was difficult to assess because of her poor concentration and distraction. Her judgement was impaired and she had no insight.

Her mental state fluctuated constantly, with her manifest symptoms changing from hypomanic to more paranoid and schizophreniform in character. It took three months for her condition to become more settled, though the staff still found it difficult to develop any meaningful rapport with her. The main medication given was haloperidol, a major tranquilliser, though amitriptyline was added later to address the depressive component of her illness.

Her family were seen and extensively involved in the situation. Mrs K's mother did not get on well with the patient's husband or his mother. Mrs K's mother was bizarre and paranoid in manner, and, at the height of her daughter's confused psychotic state she telephoned her on the ward to berate her for her behaviour. In contrast, Mrs K's mother-in-law seemed a very sensible woman, who looked after the baby when the patient was admitted.

After three months, we seemed to be getting nowhere. Though she was less floridly ill, Mrs K was still not well. We sent her home for a weekend, but whenever her mother-in-law gave her the baby, she became agitated and gave him back immediately, saying that she did not have the confidence to look after him.

It was at this point that we presented her to a problem case conference at the hospital. The case conference was attended by a consultant who had worked on a specialised mother-and-baby unit. He reported that research had shown that admission direct to a mother-and-baby unit facilitated bonding, and that patients spent less time in hospital and were more confident with their babies as a result.

Accordingly, we felt very guilty and promptly arranged for Mrs K to visit a specialised mother-and-baby unit with her husband, with the aim of then transferring her with the baby.

However, following the visit, Mrs K said that she did not want to go there. That evening she went home, pushed out her mother-in-law and replaced her with her own mother. On the Monday, she returned to the hospital in a confident state, saying that she could now manage the baby, as if she had clicked back into normality. Shortly after this, it was possible to discharge Mrs K for outpatient follow-up.

This case highlights many clinical aspects of puerperal psychosis and raises the question of how to understand Mrs K's sudden apparent recovery.

It is characteristic with puerperal psychosis to have a lucid period following delivery (Mrs K's first five days during which she appeared well). At the time of discharge from hospital, Mrs K started to become unwell with confusion. This was ignored by the obstetrics staff, as it was easier to let her be discharged. When she went home she became more disturbed, so that she had to be admitted on a formal basis.

Puerperal psychoses are unusual in presenting with symptoms of confusion, which in other circumstances is usually a symptom of an organic psychosis. The mixture of depressive, hypomanic and schizophreniform features initially makes a precise diagnosis difficult. Mrs K's psychosis eventually clarified itself as a manic depressive or affective disorder.

The resolution of Mrs K's psychosis is of interest. It seemed to be going on interminably. However, when the issue of the mother-and-baby unit was raised, Mrs K suddenly reinstated her mother in place of her mother-in-law and herself suddenly seemed to revert to normal. How is this to be understood?

Some psychiatrists have attributed sudden resolutions like this to some hormonal or biochemical imbalance post-partum that must have righted itself. We could postulate another explanation on dynamic lines. The puerperium is a particularly vulnerable time for the reawakening of any unresolved conflicts a woman may have in relation to her mother. Mrs K would seem to have denied all her confused, unresolved real feelings to her mother and instead held herself together by identifying with an adult mother figure. However, when her baby was born Mrs K became temporarily identified with her previously suppressed 'baby part'. This led to an eruption of confused manic, paranoid and depressive feelings. At the same time, after the initial eruption, she began to struggle to recompose herself.

The situation was dramatically resolved after Mrs K was confronted with the possibility of the mother-and-baby unit; perhaps this represented a priority for the needy 'baby part' of her. She opted for the alternative, displacing her 'sane' mother-in-law at the weekend, quickly reidentifying with her mother, and becoming again the 'capable adult'.

In other words, before the puerperal breakdown, Mrs K held herself together through her 'capable adult' exterior. Practically, she was capable of coping with situations. Her inner chaos was repressed and became identified with her unborn baby.

The birth of her child resulted in the eruption of undifferentiated psychotic material. The dramatic resolution of Mrs K's psychosis can be understood as a reassertion of her denial of her needy-baby part. Her caring mother-in-law, who was looking after the baby, was replaced by the patient's own mother, with whom she was immediately reidentified in the role of a 'capable adult'.

Although, to the outside world, Mrs K now appeared to be well again, the underlying psychodynamics remained as they had been before the breakdown. I will return to the question of the role of the mother-and-baby units with psychotic patients in the discussion.

A year later, I received an anxious phone call from the obstetrician. Mrs K wanted to stop her contraceptive and have another child. I said I would see her about this. When I saw Mrs K she was quite sure that she wanted to conceive again. I could only advise her to wait another year or so, so that her son had at least two years of her in a trouble-free state, before the next pregnancy. I had no idea if she would relapse, and could only point out that the general risk of relapse was one in six. I said that, while we had no way of knowing, she had been very unwell for a long time after her son was born. She felt that, as I was forewarned, and it was the second child, it would be less severe and more manageable the next time. In fact, she was right. She had another child soon after and she did have another breakdown, but it was less severe and did not last as long as the first one.

## Case 2: The risk of infanticide

Mrs J was a patient with recurrent manic depressive psychosis, who has been followed analytically over a number of years within the National Health Service. Her case is discussed at length in Chapter 14. Here I want to concentrate on issues of the psychodynamics of the puerperium, and their profound effects and sequelae. Mrs J's case also shows that while psychopathology can be handed down from one generation to the next, there is a possibility that the hand-down might be averted.

Mrs J's grandmother was the eldest of eight children born to a family living in the East End of London. After Mrs J's mother's birth, Mrs J's grandfather went off with the army to India. He returned several years later to sire seven more children. His wife was said to have been a very domineering woman. One can imagine the effects all this might have had on Mrs J's mother, and how her delusional idea of being the centre of her own mother's world would have been shattered by her father's return from India – a narcissistic blow from which she was unable to recover.

It was therefore not surprising to learn that on becoming a mother,

209

Mrs J's mother expected family life to revolve around her. She suffered from lifelong agoraphobia and depression, but was never hospitalised. She expected Mrs J to help her and not to cause problems of any kind. Mrs J's father reinforced her mother's projections by expressing the view that children should be seen and not heard. He would blame Mrs J if her mother was in a mood.

When Mrs J was 11, her mother had a stillbirth. Throughout adolescence, her mother remained very controlling and would not speak to Mrs J for a week at a time, if her instructions were not obeyed. Awareness of this background can help us to appreciate Mrs J's mental state at the time her daughter was born.

With her daughter's birth, Mrs J had her first psychotic breakdown. After the birth, she became very agitated, but was sent home. There she developed the delusion that her daughter looked like her mother's stillborn child. She had the thought that 'she was too beautiful to live'. She felt that her daughter would not have any life of her own and that she should kill her.

She had a fight to resist the impulse to kill her daughter, and in the end she cut her own wrists. With blood everywhere, and realising that she was not dying, she went round to the neighbours. She was hospitalised and given ECT.

It was with apprehension that five years later she had her son, as she did not want her daughter to be an only child. She had no breakdown at the time of his birth, but since then, she has developed recurrent manic depressive episodes. Some years later she started analysis, during which she was able to describe her experience following the daughter's birth.

Mrs J was determined that her children should have an experience different from her own. The children have no inhibitions about speaking their minds about their mother's behaviour. They seem to contain her projected life instinct. For example, on her 46th birthday, her daughter telephoned to apologise that because of a work commitment she could not be with her that day. When Mrs J responded, 'At my age birthdays mean nothing', her daughter had no inhibitions about saying, 'Well, I hope I don't think like that at your age'. Of course, by projecting the criticism into her daughter, Mrs J typically avoided the issues raised by her own attitude. However, it was also clear that her daughter was not intimidated about speaking up, in contrast to Mrs J's relationship with her own mother.

Mrs J made sure that her own children were not suppressed as she had been. For example, she insisted that her husband let her son, when young, sometimes win at the game of Monopoly. In contrast, she continues to be extremely self-depriving in attitude. Her deadly submissive relationship with

210

her mother was only too familiar to me as it was acted out daily in the transference. The power of her mother's projections and their effect on Mrs J were evident: 'If you can't beat them, join them – and squash yourself!'

In patients with this kind of psychopathology, there must always be a conflict between submitting to, and totally identifying with, the all-powerful deadening mother figure, and supporting the needy self. The conflict can be avoided by a total identification with the mother figure. However, there are times when a conflict of interests cannot be avoided. The puerperium is such a time. From total identification with a godlike mother figure, the provider of all life, in pregnancy – suddenly there are two figures on the scene when the baby is born, and the baby represents the patient's life instinct, previously neglected needs, and individuality. The way in which the underlying conflict can be brought into the open by the puerperium is what makes this a uniquely vulnerable time for a depressive psychotic breakdown – more so than any other time in the life of a woman with predisposing psychopathology.

With Mrs J it was very apparent that having her daughter brought her internal conflict into the open. Her envious and jealous internal mother would not allow her to have individual feelings. Her individual aliveness was concretely projected into her baby – who was idealised and immobilised for protection – 'too beautiful to live', reminiscent of her mother's stillborn child. Her conflict was then acted out in her struggle with herself over the question of who should survive, herself or the baby.

Like Mrs K, Mrs J required hospitalisation in the puerperium, in an acute psychotic state. However, I believe that there is a danger of underestimating the size of the problem of puerperal psychosis. Not all cases lead to admission to a psychiatric unit, and may even go undetected at the time. The third case illustrates this point.

## Case 3: The tip of an iceberg?

Mrs L came to analysis when she was in her fifties because of troublesome feelings of depression, isolation and a sense of lack of identity. She had an autistic son, for whom she had struggled to get appropriate help for twenty years. When he started to improve, she turned to her own needs.

Mrs L exhibited typical features of endogenous depression, with early morning wakening, diurnal mood-variation, lack of energy and hypochondriasis. She had headaches, which she worried might indicate a brain

211

tumour. She felt that her life was not her own, under the pressure of constant demands from her elderly mother and her autistic son.

Both Mrs L's parents had had previous marriages. Her mother, who was 33 when Mrs L was born, had a son eight years older from her first marriage. Mrs L's father was 59 when she was born. He was a retired army officer, Victorian and eccentric in his ways, but warm-hearted. Her mother was quite dismissive towards him.

When Mrs L was born, her mother had a depressive breakdown. Mrs L was sent away for three months to a nanny, who is said to have neglected her. Mrs L became ill with jaundice and gastro-enteritis. It was three months before the neglect was discovered and Mrs L returned home.

Throughout her childhood, Mrs L's mother remained predominantly in a withdrawn state in bed. However, she was very dominating and ridiculing in manner towards her daughter. Mrs L would be instructed by her grandmother not to upset her mother. She had a very lonely childhood. She lived in the countryside and would befriend the animals and plants. Her one talent was painting. Her mother was so envious of any challenge to her authority that she put kitchen rubbish on a painting of Mrs L's which had won a prize in her adolescence.

Mrs L's husband also had a difficult upbringing and had had some analysis. He was generally supportive, but preoccupied with his business, which took him away for lengthy periods. So she was often left alone again, just as she had been in childhood.

When her autistic son was born, it was a precipitate labour. After he was born, he cried perpetually for months on end. Mrs L went to stay with her mother, but her mother could not tolerate the crying baby, so Mrs L went back home on her own. She said that she had been depressed for two years, but received no treatment. It took two years before she was able to get the first specialist assessment of her son. Several years later she had her second child, a healthy daughter.

I do not wish to go further into Mrs L's history, but to make the point that here is a woman presenting with symptoms of a major depressive illness who was clearly depressed after her son's birth. However, she received no treatment – raising the issue of how many more major depressions go undetected in the puerperium.

Mrs L's opening remark at the start of her analysis was striking. She said, 'I want to be a calm sensible person with no feelings'. Since her mother had spent her time ridiculing any doubting or thinking, this statement represents Mrs L's wish to conform to her mother's requirements. Again a basic dynamic in major depression is evident, the urge to give up the sane

212

thinking-and-feeling self in order to conform to the demands of the omnipotent internal mother figure.

The lack of availability of a containing mother was graphically illustrated in a dream. In the dream Mrs L went to get food from a supermarket. There was no basket and she came out with her arms full of tin cans. Suddenly an aunt (her mother's sister) shouted from a house window: 'Where is your mother?' She dropped the cans and opened her mouth to speak. It was full of blood and bits of glass.

This dream makes the oral origins of the psychopathology very apparent. When she was severely depressed, Mrs L would also report a sensation that she had swallowed two tablets of stone that lay heavily on her stomach, that is the unresponsive stone breasts of mother. This image also evoked the Ten Commandments, not to be disobeyed.

At times Mrs L could be very self-castrating, identifying with the maternal superego. For example, she could even criticise herself for making a 'wrong' choice between two side roads to go down when in fact both were blocked with traffic.

Over the years, the material Mrs L brought to her sessions illustrated her struggle between the alternatives of submitting to and identifying with her mother, and, through the work of the analysis, her efforts to support the growth and expression of a sensitive, independent thinking-and-feeling self.

I will briefly report some sessional material to illustrate the oscillation of these two states of mind. Mrs L's daughter, now in her mid twenties, had been unhappy with her shared flat. She was talking of returning to live at home. Mrs L was unhappy with this; the house was already cramped with her husband's business office at home, without having to cope with her daughter's needs and belongings all over the place again. Her daughter was unresponsive to Mrs L's suggestion that she find another flat-share nearby, but became excited at the prospect of buying her own flat with her parents' help. Mrs L's husband's initial reaction was that they should sell their home, buy a house in the country, and buy a larger flat in London in which their daughter could also live. His response could be understood as an impractical first reaction, the result of current pressure from his self-employed business and a wish to escape.

In the subsequent session, we noted how Mrs L seemed to be ignoring her own assessment of the situation, as conveyed to me, with the conclusion that her daughter should be supported in buying her own place. Mrs L said that both her husband and daughter would have felt her to be a nuisance if she brought her views to them. She was talking to me in a very superficial style, like the grandmother who had instructed her not to trouble her mother.

When I pointed this out, she was able later to impart her views to husband and daughter, with a satisfactory outcome. However, she ended the session by saying that she felt guilty (not expanding on this).

The next day, Mrs L uncharacteristically arrived seven minutes late. She said that she had been held up by roadworks, due to installation of unnecessary extra pedestrian crossings at the top of a hill. She then said, 'Oh dear', in a contrived way. I pointed out the double message, in that, while I had taken in her frustration in a real way she also related to me as someone who should not be troubled by her genuine feelings. This reminded me of not disturbing her mother, and her reference to guilt at the end of the previous session. She then spoke of the insanity of increasing roadworks, narrowing the end of side roads to single lanes, causing further congestion, and cars dangerously waiting in the main roads to turn into side roads.

I talked about her feeling of madness at submitting to me, like her mother's stifling – as if the space for the flow of her feelings was progressively being restricted, as with the traffic – and suggested that this was not dissimilar to the previously reported problem of standing up for space for herself in her house. This reminded her of a dream she had had two days previously (when the question of her daughter's possible return was on her mind). In the dream she was standing in an underground train which was packed, giving no breathing space. An unpleasant man next to her squeezed her hand, crushing it. She was supposed to say nothing, but refused to keep quiet and shouted so that everyone could hear, 'Don't do that!'

As she spoke these words to me, they sounded quite unconvincing, like a stage act. I again referred to the switch in her voice to a stifling, accommodating mode. She referred again to the house: she liked it; it was a listed building; and she had put a lot of herself into it over the years. Nevertheless, there were space problems with it, and, while she was thinking over this at home, she heard a voice saying, 'What are you complaining about? You have nothing to complain about'. I took this as her expectation that I would react to her needs like her grandmother saying, 'What are you complaining about, regarding the space in your mother's mind? You should put up with it and like it'.

Following this, she described another reason for her continual self-stifling, apart from guilt. She was afraid that if she ceased to cling to the bad depriving object she would be exposed to an underlying state where she would be alone, with no one at all wanting her. This explains why agitation is such a prominent symptom in depressive illness.

214

Not only does identification with the omnipotent mother obviate the feelings of envy that separateness brings, but also it provides a means to avoid terrifying feelings of aloneness by remaining forever in a relationship with a bad object that blames you and that you blame.

Although the persistence of pathological relationships is an important issue in the assessment of the degree to which analytic interventions will be effective, the main reason for presenting Mrs L's material in this chapter is to illustrate that not all patients with puerperal depression are admitted to hospital. Puerperal depression, of the psychotic type, has a wide spectrum of severity, and many patients at some point will seek analytic therapy. This raises the possibility that the cases admitted to hospital are only 'the tip of the iceberg'. I will expand on this theme in the ensuing discussion.

## Discussion

In response to a leading article in the *British Medical Journal* on the mothering skills of women with mental illness, Bourne and his colleagues at the Tavistock Clinic complained about the lack of attention to the condition of postnatal neurotic depression (Bourne et al. 1993). They argued that while the incidence of psychotic illness is significantly greater after delivery than at any other time, its incidence is relatively rare (1 in 500 to 1 in 1,000 deliveries) compared with postnatal neurotic depression (10–20 per cent of mothers). Bourne et al. (1993) argue that it is the cases of neurotic depression that are dealt with (or not dealt with) mainly in the community that really matter. It is here that community workers need education in counselling skills.

I would not dispute the prevalence of postnatal neurotic depression, or the need for increased community awareness (Kumar and Robson 1984; Paykel et al. 1980). However, I would argue that the psychopathology underlying affective disorders or major depressive illness as so convincingly described by Freud (1917) and Abraham (1924) is much more common postnatally than is usually realised. In other words, those admitted to hospital with florid puerperal psychoses are only the most extreme cases, the 'tip of the iceberg'.

Reactive or neurotic depression is reckoned to be four times as common as endogenous depression (see West 1992). On that basis, if the incidence for postnatal neurotic depression is 1 in 10 deliveries, for psychotic depression it would be 1 in 40 deliveries, much higher than the oft-quoted 1 in 500 to 1,000 deliveries.

215

At any one time, the prevalence rate for endogenous (psychotic) depression is estimated at 2–9 per cent of women (see Gelder et al. 1990), and since the puerperium is such a vulnerable time for affective disorders these statistics again suggest a truer prevalence rate of at least 2 or 3 cases per 100 deliveries.

A study by Cox et al. (1993) substantiates this figure. In the study, the prime intention of which was to look at related stress in post-natal neurotic disorders, the overall incidence of depression was 9.1 per cent. However, 3.5 per cent of cases were classified as major depression (Cox et al. 1993).

The conclusion is clear. The true incidence of puerperal psychotic depression is much higher than is indicated by the 1 in 500 admission rate. The suggested incidence is more of the order of 3 in 100 deliveries. Most cases do not get admitted to hospital. They are treated in the community by general practitioners and community psychiatric nurses, or referred to psychiatric outpatient departments; or their depression goes unrecognised and they struggle through it on their own, like Mrs L.

I will now briefly consider some of the issues raised by the case presentations. All three cases highlight the pathology central to endogenous depression. Abraham (1924) succinctly summarises five roots to the psychopathology:

- a constitutional factor
- a special fixation of the libido at the oral level
- a severe injury to infantile narcissism by successive disappointments in love
- occurrence of the first disappointment pre-oedipally
- repetition of the primary disappointment in later life.

Mrs L's case includes all Abraham's points: the constitutionally inherited family history of depression; the patient's mother having a breakdown when the patient was born; the fixation of the libido at the oral level, with the sensation of having swallowed the tablets of stone breasts when depressed; the severe injury to infantile narcissism as evidenced by the mother's unresponsiveness; the first disappointment pre-oedipally, starting at birth with being left with the neglectful nanny; the repetition of the primary disappointment in later life, with her mother's lack of support at the time of the birth of the autistic child. In 'Mourning and melancholia', Freud (1917) emphasised the predominance of a narcissistic type of object-choice as the key to understanding melancholia. If there is a conflict with the loved person, who will not tolerate difference, then the relationship is maintained by a substitution of identification for object-love. The identification of the ego with the object that has forsaken them involves them giving up their own individuality.

The idealised identification so predominates that, for long periods, no sense of loss of individuality is felt. However, any situation where there is a threatened move from an 'at-oneness' to a two-person relationship is intolerable to the narcissistic object-choice.

Thus, in cases with this underlying psychopathology, any situation which highlights the existence of a needy separate ego can precipitate a major depressive breakdown. Precipitants can range from minor ailments, like influenza, to bereavement, job loss, illnesses of old age and *especially* the caesura of birth.

With birth, the violence of the conflict between the demands of the narcissistic identification and the separate needy ego, as represented by the baby, is experienced all over again. In extreme cases, the violence can lead to acts of infanticide or suicide. The law has long recognised the special circumstances to infanticide (Infanticide Act 1922, amended 1938). Infanticide is seen as a special case of diminished responsibility. Section 1 of the Act states:

> Where a woman causes the death of her child under the age of twelve months, but, at the time the balance of her mind was disturbed by reason of her not having fully recovered from the effects of childbirth or lactation consequent upon the birth of the child, she shall be guilty of not murder but infanticide.

Judges take a sympathetic view of the woman's illness, and in fact, most are referred to hospital or put on probation; only 1 per cent is sent to prison (Gelder et al. 1990). In most cases, the mother had a depressive disorder and killed the child because she imagined that she was saving it from anticipated suffering. About one-third of mothers who commit infanticide also try to take their own lives (Resnick 1969).

It is important to re-emphasise that, when we talk about a major depressive illness in the puerperium, we are referring to a psychotic illness. This means that our ordinary empathic understanding is not enough: with these cases too, we have to tune into the psychotic wavelength. In other words, events will not unfold according to our preconceived notions, as graphically illustrated by Mrs K's case.

Ordinary empathic understanding might lead us to believe that Mrs K's lack of progress, and fear of taking responsibility for her child on weekend visits, was due to our failure to support the early bonding process by arranging a placement in a mother-and-baby unit.

The way events subsequently unfolded turned these assumptions on their head. To understand them one had to tune into the wavelength on which Mrs K's psychosis operated. Her case also raises questions about the assumption that mother-and-baby units are always the preferred option for all postnatal disorders. If a mother is mentally incapable of giving full attention to her baby's needs, careful consideration should be given to the question of whether the baby is better off in a regular stable environment, say with the grandmother, or on a mother-and-baby unit. A situation where a baby has to contend with different nurses feeding him may lead to a failure to develop a healthy projective-introjective process. Psychotic breakdown processes may then predominate, with the risk of creating another generational problem. While specialist mother-and-baby and family facilities, such as the one described by Zachary (1985) at the Cassel Hospital, may be beneficial for less severe cases of postnatal neurotic depression, further thought may be needed with psychotic cases. Here it should not be assumed that the mother-and-baby unit is necessarily best, but the baby's interests should be the priority in deciding on the placement.

Depressive illness has a wide spectrum of severity, even though the basic psychodynamics remain the same, and with some patients who are quite unamenable to dynamic interventions one has to resort to purely physical treatments (Mrs K). For example, I recall one male patient, who fragmented and projected his feelings into hypochondriacal symptoms in all the organs of his body and drove his relatives mad by continually talking about his symptoms. One would literally have had to know which part of his mind had been projected into his big toe to be able to talk to him.

Other cases are amenable to analytic psychotherapy or analysis, and many will have such cases (like Mrs L) in their clinical practice. Some cases lie in between, so that both physical treatment and dynamic understandings may have their place. In general psychiatric outpatient departments, there are many cases where a prescription for antidepressant medication and the provision of dynamic understanding both prove appropriate and helpful. Such cases straddle the inter-face between biological psychiatry and psychoanalysis, raising many fascinating issues (see Chapter 16 for further discussion of these).

While we should be under no illusion that all cases of major depression are suitable for analytic psychotherapy, nevertheless I have found that even brief interventions at critical periods in such patients' lives can be therapeutic – and in the puerperium we have two lives to consider. Awareness of the conflict, and concern for the baby's interests, can be important in providing a supportive structure to mothers in vulnerable states.

One place where women with this problem may instinctively turn for support is infant observation. Very often, far more than I think is realised, the mother seeks tacit support in caring for her child from the observer's time and interest. Mothers who volunteer for infant observation have often had a depressed, unresponsive mother, and they may hope for support in helping them to avoid repeating this pattern with their child.

Welldon (1991) has described how female psychopathology can be looked at in three-generational terms: grandmother, mother, daughter. Sometimes the handing-down of the severe restrictive superego, as Welldon (1991) has argued, can be averted.

All patients who are prone to major depression must undergo a crisis of allegiance when their baby is born. Most will not come into hospital, but evidence of the conflict may be apparent to others. Understanding interventions may be therapeutic for the mother and her partner, as well as having major implications for the baby's development.

# 16

## Managing depression – psychoanalytic psychotherapy, antidepressants or both?

The severity of the psychopathology of patients with depression can vary enormously. Some may be receptive to analytic psychotherapy, while others require treatment with medication. An analytic framework of understanding still has a place in work with the latter group, and can aid general psychiatrists in relating to their depressed patients. When trying to understand and relate to patients with depression, Freud and Abraham's seminal papers remain as clinically relevant, nowadays, as when they were first written (Abraham 1924; Freud 1917). Analytic thinking can help us to make sense of many of the symptoms of depression, including early morning wakening, diurnal mood variation, agoraphobia and hypochondriasis. It is also important to help the supportive relative with their countertransference experiences, when their partner is undergoing a depressive episode.

In this chapter I conceptualise depression as a situation where a pathological ego-destructive superego has taken over the driving seat (O'Shaughnessy 1999). In the treatment of depression, we aim to unseat this pathological superego and replace it with a more benign and mature superego that fosters ego development. Understanding depression in this way can provide an overall framework of approach to the treatment of this debilitating condition, whether we are treating the patient with antidepressant medication, psychotherapy or both.

In order to understand depressive illness, we also need to distinguish it from other causes of low mood and recognise its special psychopathology. Freud's seminal paper, 'Mourning and melancholia' (1917), helps us to go beyond ordinary empathy by recognising the underlying narcissistic structure. However, Freud's insights are usually not incorporated within general psychiatric training and practice. Conversely, I would argue that psychoanalytic therapists do not think enough about depression in terms of a psychotic disorder, nor, as a rule, do they consider when medication might be needed in this context.

## Different meanings of depression

We need to be aware that there are four quite different ways that we may talk about depression. Edith Jacobson (1978), in her studies on depression, referred to them as normal, neurotic, psychotic and grief reactions.

### *Normal depression*

Jacobson's normal depression is akin to what Melanie Klein referred to as the depressive position. It is essentially a state of health, a capacity to bear guilt, stay in touch with mental pain and emotional problems and bring thinking to bear on situations. In Kleinian terms, we oscillate between our ability to stay with painful situations or seek temporary relief through splitting and projection, returning to the paranoid–schizoid position, or flight into manic idealisations (Segal 1973b).

### *Neurotic depression*

Neurotic or reactive depression can be understood, simplistically speaking, as an exaggerated response to stress due to low ego strength combined with a failure of the external support system. Such depression is basically a cry for help.

An asylum seeker was admitted to hospital after running in front of cars. A flatmate reported that he had tried to jump out of a window until he was restrained and then took a few paracetamol tablets. He clinically presented in a withdrawn and retarded state, as if undergoing a severe depressive episode, but was fine the next day after we indicated that, if

221

contacted by his solicitors, we would write a supportive asylum appeal letter.

Suicide attempts in cases of reactive depression can be seen as a wish for temporary oblivion and a cry for help in relation to clear external precipitants, such as a family row or break-up with a boy-friend. In such cases a supportive response from the carers can be sufficient to deal with the crisis and medication is not indicated. In contrast, in suicide attempts by patients with features of psychotic depression, who are typically older, there is a real intention to kill themselves, and the treatment would typically involve medication and admission to a psychiatric hospital (Lucas 1994; Stengel 1964).

## Grief reactions

In 'Mourning and melancholia', Freud (1917) movingly described the process of mourning. In grief we try to turn away from reality and cling onto the lost object through a hallucinatory wishful psychosis, such as hearing the voice of our lost loved one. However, in submission to the reality principle we eventually have to relinquish the external object and reinstate it as a memory inside us. To do this we have to go through the work of mourning (Freud 1917).

Freud highlighted the similarities of mourning with melancholia, a condition that would now be referred to as a severe depressive episode (ICD-10: WHO 1994). In melancholia too, Freud surmised that a loss must have taken place; however, the nature of the loss in melancholia is more difficult to discern. He concluded that it therefore must have been an internal narcissistic loss, occurring at an unconscious level, and requiring to be understood in its own right (Freud 1917).

## Psychotic depression

In modern day terminology, Jacobson's psychotic depression would be termed a severe depressive episode with psychotic symptoms (ICD-10: WHO 1994). Depression is, in fact, a very common condition. Some 3 per cent of the population are seeking help at any one time, another 3 per cent who remain undetected are struggling on their own in the community, while 10 per cent also undergo manic

222

episodes. In manic depression, there is a 15 per cent risk of suicide, and up to 50 per cent of patients may have visited their GPs in the few weeks preceding suicide (Gelder et al. 2001).

It is useful to be familiar with the clinical presentation, as otherwise, if the patient does not complain of depression but only emphasises one of the many commonly experienced symptoms, one may fail to realise that the symptom is part of an underlying syndrome. The typical symptoms, familiar to all practicing psychiatrists, include the following: diurnal mood variation, early morning wakening, and psychomotor retardation − a slowing up of all physical and mental processes − with resulting loss of appetite and weight, decreased libido, amenorrhoea, constipation and retardation (stupor). Other features include agitation (a ceaseless roundabout of painful thoughts), poor concentration (depressive pseudo-dementia), agoraphobia, depersonalisation and derealisation, a loss of energy (mimicking anaemia) and hypochondriacal features including headaches, chest pain, stomach pains with associated cancer phobia, and atypical facial pain (depressive equivalents) and suicidal thoughts (Gelder et al. 2001).

There are compelling arguments in favour of regarding depressive illness as a biological disorder. Many psychiatrists see the symptoms of a slowing up of psychological and bodily processes as indicative of a medical disorder that requires physical treatment. Also in depression, common neurotransmitters in the brain are depleted, and antidepressants work by raising their levels, supporting the view of a biochemical disorder. According to traditional psychiatric teaching there is no place for psychotherapy, other than of a supportive kind, while the patient takes his medication and recovers from the episode. However, I would argue that the usefulness of psychoanalytic thinking is not restricted to the less severe cases.

## The psychoanalytic understanding of depression

It is impossible to do justice in a précis to the richness of Freud's (1917) paper, 'Mourning and melancholia'. Freud points out that, in depression, the dominating internal relationship is with an object demanding total obedience, with the associated illusion of being totally looked after by the object. This absolute identification breaks down when needs arise, but not completely, so that the identification with the idealised object still remains, and the ideal object is criticised for having let one down. As Freud put it, 'an object loss was transformed into an ego loss' (Freud 1917, p. 249). So, when the patient announces to the world that they are useless, they are not really criticising themselves, but a purported ideal that has temporarily let them down. Their apparent self-tormenting can then be understood as a tormenting of the ideal object that is felt to have abandoned them at a time of need. The sadomasochistic process of self-criticism that characterises depressive episodes continues in a relentless fashion until it has run its course.

Some experienced nursing staff will have no difficulty in intuitively understanding the need to let this process run its course in hospital, without demanding excessive physical interventions.

In depression no true mourning, which would involve relinquishing the object, can occur because of the unresolved ambivalent dependence on an ideal object. It is striking how, after months of self-berating, patients may recover their former composure without showing the slightest curiosity about their whole recent experience in hospital.

Freud emphasised the oral roots to the psychopathology of depression, with regression to oral narcissism, as evidenced by a patient's refusal to eat when in a severely depressed state (Freud 1917). Expanding on this theme, Abraham (1924) brilliantly and succinctly summarised the dynamic factors underlying depression, as follows:

- a constitutional factor of an overaccentuation of oral eroticism
- a special fixation of the libido at the oral stage
- a severe injury to infantile narcissism
- occurrence of the primary disappointment pre-oedipally
- repetition of the primary disappointment in later life.

The case of Mrs L described in Chapter 15 offers a particularly clear illustration of these dynamic factors at work. Freud initially referred to melancholia as a narcissistic neurosis. After the introduction of the structural model, he described it as a disease of the critical agency or superego (Freud 1917, 1923).

In his paper 'On narcissism', Freud compared the healthy state of taking in mental food from parental figures, the anaclitic state, with a self-centred state in which no development occurs, the narcissistic state (Freud 1914). In depression, the narcissistic state predominates and takes the form of a delusion of not only being at one with an all-providing primitive godlike superego, but also living in fear of being cast out, as though from the Garden of Eden, if any questioning or curiosity develops.

If one develops any need, whether emotional or physical, such as a bout of flu, this is felt to be a criticism of the primitive god-like superego, who should have prevented it happening, or of oneself for not following the correct path to prevent getting ill in the first place and this may trigger another depressive episode of self-berating.

The commonest symptom of depression is extreme agitation, as at the moment of curiosity or questioning, one feels separated from the godlike superego. This results in a feeling of being completely unheld, like a newly born baby left on a changing mat shaking with the 'Moro reflex'.

This central insecurity, which the patient experiences at the slightest challenge to their total submission to the narcissistic object, explains why anxiety is the most prominent of all symptoms of depression, and why general psychiatrists often use the overall term 'agitated depression'.

In her paper 'Mourning and its relation to manic depressive states', Klein (1940) also emphasised a central theme of insecurity in individuals with depression, explaining it in terms of their inability in childhood to establish their good objects and so feel secure in their inner world.

Bion's insights on the role of the maternal container add further depth to our appreciation of the nature of the agitation:

> Normal development follows if the relationship between infant and breast permits the infant to project a feeling, say, that it is dying into the mother and to reintroject it after its sojourn in the breast has made it tolerable to the infant psyche. If the projection is not accepted by the mother, the infant feels that its feeling that it is dying is stripped of such meaning as it has. It therefore reintrojects, not a fear of dying made tolerable, but a nameless dread.
>
> (Bion 1967, p. 116)

Each of the various symptoms of depression invites consideration from a dynamic perspective. Agoraphobia might be understood in terms of fear of separation from the idealised identification, since having any separate identity would bring down the wrath of a jealous

225

god. An analytic patient of mine, when depressed, would develop agoraphobia, linked to fears of having developed a shape to her body, as if this represented individuality and would draw hostile notice to her.

Symptoms akin to mourning can be understood in terms of the feeling that the ideal object has been lost, with both the self (depersonalisation) and the outer world (derealisation) feeling unreal. Patients with depression typically wake early and feel worse in the morning, feeling better as the day goes on. Biological psychiatry has unsuccessfully tried to explain these features in terms of diurnal variations in steroid levels, but the symptoms can be also considered at an analytic level.

A man with severe unrelenting depression, whom I saw supportively for a year, came weekly to the outpatient clinic accompanied by his wife. After I had left, he was admitted and received ECT, but sadly then took his own life. His problem was that he could not come to terms with the fact that, in a fit of rage during the war, he had killed a Japanese soldier who was on the point of surrendering, because the Japanese soldier had recently killed his friend, whom he had found with his head smashed open. He would wake up early from a recurring nightmare. In the dream, a man had been shot in the head. His skull was open and he was dying. The patient was holding him, waiting for the doctor to come. The man died just before the doctor came.

There were of course many striking aspects of this case, including the impossibility of reparation, as the patient could never forgive himself for having committed his murderous attack. However, the point that I wish to highlight here is the patient's waking early with the recurrent nightmare and then feeling worse in the morning, but improving as the day went on, that is his symptoms of early morning wakening and diurnal mood variation.

We have an internal as well as an external world, and this helps to make sense of the patient's experience at a psychological level. The patient wakes up early in order to escape a terrifying and critical internal world. Patients with depression feel worse on wakening as they find themselves totally dominated by their unforgiving internal world. As the day progresses they start to feel better, since the external world is a far more humanly responsive one than their internal world. Consideration of this dynamic may also introduce a way of talking with patients and their relatives about the internal experience.

## The place for medication

Since the godlike primitive superego of patients with depression demands that all feelings or other signs of need be repressed, these feelings may be projected into the body and felt only as physical sensations, referred to as 'depressive equivalents'. While depression raises fascinating questions about the relationship between the mind and bodily experiences, as transmitted through neuronal networks, at the end of the day, we may be left with a patient with no insight seeking relief from very distressing physical symptoms. This is where antidepressant and anxiolytic medication enter the picture.

A patient gave a history of being a corporal in the army many years ago. When he was 30, he had an attack of pericarditis. This destroyed his delusion of immortality. He held on to this belief by projecting his anger at the loss into his body. He became consumed with hypochondriasis, complaining of pain in every organ. If visitors came round to see his family, he would dominate the conversation and talk of pain from his big toe to his testis, abdomen, chest and head.

If his behaviour became too much for the family, he would be admitted to give them respite and he would receive medication or ECT. I inherited him when he was in his sixties. On admission, he again talked incessantly about his symptoms. However, I was struck by the way he managed to chase the female nurses round the ward with his walking stick, in a sexually provocative way. Interestingly on the morning of his birthday, his mind temporarily returned to his head. He behaved normally, in a patients' group, inquiring about other patients' welfare. However, he then reverted to his former ways. This patient lacked any insight and all treatment inevitably remained at a physical level. However, we can still take a psychoanalytic interest in the way his mind was functioning.

One has to accept that, for some people, the severity of their psychopathology is such that one can treat them only at a physical level. Others, whose psychopathology might not be so severe, may come for psychotherapy while taking medication, while others may opt for a purely psychotherapeutic approach.

When working with patients in psychotherapy, medication can be utilised to reduce the intensity of symptoms when these threaten to become incapacitating, for example, when patients are unable to get up in the morning to attend their sessions or when their suicidal

227

feelings threaten to become overwhelming. The doctor prescribing the medication, whether the general practitioner or specialist, can work in harmony with the analytic psychotherapist, provided that they share an understanding of the patient's condition and agree on the purpose of each aspect of the treatment plan.

It is very important to include the patient's spouse or partner in the management of all cases of severe depression. The partner needs support and education in the dynamics of the disorder in order to help them to endure extended periods where the patient will not listen to their advice. Understanding the transference and counter-transference issues in depression can help the patients and their relatives as well as the professionals to understand and cope with the experience.

## The transference and countertransference in depression

### *The transference*

If one conceptualises a major depressive episode as a psychotic epi-sode, then one cannot rely on one's ordinary empathy. It is necessary once more to tune into the psychotic wavelength in order to make sense of the disorder and understand the transference phenomena.

The patient has a belief that things should never have gone wrong. Their object relationship is to a god–like figure. If anything goes wrong, someone is to blame because it could have always been pre-vented from happening in the first place. There is no desire for under-standing, only a wish to return to a previous trouble-free state.

> An example would be a man driving a car who knocks over another man riding a motorbike. The motorcyclist is lying on the ground uncon-scious. His motorbike is in flames. The driver gets out of his car and beats himself on his chest, saying to himself, look what a terrible person you are for what you have done, but he does not lift a finger to help the motorcyclist.

This leads on to the countertransference experience for those trying to help the patient, whether psychiatrists, analytical therapists or relatives.

## The countertransference

The first issue to be appreciated is the clash of interest between the patient and the carers. Patients are not interested in gaining insight; their only concern is to find a way to regain their previous illusion of perfection. The therapist or relative, on the other hand, tries to persuade the patient not to be so demanding and critical of themselves and to take a more reasoned, forgiving and understanding approach. The countertransference feelings experienced by the carer are frustration and irritation, as anything that is offered in terms of helpful advice is rejected, while the patient persists in remaining in a troubled state.

While the process of self-berating goes on, it feels to the professionals and carers as though there is no sign of light at the end of the tunnel and that the process will go on forever. Often patients themselves will ask if their state of depression will ever end. The carers need help to appreciate that patients' self-berating over the loss of their illusion of perfection is an internal process that will go on with a momentum of its own until it abates. The carers may need help to understand that they should not take the patient's rejections of their offers of help personally.

The relatives' need for support becomes much more pressing when manic states arise (see Chapter 14), which involve an element of triumphing over the object of dependency. This is projected onto the nearest relative, with acting out behaviour of verbal abuse and sexual affairs. Such behaviour is potentially very destructive of relationships and once patients have come down from their manic state, there can be a real risk of suicidal behaviour. In such circumstances, it is even more important to help and support the relatives in understanding and coping with their countertransference feelings.

I will conclude with a discussion of the two superegos, the mature benign reflective superego and the ego-destructive superego that takes over in depression, as this can provide us with an overall framework for thinking about depression.

## The superego in depression

Freud (1923) introduced the concept of the superego in *The Ego and the Id*. He described how one part of the ego sets itself over against the other and judges it critically. The superego incorporated Freud's previous concepts of the dream censor, the special agency in the ego, ego ideal and unconscious sense of guilt (Laplanche and Pontalis 1973).

Klein described an early pre-oedipal stage to the formation of the superego. She thought that a very harsh superego was already in evidence at the oral stage, which becomes modified over time, with experience, gradually becoming more benign, less demanding and more tolerant of human frailty (Segal 1973a).

Freud commented on the particular characteristics of the superego in melancholia, noting an 'extraordinary harshness and severity towards the ego' in both obsessional neurosis and melancholia (Freud 1923, p. 53). However, the superego was more dangerous in melancholia where it could be seen as 'a pure culture of the death instinct [which] often succeeds in driving the ego into death' (Freud 1923, p. 53).

Klein also referred to an early very harsh superego, formed as a result of a defusion of the instincts, which stood apart and was unmodified by the normal processes of growth (M. Klein 1958; O'Shaughnessy 1999). It is necessary to take the operation of this abnormal superego into account in cases of depression.

Bion outlined the characteristics of this ego-destructive superego in the following way: 'It is a super-ego that has hardly any characteristics of the super-ego as understood in psychoanalysis: it is "super" ego. It is an envious assertion of moral superiority without any morals' (Bion 1962, p. 97). He further comments,

> In so far as its resemblance to the super-ego is concerned [it] shows itself as a superior object asserting its superiority by finding fault with everything. The most important characteristic is its hatred of any new development in the personality as if the new development were a rival to be destroyed.
>
> (Bion 1962, p. 98)

The following example illustrates the extraordinarily murderous character of the ego-destructive superego.

A patient with a long history of depression had reached mid-life. He had no previous history of self-harm. He had never worked and had lived with his mother until she died two years previously, when he went to live with his single brother, who went to work. He spent his days visiting different sisters,

230

who remained very loving and supportive. He had recently become somewhat more agitated, but persistently denied suicidal feelings, including on
the very day that he actually committed suicide by repeatedly stabbing
himself with a kitchen knife, with his brother returning from work to find
him dead.

His family needed help to understand that their loving feelings had
been appropriately directed in supporting a dependent part of the
patient that had never been allowed to develop by his ego–destructive
superego. When the patient reached mid-life and this murderous part
of him was called to account for its destructiveness in never having
allowed the patient to develop a life, it turned on the ego and killed it.
In my discussion with the patient's relatives in the aftermath of his
suicide, one of his sisters recalled how months previously, he had said
that his body was tired of living, which suggested that his ego had
been located in his body where it could be attacked by the superego.

Bion thought that the pathological superego arose out of early
failures in communication between the infant and mother. In depression, the ego–destructive superego takes over the driving seat
and attacks the self. In such a situation, O'Shaughnessy (1999)
summarises:

> No working through can take place, only an impoverishment and
> deterioration of relations, with an escalation of hatred and anxiety
> that results in psychotic panic or despair. In this dangerous situ-
> ation, the significant event for the patient is to be enabled to move
> away from his abnormal superego, return to his object, and so
> experience the analyst as an object with a normal superego.
>
> (O'Shaughnessy 1999, p. 861)

To end on a more positive note, in contrast to the previous
example, there are also cases where patients may actively seek help
through analytic psychotherapy.

A young woman came to therapy with a five-year history of disabling
depression. She had been hospitalised early in the illness and had been on
antidepressant medication for a number of years. She came from a strict
religious background. She wished to develop her own mind, while facing
up to the guilt of developing a different attitude to her parents. She was
determined to come off medication. She described her feelings in therapy

as going round and round in reflecting on painful events; however, the movement was like a spiral rather than a circle, so that there was a gradual forward movement. The active involvement of the therapist on the side of a mature reflective superego helped lessen the effects of the patient's ego-destructive superego and support the development of her own mind.

Prior to analytic therapy, this young woman would typically wake in an exhausted and tense state, often unable to get up for the day, and recalling recurring nightmares of being chased by gunmen. After some time in the therapy, she had a different dream in which I was associated with helping her with her internal world. She reported waking from this dream in quite a different state of mind, with a pleasant feeling rather than an exhausted one.

## Summary

It is vital to distinguish major depressive episodes from low mood. If we regard major depressive episodes as manifestations of an under-lying psychotic disorder, we need to make a special effort to tune into the wavelength of the psychopathology in order to understand it and become empathic to the ongoing process.

Psychoanalysis as well as biological psychiatry has much to contribute in the understanding and management of depression. A biological and a psychoanalytic approach are not necessarily mutually incompatible.

The psychoanalytic theory of an abnormal ego–destructive super-ego operating in depression has implications for the overall framework of approach to treatment of this condition. The priority in treatment, whether through medication or analytic psychotherapy, is to unseat the primitive ego-destructive superego and gradually enable its place to be taken by a more mature and reflective superego. Only when the reflective superego is back in place can any meaningful analytic work be done to strengthen the patient's ego or individuality.

## PART FIVE

# Implications for Management
# and Education

# 17

## Developing an exoskeleton

### Introduction

The onset of a schizophrenic breakdown in an adolescent is an alarming state of affairs. The psychosis may have been hidden through projective identification, with the parents acting as the container, until emotional separation in late adolescence results in a massive fragmentation of the personality. In this situation what is urgently needed is to build up what I would call an exoskeleton around the patient, that is, a containing structure that is responsive to the patient's needs, takes in his or her projections and responds to them in a containing way.

It can take years to build an effective exoskeleton around the patient. This containing structure may involve family, committed professionals, a day centre, or possibly a group home with the back-up of the inpatient ward as a safety net.

The aim of this chapter is to underline the patient's chaotic and dangerous state of mind during the first years after the emergence of a severe psychotic disorder like schizophrenia. I will discuss the problems that the patient's relatives may encounter in their attempts to mobilise the relevant psychiatric services into a committed team to develop an effective containing exoskeleton. I will use material from a particular clinical case to illustrate the difficulties. This case also raises the issue of what psychoanalysis has to offer within this context.

### The early years of schizophrenia: living with the unbearable

I want to use the history given by the mother of a young man who was developing schizophrenia, who shared her concerns with me during those early most difficult years. This case raises important issues for further consideration.

This family's history poses a challenge to the current widely expressed views that schizophrenia is not an illness, but rather an invention, that the concept should be abandoned, that it can be prevented by creating the conditions for saner societies, and that in first-onset psychosis the emphasis should be on non-hospital, non-drug intervention (Bentall 2004; Davies and Burdett 2004; Read 2004; Read et al. 2004).

> Mr M was a young man of 25. He had started to become ill five years previously. He became psychotic, left home, took drugs and took to wandering round the country, and then to wandering around abroad while he was unwell. Mr M's parents were very intelligent, sensitive people, he had a sister who was quite well and there was no family history of schizophrenia. His mother at this time was trying to cope with this nightmare on her own.
>
> In those early years when Mr M took to wandering around England it was clear to his mother that he was very ill. In fact he had been ill for several years before she was able to get professional help for him. The professionals were not prepared to take responsibility for sectioning him. They seemed unwilling to listen to his parents. Many professionals along the way gave Mr M's age as the reason for their failure to intervene, telling his parents that it was up to their son whether he accepted help or not. His mother described this viewpoint as in itself completely mad, and another way to allow his GP and the Social Services to distance themselves from becoming involved in his care.
>
> During Mr M's wanderings in England he was repeatedly seen and observed to be ill, but no one would take responsibility for his condition. For his parents it was like trying to get blood out of a stone to get the professionals to give them any information about their son. Mr M's age and issues of confidentiality were repeatedly used to justify their refusal to discuss his state with them.
>
> Mr M then went off to France, where within twenty-four hours his illness was recognised and he was repatriated. When his mother was able to identify that he was returning to England, she managed to alert the professionals and finally, with the aid of a social worker, succeeded in having him admitted to a hospital on a section and then transferred to the local psychiatric service. He was in a florid psychotic state. It was very upsetting for his mother, as at first he was very hostile towards her, saying that he would never return home again.

He eventually settled with medication and returned home. He continued to see his local psychiatric consultant for outpatient follow-up and was prescribed oral and depot medication. His parents also arranged analysis for him, though this involved considerable travelling from the countryside for daily sessions.

Before exhibiting any psychotic features Mr M had presented a picture of a troubled adolescent, and at that time his mother had turned to a very experienced, but non-medical, adolescent psychoanalyst for advice. When he subsequently became psychotic, the analyst told her to sit with him twenty-four hours a day. This advice made her upset and angry as she felt that it failed to address the issue of how frightening the situation had become for her.

After Mr M's initial admission, his mother tried to get him involved in a variety of activities during the day. At this stage, she did not feel that his being in an environment daily with patients with chronic psychoses would be therapeutic and the professional staff did not have any suitable alternative day facilities to offer. Initially Mr M responded to her suggestions of activities or studies with great enthusiasm, but this quickly turned to avoidance. He soon became socially isolated.

Early on in his illness, Mr M had stood on the banister rail, at the top of the stairwell, threatening to jump. He then laughed at his mother saying, 'I'm only doing it to frighten you!' He had also said that he didn't want to grow up but wanted to remain an 8-year-old boy.

His behaviour became totally draining. For example, when his mother would pick him up in the car after his analytic sessions, he would drag her through some alarming paranoid state of mind and after an hour calm down again, by which time she would be thoroughly exhausted. These episodes also occurred at other times of day, such as in the evening at home, and increased in frequency.

If his parents left him to get up in the morning, he would often stay in his bedroom till the afternoon. He would passively agree to any idea suggested, but imparted no conviction of a real involvement. His father became so concerned by his state that he felt unable to leave him on his own. He would sit with his son as if he was undergoing a physical crisis, waiting for the crisis to remit, as advocated by his first analyst. His mother did not agree with this approach and felt that there was a need to make the professionals more aware of Mr M's alarming states of mind so that they would intervene.

Mr M's disturbing states intensified. When the relatively innocuous step of arranging for him to attend a fortnightly befriender's group led to an acute psychotic reaction, in which he experienced worms eating into his body, his mother felt that she could no longer manage him by herself.

When she managed to get hold of Mr M's community nurse to see him while he was in this state, the community nurse arranged a review meeting with his psychiatrist. For some time, his mother had been worried about potential suicide, but felt that there had been no choice other than to live with the risk and manage her son's moods on a day-to-day basis.

His consultant psychiatrist was also worried about his state and thought that he should come into hospital for a few weeks, to get his medication adjusted. It transpired that this primarily meant the addition of antidepressant medication. His mother felt guilty about the need for admission, as if she was abandoning Mr M. At first the hospital reminded her of an old Victorian institution, and she imagined her son being institutionalised and lost forever in depressing Dickensian surroundings.

At the same time, with his admission she felt a great weight being taken off her shoulders and her overriding memory afterwards of the time he spent there was that she had been very impressed by the Victorian hospital. It seemed to her to have been the only proper place of sanctuary offered to her son, a physical structure that could contain him.

A few days after admission, Mr M's named nurse, whom his mother felt was involved with his case and knew what was going on, went away for a few days. When his mother next visited him, she found that he had stayed in bed for the last two days. The bed was in a mess and the room didn't appear to have been cleaned. Her son didn't appear to mind at all. He talked of there being nothing left in life and he was preoccupied with thoughts of hanging himself.

At the same time, he didn't want his mother to speak to the nurses. It seemed that this was as much because he did not want their attention drawn to the state of his room as because of his suicidal risk. In fact, a few hours later, he phoned his mother on her mobile to let her know that he was no longer feeling suicidal and was feeling much better. The next day, he was pleased to relate to his mother that the nurses had taken custody of his razor and cigarette lighter, as if being designated ill had exempted him from any responsibilities.

His mother had had anxiety dreams during the week of Mr M's admission, indicative of the stress that she was carrying. One was of a fruit bowl that was full to overflowing with too many items; all were items she needed to attend to. The other dream was simply a picture of manicured nails, which seemed to represent her attempts to keep her feelings to herself, in a manicured state, until this became unbearable.

I have described these events in some detail in order to convey an authentic picture of what it is like to be the parent of a young person who has been overtaken by a schizophrenic illness. They have lost the person that they once knew. The situation is a nightmare. There is worry about potential suicide. There is a struggle to try to make sense of the situation, as well as attempts to find temporary relief by blaming oneself or the institution for its shortcomings.

I think that it would be misleading to blame the facilities available or the degree of coordination between the professionals, as it inevitably took time for the situation they were facing to unfold. Medication had been given and activity placements had been tried. Indeed, in the early years of Mr M's illness, he was regarded as too well to attend a day centre for chronic states. I have learned over the years that it is important when coping with protracted psychotic episodes to think in terms of it being nobody's fault but view the illness as having its own autonomy. This helps to free us in our attitude to our work. In Chapter 14 I discussed a patient with recurrent manic depressive episodes whom I followed analytically in the health service over many years, whose case also illustrates the need to think in this way.

## Underlying dynamics

### *Tuning into the psychotic wavelength*

To make sense of what has been happening with this patient we must first tune in to the psychotic wavelength. We have be aware of the dominance of the psychotic part of Mr M's mind, which is intolerant of frustration and uses the mind as a muscular organ to evacuate the thinking undertaken by the non-psychotic part of the mind. The psychotic part is driven by deadly anti-life forces. Having evacuated the concerns arrived at by the non-psychotic part, the psychotic part fills the gap with denial and rationalisations, and then presents itself to the outside world as if very reasonable in attitude.

### *Who makes the diagnosis of a psychotic disorder?*

In ordinary circumstances, patients take themselves to the doctor with troublesome symptoms. The doctor makes a diagnosis, decides on the severity of the condition and prescribes treatment. In major psychotic disorders, the situation is the reverse of normal. The relative or partner makes the diagnosis and goes to the professionals. It is then a question of whether they are going to be believed.

This places an enormous strain on the relatives, here Mr M's mother in particular. She is the one who realises Mr M's condition in the first place and his later deterioration and she then has to alert and convince the professionals to become involved.

### Issues of confidentiality

Mr M had told his mother not to divulge to the nursing staff that he was preoccupied with suicidal thoughts. She, of course, did tell the staff. However, perhaps the 'of course' is not so obvious. Professionals sometimes misguidedly maintain the same respect for patient confidentiality when working with individuals with psychotic disorders as they would with non-psychotic patients. Psychotherapists normally regard their involvement with patients as private and sacrosanct, but if a patient is exhibiting suicidal or homicidal features, it can become important to share concerns.

The issue of confidentiality again raises the issue of needing to be clear in one's mind about whether one is working with a patient with a neurosis or a psychosis. Mr M's mother graphically described how, for several years, at the onset of his illness, the professionals refused to divulge information or listen properly to his parents' concerns because of his age, and did not accept that there should be a difference of approach in relating to psychosis as opposed to neurosis. When working with psychotic patients, issues of safety, whether for the patient or the public, should always override issues of confidentiality.

### The multidisciplinary approach

Clearly, if concerns about the management of patients in psychotic states are to be shared, there has to be freedom of communication between the responsible professionals. The South Devon Homicide Inquiry into the murder of an occupational therapist concluded that tragedies were less likely to happen, even if many cannot be prevented, when there is a good supportive morale and when professionals from different disciplines are able to communicate openly about their concerns without misguided restraints over confidentiality (Blom-Cooper et al. 1996).

Since patients in psychotic states tend to project their difficulties and it is the relatives or professionals who first pick these projections up, it is important for the involved professionals and relatives to get together. This means that a multidisciplinary approach where every participant's information is afforded equal respect is essential. It is like putting together a jigsaw puzzle: we cannot know in advance who may have the missing link that will enable us to clarify the picture.

No piece of information should be regarded as sacrosanct. We have to create an atmosphere that will enable us to share and discuss our anxieties freely as a team, especially when faced with potentially suicidal states of mind.

### Addressing suicidal states of mind

When addressing suicidal states in psychosis, we have to consider whether to try to understand the act using our ordinary empathic feelings or whether we need to tune into a different wavelength. The ordinary way of understanding such states of mind would be to say that we can all become depressed at times, and we could understand that someone in Mr M's position might feel like ending it all. The approach that would follow from understanding his case in this way would be to contain the patient in hospital and give him antidepressant medication until he started to feel better, as his psychiatrist initially suggested to his mother. While this view of Mr M as in need of treatment for depression is understandable, the question arises of whether it is the only way to explain Mr M's alarmingly fluctuating suicidal state.

An alternative framework would be to understand Mr M's suicidality in terms of a psychotic part of his personality that sometimes threatens to attack or even murder the healthy part in order to prevent exposure of its self-destructive behaviour.

## Approach to the hospitalised patient

We can now use the above considerations to guide our approach to a patient like Mr M, a young man with schizophrenia who is expressing suicidal ideation.

It seems to make intuitive sense to see Mr M as primarily going through a depressive phase with difficulty getting up in the morning that should respond to treatment with antidepressant medication. However, this does not fit in with his mother's report that it has been hard to get him out of bed for years. She was not impressed with the above formulation.

By thinking in terms of the psychodynamics underlying psychosis, we arrive at a different perspective. When the patient does not get out of bed in hospital and keeps his room in a mess, while his key nurse is on leave, his mood is triumphant. He is enjoying himself while he negates everything in life and contemplates ways to kill himself.

There are two parts to his personality; the psychotic part had taken over while his key nurse, who would support the life forces in him in standing up to this part of his personality, was away. The psychotic part triumphed over the life forces in the patient, reducing him to staying in bed, neglecting to eat or care for himself and idealising self-destructiveness. His fear of being on the receiving end of this manic murderousness was projected so that it was his mother who was left to carry the worry about his state, as indeed she had been prior to the admission. The psychotic part of Mr M did not want its way of behaving exposed, so tried to intimidate his mother by telling her not to communicate with the nurses.

Later the patient tried to play down his behaviour as a passing mood, rather than a persistent way of being, by ringing his mother on her mobile to reassure her that he was now feeling better. However, by now, his mother was not prepared to accept his rationalised explanation of his behaviour. At this point it was important to confront the patient with the operation of this powerful part of his personality with its deadening ways which, fuelled by grandiosity and indiscriminate envy, would rather murder himself to remove the evidence of his behaviour than be exposed for questioning. The patient also needed to be helped to realise that it was his parents who were left to contain the frightened feelings of the projected healthy part of himself that was on the receiving end of the threatened attack.

The psychotic part of Mr M derived a cruel enjoyment from frightening his parents. Of course, the consequence of his behaviour was that he remained in a dependent state and never had to face growing up, as he had spelled out when he said that he wanted to remain a little boy forever. Powerful forces are operating to maintain this state of affairs.

For movement forward to occur, all the carers needed to respond to the presenting situation, first by grasping the true state of affairs, and then by planning a joint strategy with a logical coherence. The patient then needed to be confronted with this plan. Mr M would need to be repeatedly confronted with the negative ways in which a part of his mind could work, undermining therapeutic initiatives, and how he kept trying to seduce others into accepting his ways as reasonable, for example on the ward where he initially succeeded in having his occupational therapy (OT) programme arranged for the afternoon because he couldn't get up in the morning.

As Bion (1957a) described, in schizophrenia there is a never-decided conflict between the life and death instincts. In working with such patients one should not be thinking in terms of bringing about a cure; rather, the professionals need to engage alongside the patient's family in a lifelong struggle against the powerful negating forces at work in him, starting with the immediate worry of the risk of suicide if the destructive forces were left unaddressed. An ongoing concern in working with Mr M was that as soon as anything positive was instigated, like the befriender's group, it led to a frightening backlash from the psychotic part. This situation was understandably too much for his parents to manage on their own. A whole team needed to be involved, and in planning his care it was important to consider whether he might benefit from placement in a well-organised group home with in-built structured activities, if one was available.

This may all sound terribly obvious, but when it comes to dealing with psychosis, nothing is straightforward or can be taken for granted. For example, it had been felt that the patient was too depressed to get up and go to OT in the mornings. A few days later, when he was out on leave with his parents for lunch in the local town, he suddenly walked into the road in front of a car, so that his mother had to pull him back. When she then chastised him, he had a paranoid outburst, got out of the car while it was moving, and made his own way back to the hospital. A tranquilliser was added to his medication to calm him down. The next morning he got up and went to OT, presumably afraid of what the staff's reactions might be to his destructive behaviour of the day before.

## Living with unbearable anxieties

It is important to appreciate how difficult it is for the professionals as well as the family to live with unbearable anxieties, when a patient presents in an unpredictable acute psychotic state. We can give more tranquillisers as an interim measure to make both ourselves and the patient feel better. We can look for an ideal solution, for example by pinning our hopes on clozapine, a drug that is prescribed for cases that have proved refractory to other medication.

However, we must also remember to ask ourselves whether our overwhelming need to find an answer does not represent a psychotic reaction to unbearable pressure that leads us to play down the over-all difficulties and concentrate on one aspect in the hope of finding a definitive solution. This might take the form of advocating the primacy of medication, a behavioural approach or psychoanalysis, or one may be played off as superior to the other. We are then in danger of developing a closed mind rather than achieving an integrated approach.

## Further developments

In time, Mr M's mental state settled sufficiently to enable his return to the community. He chose to immerse himself in the church. While there was concern about his over-identification with religion as a substitute for his own growth, at the same time the church community provided a warm, socially supportive atmosphere for him. In time he found a partner, also somewhat fragile with her own mental health problems, and they were accommodated together in supportive accommodation. Mr M received supervised medication and ongoing monitoring from his parents and the professional staff, so that an effective exoskeleton supporting him was now in place.

The establishment of this supportive exoskeleton took many years of hard work, especially by his mother, who had to learn what it meant to have his condition and find a way of communicating effectively with the professionals. However, lifelong monitoring would need to remain in place.

Finally it is interesting to consider the place of analysis in Mr M's case. Mr M's mother had sought help from all possible sources, including analytic help, especially early on. She found the advice of the non-medical adolescent psychoanalyst at the time when Mr M first broke down unhelpful. He needed admission, not a misguided attempt to contain his psychosis by sitting with him twenty-four hours a day. Later, still in the initial stages of his illness, Mr M underwent several years of individual analysis. This was a very difficult time for his mother, as he had to be driven a considerable distance to his sessions and he would often have disturbed episodes in the car on the way home.

As a supportive exoskeleton started to take shape in the local community, together with logistical difficulties in managing to fit in the travel to sessions while attending local activities, Mr M became resistant to continuing with his analysis and his mother decided that it was the right time for him to stop. Mr M's analyst told her that continued analysis was the only hope for his future. His mother again required strength of character to not accept that this was the case.

It is important to consider the place of psychoanalysis in the early management of this patient's schizophrenic illness. Early on in his illness, his mother turned to analysis for help and support in addressing Mr M's psychotic state and encouraging his capacity for thinking. The aim of individual analysis would be to contain fragmented states of mind and strengthen the non-psychotic part's capacity for reflection. However, it would be a mistake to believe that individual psychoanalysis was the only thing that mattered for progress. In the early years of the illness, the most important thing is the gradual establishment of an effective exoskeleton of local supportive services. Applied analytic thinking has a place in considering what needs to be built into the supportive framework, and in making sense of states of relapse, but when working with psychosis one should not fall into the trap of placing all one's eggs in one basket, and becoming morally judgemental about all other initiatives.

## Summary

The onset of a severe schizophrenic illness is a frightening state of affairs, with unpredictable acting out behaviour. Typically it is the parents who have to cope with this state of affairs emerging in their late adolescent child and alert the professionals. It may take something like five years for the patient's mental state to settle down. During this period, it is vital to build up a supportive exoskeleton, a team composed of carers and professionals who are reliably available to contain and respond to the patient's needs. While medication, psychological interventions and occupational activities are important, the priority in the early years of the illness remains the recognition of the need to build up an ongoing supportive network, for responding to situations that the psychotic part of the mind cannot deal with if left to itself.

Later on, the patient may relapse if the supportive exoskeleton breaks down. In these relapses the patient may produce delusions, with the associated affect being projected into the carers. The need for the carers to process their countertransference experiences in order to make sense of the delusions is discussed in Chapters 12 and 13.

# 18

# Destructive attacks on reality and the self

## Introduction

The focus of this chapter is the destructive attacks on reality and the self encountered in work with patients in everyday general psychiatry. Psychoanalytic insight can help us to understand the underlying psychopathology, and assist us as we try to understand and cope with the tragedies that can result from these violent attacks. There are three areas of particular concern: violence directed at the self (suicidal acts), violence directed at others (murderous attacks) and the effect of such incidents on staff morale.

We need a framework of understanding to help us cope when we are presented with either potentially or actually destructive actions. Constant risk assessment is required to work with patients with unpredictably fluctuating states of mind (Lucas 2003b). This chapter describes the author's development of a framework of understanding linked to clinical experiences, and contrasts this approach with the more prescriptive approach to management through the use of risk assessment forms.

## The overall assessment of risk

Since the mid 1990s momentous changes have occurred within the National Health Service in the UK, with the closure of the large asylums and a shift of emphasis to community care in conjunction with district hospitals. Subsequently tragedies have occurred, like the Christopher Clunis case where a man with paranoid schizophrenia and a history of past aggression was left unsupervised in the

247

community and killed a stranger while he was in a deluded state. Such tragedies have led to the creation of more medium secure units but not more general psychiatric facilities.

Management's anxiety over containing disturbed behaviour has replaced asylum walls with 'walls of paper', namely the Care Programme Approach (CPA) form and the risk assessment form. The problem with forms can be that they encourage a psychotic belief that everything would have been all right if only one had followed the form. However, review and research articles continue to reinforce the view that there is no foolproof way to prevent tragedies. Proulx et al. (1997) conducted a study of 100 inpatient suicides and concluded that 'inpatient suicides remain a relatively rare phenomenon difficult to predict, and that all the signs of a potentially impending suicide can be identified more easily with the benefit of hindsight' (Proulx et al. 1997: 250). If used retrospectively, suicide risk scales tended to identify a large number of false positives. This study did not find any specific item which would improve the specificity of such scales.

However, the government-driven desire to achieve an anxiety-free state about the risk of violence to self or others, has resulted in a trend towards giving undue weight to risk assessment forms. The statistics from Appleby's National Confidential Inquiry into homicides and suicides revealed that 24 per cent of suicide cases, some 1,200, had had previous contact with mental health services. Half of these had contact with mental health services in the week before their death, but in 85 per cent of cases the risk was not perceived. Among the recommendations for improvement was a thorough overhaul of the CPA, and training in risk assessment (Appleby 1997; Thompson 1999). This preoccupation with forms seems illogical as the patients were actually receiving medical attention at the time of suicide. The proper conclusion is that when it comes to individual cases, we still have to rely on our own sensitivities and clinical acumen, and learn from experience.

The following serves as an example of what I would call a delusional belief in the power of forms over feelings. It comes from a monthly Trust review on violent incidents and the recommended lessons to be learned. It is typical of many others.

Incident: Doctor kicked on the shin while assessing a patient in the emergency reception centre.

Recommendation: Training on risk assessment required.

Lessons learnt: Completion of risk assessment forms on all patients.

Forms do of course have their uses. It is always important to record suicidal ideation in the medical or nursing notes. Perhaps the CPA's best feature is the requirement to designate a key worker responsible for coordinating follow-up care. The risk assessment's best feature is an invitation to look through past psychiatric records to alert one to previous alarming states of mind and acting out behaviour. However, spending time filling out 120 boxes on a risk assessment form not only is unnecessary bureaucracy, but also takes valuable time away from the nurses' contact with their patients. Forms will never be a substitute for learning from actual clinical experience and acquiring relevant frameworks of understanding is an ongoing individual learning curve for all of us.

As I have argued in earlier chapters, when relating to the destructive attacks on reality associated with major psychiatric disorders, one needs to think in terms of two separate parts to the personality, and to bear in mind that that the psychotic part is the dominating force. It is resistant to change and, at times when it feels under threat, can produce a dangerous backlash. Since there is an intimate relationship between the mind and the body, the non-psychotic part of the personality can be projected into the body and the body then attacked. This situation, arising in major psychotic disorders, is to be distinguished from the self-harm characteristic of borderline states, where a suffocating object might be projected into the body and temporary relief of tension sought through cutting.

## Violence to self

This psychoanalytic framework of understanding can help us to comprehend suicidal states of mind and to manage both our own anxieties, and those of staff, relatives and management. The following two examples illustrate how experience gained from one suicide helped to make sense of a subsequent suicide through the application of this framework for understanding.

# Case 1: An inpatient suicide

Mrs N was a middle-aged woman with a ten-year history of unremitting chronic severe psychotic depression. Many years ago, she had jumped on a railway line and lost both legs. Since then, she had made further suicide attempts by taking overdoses. Following the overdoses, she was admitted into hospital on section. She would never discuss her suicide attempts. She would just fixate me with a chillingly murderous stare. She would also have screaming fits on the ward that were not amenable to discussion, but would subside prior to discharge back into the community.

We spoke at length with her husband about her outlook, and the likelihood that she would one day succeed in killing herself. We agreed we could only do our best. While in hospital, the nursing staff and occupational therapist found it hard to engage her in any activity. The only sign of life she gave was her interest in playing games of Scrabble. My countertransference feelings of being at the receiving end of her chilling stare led me to think about the underlying dynamics in terms of a dominating murderous psychotic part that had imprisoned another part of her, a part that did want human contact, that is through the games of Scrabble.

In other words, it was important to think about Mrs N in terms of two totally separate parts of her personality. The powerful psychotic part is never to be contradicted. Fuelled by the death instinct, nothing is allowed to change or develop. It is never to be challenged or criticised, and any attempt to change this state of affairs will lead to a murderous backlash. The psychotic part keeps another part of the personality imprisoned, the non-psychotic part that longs for companionship and support for development and freedom of expression. It was my countertransference experience at the time that alerted me to this underlying dynamic of a powerful psychotic part keeping the non-psychotic part in an imprisoned state.

When Mrs N returned home, she would lie downstairs with her elderly mother in attendance until the next admission. I put to her that there was an imprisoned part of her mind that wanted us to help bring some variety into her life when out of hospital, and a tear trickled down her cheek. She said that she would like to be taken swimming. We said that we would make arrangements for a befriender to take her swimming when she was settled enough to return home. The CPA programme was fully in place and recorded.

Two weeks before her death, she was left behind while other patients went on a day-trip by bus to the seaside because the bus could not accommodate her wheelchair. She appeared angry. Afterwards, when she was having a bath, the nurse bathing her left her briefly to fetch a towel. The nurse returned to find her submerged under water, giving the nurse a fright as she pulled her up. This bathroom also contained the only toilet on the ward wide enough to accommodate her wheelchair from which she could get independently onto the toilet. Her mood settled over the next twenty-four hours. She continued, as previously, to go independently to that toilet. Within two weeks, it was felt that she was ready for a trial weekend at home. But when her husband came to collect her on the Saturday morning, she had gone to the toilet, turned on the bath and drowned herself.

The aftermath of this event is of particular interest. I had been away on leave and returned to face an internal hospital inquiry to investigate and look for any lessons to be learned. For example, was the CPA form completed and had it been reviewed recently? Did everyone know its content? Did another nurse become the key worker if the key worker was not on duty? Was there adequate interdisciplinary communication? Could the ward be altered in design to enhance safety? However, with the anxiety engendered, and pressures to produce a report with recommendations, there is a danger of falling into the trap of believing that answering these sorts of questions can furnish explanations for the tragedy. The nursing staff, who had cared for the patient and were devastated by her death, gave flowers and went to her funeral, inevitably then felt as though they were on the receiving end of a clinical inquiry.

Freud (1920) thought that both self-preservative life forces and self-destructive forces exist in all of us, the latter being linked with his concept of an innate death instinct. Usually our emotional states contain a mixture of positive and negative feelings. However, at times of suicidal and violent acts, there is a diffusion of the two forces, with the destructive force in the ascendant. It can also be helpful to think in Bion's terms of two separate parts of the personality, the psychotic and non-psychotic parts (Bion 1957a). In some cases of suicide, one might view the psychotic part of the mind as killing the non-psychotic part in order to avoid having to account for its own destructiveness. One might understand this case of inpatient suicide in these terms. The more open, healthy state of mind that emerged with Mrs N's tears made her vulnerable to a deadly defensive backlash.

In his classic paper 'Mourning and melancholia', Freud (1917) described how we all have to go through the work of mourning after the loss of loved ones. We have to accept their death and through

251

mourning we reinstate them inside us in our memory. However, the finality of the suicide act can incline us to more melancholic reactions, where we blame ourselves or others due to the unbearable pain of the situation. *The superego plays a leading role at every stage of the process, from the patient's illness and suicide to the consequences afterwards, and for the participants at every level of involvement, the family, the consultant and other professionals and the organisations involved.*

As the consultant I saw my role as offering support to the nursing staff by attempting to bring in a balanced perspective; namely that while an inquiry must be made and any lessons learned, the tragedy was nobody's fault and could not have been prevented. It was interesting to consider my superego or critical conscience, which I felt answerable to in that situation, as the consultant. In my mind, the arbitrator would be an understanding coroner.

Unfortunately, as both this case and the next one illustrate, it is not always possible to enable the patient to reinstate the more benign superego, and prevent the deadly attack on the ego. In this case, the coroner represented the reinstatement of a more benign mature reflective superego that tolerated the complexities of life, rather than blaming the staff.

All suicides challenge our omnipotent belief that we can help everyone and that tragedy is always preventable if we carry out correct practice. Thus, cases of suicide expose those involved to accusations from harsh superego representations. Suicides are particularly hard on nursing staff, who have given loving care to a patient over many admissions, and have to try to come to terms with a suicide at the same time as answering an immediate internal inquiry centred on CPA and risk assessment forms. Fortunately, in this case, the coroner proved to be non-judgemental. He apportioned no blame or criticism, just sympathy to all those affected by the tragedy. He approached me afterwards and told me that he felt that the patient's condition was untreatable.

## Case 2: A suicide in the community

The lessons I learned from this experience helped me when I later had to face an even more horrendous situation.

Mr P was 39 years old. His psychiatric notes described two brief admissions in his early twenties in a paranoid state. He was diagnosed with schizophrenia and placed on depot medication, which he had taken ever since. He had never worked. His father had died many years ago, and for decades he lived with his mother. Recently there was a suggestion that he had been experiencing mild mood swings, but there had been no admissions for over fifteen years. He had no history of self-harm.

Mr P had a very supportive family of four sisters and a brother, and a community mental health nurse (CMHN) monitoring the situation. He preferred to do his own thing rather than attend a day centre. When his mother died, he moved into joint accommodation with his single brother, who went to work. He would visit his sisters during the day and one married sister was particularly supportive.

He moved into our catchment area and it was noted that he had developed an agitated depression. His CMHN became concerned and felt that he needed medical attention, and she referred him to me. I saw him in the middle of a busy new patient clinic. He was clearly in an agitated and preoccupied state. However, while he accepted antidepressant medication, he refused an offer of admission. He also refused the offer of attending the day hospital, saying that he would think about it. He denied any suicidal feelings, but conveyed a distressed state and he was also informed of the Emergency Reception Centre facility.

At the time I did not think that he was sectionable, or that his family would have supported admission. I therefore arranged to review him at my next outpatient clinic, and told him to bring a relative along. Although he was clearly unwell, he refused all offers of help before I had to terminate the interview.

On Monday morning I was informed that he had committed suicide on the previous Friday afternoon. He had come to the hospital on Friday at midday to collect his tablets and had bumped into his CMHN, who used the opportunity to check on his mental state. He had not slept the night before, but had then slept to midday. When asked he denied feeling suicidal. The CMHN advised him to go round to his sister, until his brother returned from work. His brother had also ascertained that Mr P had not slept the night before, advised him to sleep to midday and then go round to his sister. Again he denied suicidal feelings. When he returned from work that afternoon, his brother found Mr P lying dead, with blood everywhere. He had cut his throat, wrists, body and legs, and had walked round the flat until he died. There was an open empty medicine bottle on the floor.

Mr P's suicide was a severe shock to both relatives and professionals. His eldest sister rang up saying that the family wanted help to understand and make sense of it. They did not blame anyone. I was left trying to process this on a typical very demanding NHS Monday morning. In the midst of my many commitments, as the consultant, I had to cope with my own feelings of guilt, with the immediate effect on the supporting staff, and attempt to process and make sense of the tragedy for the meeting arranged with Mr P's family and CMHN.

I had to come to an understanding of what had happened that would convince me and help Mr P's relatives. In my formulation I drew on my experience from the inpatient suicide and the love shown by the nurses who had attended Mrs N's funeral and sent flowers. My understanding was based on the idea that the suicidal patient splits mind and body, equates the healthy part of their mind with the bad object and projects it into their body. Their body becomes identified with the bad object, which is then murderously attacked (Bell 2001). I felt that there was a split between two parts of the patient's mind, the healthy part, which had responded to his family's love and appreciated their love and care, and the ill, very secretive part that had hidden his suicidal intentions.

The suicide of a relative is beyond ordinary comprehension and empathy alone was not enough. I had to help the relatives to understand that the patient, on reaching mid-life and separated from his mother, was having to face up to the destructiveness of the psychotic part of his mind and how it had prevented him from living. When internally brought to account, the psychotic part murderously attacked the evidence by killing itself. When I shared these thoughts with his sisters, one of them recalled the patient saying three months previously, 'My body is tired of living'. I was then able to share with them my own countertransference feelings of guilt and helplessness. These understandings enabled the relatives to begin to express more ordinary guilt feelings, such as 'If only I'd done that' and to understand how he had been sick and why he appeared to have rejected all their love and support.

On this occasion, unlike the previous clinical example of Mrs N, the family and I had not been sufficiently aware of the patient's underlying murderous state of mind before the tragedy. After I had seen the patient, I was only left with a feeling of general unease, and impatience over his having presented in a distressed state, while refusing to accept my offers of help. Only after the suicide was I able to recognise how destructive he had been and the compulsion to destroy that recognition. I then found myself able to draw on my experience with Mrs N, with the two separate parts of the personality, to help make sense of what had happened. The non-psychotic part had come to me in search of help and protection from the destructive power of the psychotic part. The struggle between the two forces had led to my countertransference feeling of an impasse towards making any progress, when I tried to clarify his presenting state of mind. This time I did not have such a clear picture of an imprisoned part of the patient's mind, as through projection I also felt imprisoned in the impasse. Only after the tragedy, with wisdom of hindsight, was I able to fully appreciate the experience that I had undergone.

This experience left me with feelings of gratitude to my psychoanalytic thinking which, together with my previous experience, had helped me to arrive at a formulation that proved helpful to the relatives. I was of course still left with my own superego telling me that if I had spent more time with the patient or had been more sympathetic, the tragedy might not have happened.

It is not surprising to hear about burnout and early retirement from general psychiatric posts, or psychiatrists opting for quieter specialities with less demanding workloads. However, psychoanalytic thinking can provide us with invaluable support and understanding as we continue to work in the 'impossible profession'.

## Violence to others: identifying the psychotic wavelength

Many interesting statistics have arisen from the National Confidential Inquiry into Suicide and Homicide by People with Mental Illness (Appleby 1997; Thompson 1999). Of the homicides, the majority had personality disorders, often abetted by drug or alcohol abuse, fewer had schizophrenia. Most victims were from within the family or the patient's circle of acquaintance. However, within the field of general psychiatry, it is the patients with psychosis that present the challenge, when trying to determine the risk of potential violence. The violent act might be to a complete stranger. If persecutory or depressive feelings become unbearable, in the psychotic state, the patient may project the problem concretely into a stranger and then seek relief by attacking the stranger. Leslie Sohn (1997) described the process in detail with an analytic study of patients who attempted to push strangers onto railway lines.

While risk assessment takes place every time a patient with a history of psychosis is seen clinically, there are two particular settings where this is the central feature of the proceedings. These are when assessing the grounds for a formal hospital admission and when a hospital tribunal is considering whether it is safe to lift a patient's restriction order.

Admission of a patient on a compulsory basis under the Mental Health Act 1983 requires a recommendation from two doctors. Ideally one should be the patient's general practitioner, who knows the patient well, and the other should be a specialist in psychiatry, ideally the responsible consultant. After speaking with the nearest relative and seeing the patient, the approved social worker then decides whether to complete the section. In most cases, there must be full agreement on the necessity for a formal admission. Only in cases where problems have arisen can lessons be learned. The following case serves as an illustration.

## Case 3: The consequences of failure to listen to a relative

The mother of a patient with a previous record of admission in a violent psychotic state noticed that her son seemed to be deteriorating. Mr R had stopped complying with his medication. He would no longer allow her access to his home and when she looked through his window, she noticed broken dishes in his bedroom. His mother notified his community mental health nurse (CMHN). Mr R threatened to harm the CMHN if she attempted to visit.

The CMHN notified the GP and as the responsible psychiatric consultant, I was asked to visit the patient at home. Mr R was clearly in a guarded and paranoid state, allowing only a limited dialogue in the hallway. I completed my part of a compulsory order. The GP did not visit, as the patient's current residence was some distance from his practice. The ASW came with another doctor, who was approved under the Mental Health Act 1983 but unfamiliar with the patient. The patient was still guarded in manner, refusing access to his room and arguing that his privacy should be respected. He said that his mother did not understand his needs, but agreed that he should not have spoken threateningly to the CMHN.

Mr R assured the ASW that he would visit his GP that week to collect further medication and that he would comply with outpatient attendance. In this situation, it was felt that the order could not be completed. The ASW also suggested that the mother might need help to improve her understanding of her son. However, the next day he was formally admitted after an unprovoked violent attack on a stranger.

Mr R had thrown bleach in the face of a young woman who was waiting to collect her young child from a school opposite to where he lived. Fortunately his attack caused no permanent disfiguration or blindness, but he said at the time that his aim had been to scar her. His action could be understood in terms of the wish of the psychotic part of his personality to avoid any reflection on his current mental state. Mr R envied the child, who seemingly had no problems as he was going to be totally looked after by his mother. The psychotic part of his personality wished to ensure that any current self-criticisms were projected and disowned into the mother, so that he could remain in an omnipotent state of mind.

This brief vignette raises several issues for consideration aside from the immediate points that the GP who knew the patient was not able to be part of the assessment team and that the ASW had not spoken directly with the consultant before arriving at his decision.

Patients with psychotic disorders project and disown their problematic states of mind, especially when relapsing. As discussed in earlier chapters, the commonest presenting symptom of psychosis is not hallucinations or delusions but lack of insight presenting as denial and rationalisation (Gelder et al. 1998). Bion's theory provides an analytic framework that can help us to understand this vignette. While the non–psychotic part of the mind is capable of reflection, the psychotic part, fuelled by envy and hatred of psychic reality, operates by evacuating troublesome feelings, thereby creating hallucinations and delusions. The psychotic part then covers up its murderous activity, by appearing calm and reasonable. Whenever we have to make an assessment of a patient with a possible history of psychosis, we must consider whether we are listening to a straightforward communication from the non–psychotic part or a rationalisation from the psychotic part.

In physical illnesses it is the doctor who makes the diagnosis. With relapse of psychosis, it is usually the relative who first makes the diagnosis. Then it is a case of whether the professionals believe the relatives or the patient's denial of illness and rationalised explanations for the reported disturbed behaviour. Without Bion's model in mind, one may be forced into a position, as in this case, of adopting a moral stance where the relative is held to be in the wrong, and consequently the degree of the patient's potential violence is underestimated.

257

The other situation where risk assessment in relation to potential violence arises is at mental health tribunals where a patient appeals against continuing detention in hospital. Tribunals can get into dreadful muddles if they lack the framework of understanding that will enable them to recognise the operation of a separate psychotic part of the patient's mind, which is capable of disguise and rationalisation.

### Case 4: The power of rationalisation

The parents of Mr S eventually had him admitted to hospital because he was living as a recluse at home, refusing to collect his benefits, and his parents had to do everything for him. His room was in such a state of neglect that they had to remove the door and replace it with a curtain in order to gain access to clean it. Mr S had the delusion that he was a film producer. He would say that he had a team under him but would never be able to substantiate this claim. In hospital he dressed soberly, wearing a sports jacket and tie, and his assertions sounded convincing. When he appealed against his section he insisted that his parents did not attend the tribunal. The tribunal sat for five hours but could not make up their minds about whether or not Mr S was a film producer as he claimed. They adjourned pending the patient bringing in a film and asking for a professional film producer to come and evaluate it.

I attended a second outside tribunal. This time his parents' views were heard, and the section was upheld.

This case illustrates the powerful persuasiveness of rationalisation and highlights the need to obtain and carefully consider the relatives' views in all cases of risk assessment relating to psychosis. The patient's very powerful projective identification of his madness into the listener can result in the listener feeling that they must be mad because the other person seems so rational. One is then left either having to negate one's doubts, or seek help from others who know more about the person's background and history.

### Summary

Risk assessment requires more than completion of the appropriate forms. Each presenting clinical case needs assessment in its own right.

Psychoanalytic insights on the working of the mind have an important contribution to make in the individual assessment of dangerous states of mind. We have to rely on our own sensitivities and clinical acumen and learn what we can from unforeseen tragedies like the cases described above. A review of major inquiries concluded that most tragedies were 'inherently unpredictable' (Blom-Cooper 1995). Good practice relied on good morale. In other words, the management and clinicians needed to support and respect each other and work as a team. A good working relationship between the involved members of the clinical team is the most important factor when trying to reduce the risk of tragedies, although it is not always possible to prevent them from happening. When tragedies occur, the team of professionals needs to make sense of the situation, and support each other and the relatives. Continued development of our own analytic sensitivities and clinical skills remains the real challenge in the field of risk assessment.

# 19

## The role of psychotherapy in reducing the risk of suicide in affective disorders
## A case study

This chapter was originally published as a joint article with Caroline Taylor-Thomas, who brought the patient for supervision.[5] I am grateful to Mrs Taylor-Thomas, an experienced psychoanalytic psychotherapist, for permission to republish the article and for her contribution. Material is presented from a patient with a diagnosis of a recurrent affective disorder who exhibited resistance to engaging in the work of therapy alongside the emergence of active suicidal intent. The case shows how supervision can help in containing intensely disturbing feelings in the therapist and aid in identifying the underlying psychosis. Through exploration of their counter-transference feelings, the therapist can become attuned to a playing down of the psychosis by the patient and alert other involved professionals. Technically, the challenge remains one of how to make an impact in the sessions by converting a psychotic monologue into a dialogue. The case illustrates the role that psychoanalytic psychotherapy can play in helping to reduce suicide risk in a depressed patient.

### Introduction

As I have argued in previous chapters, in affective disorders, as distinct from other causes of depressed states, there is a hidden psychosis. With such cases, tuning into the psychotic wavelength is necessary in order to make a significant impact. The case described in this chapter illustrates some of the features that can obscure appreciation of this underlying psychopathology.

For the psychotherapist working with a suicidally minded patient, access to regular supervision can be crucial, not only in helping the therapist to contain the intensely disturbing feelings that occur when engaging with a patient whose life is at risk, but also in helping them to process their own superego reactions.

The therapist needs support in moving from domination by a critical superego, instigated by the patient, to develop a more reflective superego. This in turn helps the patient to move into a more reflective rather than self-critical mode of functioning. Through this process, the patient comes to be able to entertain the idea of being ill rather than bad and this produces a palpable relief. The patient is gradually less dominated by self-reproach, and the difficulties encountered in making any real impact on the patient can start to be addressed. Material taken from the psychotherapy and supervision of a 36-year-old suicidal patient will be described, followed in the discussion section by a review of some of the theoretical and clinical issues raised by the material.

## Background history

Mrs T was referred for psychotherapy through a low-fee clinic scheme, suffering from depression. She was already under psychiatric care for her ongoing affective disorder. The case described is not one where the risk of suicide was only a theoretical consideration. Mrs T kept a rope in the loft in her home, contemplating using it to hang herself.

During eight years in twice-weekly psychotherapy, she has taken two overdoses and had three hospital admissions. There have been numerous threats of suicide and episodes of cutting and burning herself. Over the years Mrs T has also been on a variety of antidepressants and mood stabilisers, including lithium carbonate. At the time of writing the therapy was ongoing and Mrs T had not been readmitted to hospital for more than two years.

Mrs T is a married woman and mother of two young children. The youngest of three children herself, in childhood she was brought up in a household dominated by a recurrent physical illness of her mother and also by adherence to fundamentalist religious convictions that had run in the family for generations. Father was a 'spare the rod, spoil the child' disciplinarian who would hit the children with a stick, which he kept behind a cupboard by the stairs. The experience of growing up in this culture left Mrs T feeling that she did not exist. Religious rules substituted for her developing a mind of her own. Mrs T went on to marry a man from a similar religious background. After rising to departmental head within a caring institutional setting, she was subsequently given early retirement as her depressive illness took a grip on her.

## The treatment

The treatment will be described in three phases linked to progressive changes occurring in the therapy. In the first phase there seemed to be no hope of making any meaningful contact with Mrs T, leading the therapist to think that the therapy should be ended. In the second phase, the real nature of Mrs T's problems became apparent, first to the therapist and then to the patient, with both then becoming interested and engaged with the underlying pathology. In the third phase Mrs T showed striking changes in her thinking and a growing capacity to understand how her mind was working. However, a central question remains for the therapist with such a patient about whether any lasting purchase is gained on self- destructive aspects and whether related insights are internalised rather than evacuated. This issue will be considered further in the discussion.

### The first phase

The first phase was characterised by an increasing conviction in the therapist that there was nothing happening in the therapy and that it was going nowhere. Mrs T seemed to show no interest in knowing about or attempting to understand her mental state. It appeared that she wanted to cling to the therapist and use the space provided by her sessions in order to evacuate her mental contents rather than seek any meaning in them. This took the form of monotonous and repetitious complaints about herself and her lack of worthiness as a Christian, a wife, a mother and a patient. These self-reproaches were interspersed with threats against herself, sometimes vague and at other times more specific, which she would then quickly disown. Interpretations made no impact, and her responses to any attempts to instigate symbolic thinking were very concrete in quality.

There was uncertainty and confusion about the precise nature and

262

severity of Mrs T's problems. On the one hand she presented as someone oscillating between suicidal depression and 'highs' where she could look after everybody and do everything in a perfect way. At the same time she would confide in her therapist that she was over-dramatising her accounts of her depression and suicidal thoughts in order to manipulate her GP and psychiatrist, because of her need for respite through hospital admission. She needed the respite because when she was God's helper, it all became too much for her. She would either become suicidal or long for a respite in hospital.

This led to uncertainty in the therapist's mind as to whether the patient was providing a true or fictional version of her state in her sessions. It also resulted in confusion, and sometimes exasperation, in all those treating her, with the patient feeling that she got the attention she craved only by fraudulently exaggerating her suffering.

The following clinical material from a session approximately two years into the work is fairly typical of this early stage of the work.

Mrs T arrived a few minutes early, sat in the waiting room and when invited, tentatively entered the consulting room, searching around with her eyes. Her characteristically long opening silence gave the therapist the opportunity to observe how her ubiquitous soft shapeless clothes folded around her like baby's clothes on a toddler. Her trainer-clad feet relaxed into their pigeon-toed resting position, adding to the impression of a rather childlike figure. Although she said nothing, she managed to convey, as she often did, the impression of someone who was apprehensive but at the same time full up and brimming over.

The therapist noticed with irritation that her eyes were drawn to the clock, as they usually were at this point in the session. It confirmed as always, that only a few minutes had passed. Once again, with irritation, she became aware of a familiar predicament – one that she had spoken to the patient about before. Should she break the silence with one of the interpretations she had used so often before, and which had begun to sound so mechanical? Or should she wait, feeling guilty that she was failing to rescue an anxious patient from her suffering – something she had also voiced before.

As the silence wore on, the therapist became uncomfortable with thoughts about whether Mrs T was dramatising her presentation. In a recent session she had confided exaggerating her situation to her doctor in order to get more sympathy and attention. She claimed that this was not something that happened in her sessions. The therapist was not so sure. 'It's difficult to start,' Mrs T said at last. Looking around the consulting room, she added mournfully, as if it hurt her, 'The flowers are beautiful.'

After a long pause, when it became clear there would be nothing more, the therapist said that Mrs T expressed appreciation of her arrangements here, but that she got the impression something pained her. She wondered if the break since the last session left her feeling like a flower with severed roots, making it difficult to reconnect with the therapist and start again. Mrs T responded in a way that was characteristic:

'I feel it's my fault, that with coming here, and the doctors, I get so much help that I should be better by now. I'm sure there are lots of people in a worse state than me who would be able to use all this properly.'

The therapist observed that Mrs T had moved into castigating herself, as she often did, and that she probably felt that the therapist was irritable and angry with her. She said to Mrs T that she thought this might be preferable to facing reproachful feelings towards her therapist and her doctors for failing to remove her difficulties, but Mrs T was adamant: 'I just feel that I'm being selfish taking space here when other people are much worse than me.'

The therapist said that Mrs T was inviting her to come in and reassure her that it was legitimate for her to have therapy, but she did not think that such reassurance would help. She said that she had the impression that Mrs T's self-reproaches were like a mantra she repeated over and over, designed to keep her and her therapist away from any real thought about her and what she was going through. After a pause Mrs T said:

'I feel that everyone wants me to get better – you, Dr X [her GP] and my family. But if I do, it just means that I'll have to be a wife and mother and look after the people at church and that I'll have no help at all. I'd rather stay as I am. At least I get some attention.'

Any further attempt to interest her in thinking about this situation proved fruitless. She often attributed her depression to her shortcomings as a Christian, saying that if she prayed harder or better, it would lift. Over time Mrs T made it clear that she wanted peace rather than having to think. Having a mind involved having dirty, messy and sinful thoughts and feelings. 'We believe it's bad to be angry, that if you're a good Christian you shouldn't get angry', she had told the therapist on a number of occasions.

Life without a mind and without feelings was felt to be preferable. Mrs T made it clear that she had no intention of using the therapy space for reflection or the development of understanding. She just wanted someone to

264

make her difficult, depressed feelings go away. The atmosphere created was of someone who exaggerated her state in a histrionic way in order to obtain and secure the attention she craved. Once she had it, her ambition was to hang on to it.

The therapist's feelings of irritation and boredom mounted unbearably as the therapy wore on. These feelings were attended by guilt over an absence of empathy for Mrs T and the stuck nature of the work. The patient claimed she suffered but her therapist did not really believe her. She felt disheartened and began to question both her competence and abilities as a psychotherapist.

The uncharacteristic intensity of the feelings the therapist experienced towards the patient, particularly her wish to put an end to the therapy and get rid of Mrs T, alerted her into recognising that she was having difficulty distinguishing what belonged to her and what belonged to the patient. This alarmed her and led her to seek more intensive supervision of her work with Mrs T.

This move opened up the interesting, but at the same time frightening, second phase of the work. It also generated new life in the sessions.

### The second phase

As a result of the supervision, the therapist was able to think about the situation from a different perspective, something she had previously been unable to do with this patient. This involved exploring the meaning of her negative feelings towards Mrs T and the extent to which Mrs T's punitive superego was impacting on her own vulnerabilities in this area. It also involved questioning whether patient and therapist had been unconsciously treating the wrong patient – seemingly a controlling, manipulative histrionic – who stimulated a contagious primitive superego in them both.

With supervision, it became possible to tune into a different wavelength and to recognise that Mrs T's rather histrionic presentation served to obscure a more serious and complex underlying situation, in which Mrs T was in the grip of an affective disorder over which she had no control. It became apparent over time that Mrs T preferred to see herself as someone who manipulated and exaggerated her distress in order to maintain her illusion that she was in control of the situation, as though she could stop being ill if she chose to.

Once this shift in attitude had occurred within the therapist, it made a

265

dramatic difference to the work, particularly in her emotional response to the patient. As the therapist's own superego modified as a result of her new understanding, her countertransference changed from chilly disbelief and impatience into interest, concern and sometimes alarm. As a result, the tone of the sessions began to change as Mrs T and the therapist were able to begin to face together the more disturbing underlying aspects that had been disguised by her initial presentation.

The following material from this phase conveys something of Mrs T's manically driven state, and the impossibility of her preventing its eventual inevitable collapse into depression.

'Sometimes I feel I'm going up a sand dune and that as I get nearer to the top I'm sliding back and getting more and more exhausted.' Crying, she went on to describe the punitive aspect within herself that she was up against.

'At the bottom of the sand hill there are lots of people saying that I should be doing this or that, and that they're in a worse state than me and they're not getting all the help that I get. I just feel that I'd be all right if I could get to the top of the hill.'

The scale and power of what she was up against internally was vividly conveyed by something she said just prior to her first hospital admission. 'I feel that I've got this war going on in my head – but I don't know what it's about. It's not like single bullets going off – it's like I'm standing in front of two tanks and I just want to get away.' At this time Mrs T regarded death as a friend, an idealised state defined by the presence of peace through the absence of suffering. Although on this occasion Mrs T made no actual attempt on her life, her suicidal thoughts increased, with plans for using the rope in the attic, or getting drunk and overdosing on pills.

At the same time it became clear that Mrs T enjoyed a fantasy that she would survive her death, a fantasy which was particularly dangerous since she believed she would go to a heavenly better place and become at one with a perfect object who would look after her forever. On one occasion when the therapist had been talking about the ubiquitous conflict in Mrs T between lively and self-destructive aspects, she responded, 'When you talk about it, self-destructive has a hostile sound to it. I'm not aware of feeling anything like that. I see death as peaceful, with no stress. A sort of back to the womb situation.' She added: 'It feels like something good and peaceful, with a road stretching out from it.'

266

Later she talked about death as a sleepy, unconscious state where she could remove herself from any thoughts, feelings or conflicts: 'I suppose I see it as a kind of Nirvana'. She often spoke about her fantasies of suicide in a dissociated way:

'I was thinking of trying something next week, but I thought it was a bit close to our holidays, so I thought maybe when we get back from holidays and when my daughter is away at camp, she gets very upset if anything happens to me.'

Squaring her suicidal impulses with her religious convictions presented no problems for Mrs T. She said, 'I've given some thought to God's attitude towards people who take their own lives and I think probably that he'd forgive one sin at the end'. Her family, she reasoned, would be better off without her. However, following time in therapy, some evidence arose that Mrs T was becoming frightened by what she was up against inside herself. After a serious overdose that led to her second admission to hospital, Mrs T spoke about her fear that she had succeeded in taking a fatal overdose and how this had coincided with the realisation that she did not really want to die.

Links between suicide attempts and revenge on an unresponsive object emerged. After her release from hospital she told the therapist, 'They have to take notice of you if you try suicide.' It transpired that before she took the overdose, Mrs T had been unsuccessfully trying to see a key worker or a doctor at the day hospital she attended in order to let them know how depressed she was feeling. She was also clear about at least one function of her self-mutilation, which involved cutting her arms and burning them with cigarettes (she does not smoke). She said that she did not want to stop. 'I suppose I don't want to stop using my body to shout at people,' she explained.

Mrs T was profoundly shocked when a family friend succeeded in killing herself, saying 'I would have liked to put out my arms and held her.' Nevertheless, she was fascinated by the event, particularly about what might have actually tipped the woman into committing suicide.

During this second phase she began to articulate the burden she felt that her children, her husband and the members of her church congregation placed on her. On the one hand she perceived them as getting in the way of ridding herself of her conflicts by killing herself, and on the other hand she experienced them as greedily demanding that she give over everything of herself to them. She spoke with contempt about the congregation's response to her admission of praying for her recovery, but at the same time

267

experienced this as a pressure on her to be well and felt that she was a failure for not managing to respond to their prayers.

She was plagued by fear that she might improve or get better. In her black and white state of mind, if she improved it meant that there was no room to be a patient. This presented a problem, because if there was to be no patient, there could be no help. She would be back alone in the grip of aspects of a self that demanded she gave over everything to others. In turn this meant that she had nothing for herself and that her life was not worth living.

A dream just before she went into hospital, for the third and final reported occasion, illustrated her black and white manic state. In the session she said:

'I've been having lots of dreams, but I can only remember one of them. It was very frightening. I was being pushed into a plane. It was black and white and looked very familiar – but I was aware that it went very fast and I was frightened. A friend's husband was the pilot. I think it was one of those stealth planes that flies undetected and then dumps its deadly load.'

She awoke feeling very frightened. As the result of the dream, it was possible to explore with Mrs T both the fear and attraction of her driven state, and the feelings of helplessness that accompanied it.

The theme of stealth, secrecy and trickiness was a strand that ran throughout the therapy, with Mrs T covering up the extent of her disturbance, in the same way she covered the gashes on her arm with the sleeve of her shirt, leading people to believe she was exaggerating the seriousness of her psychopathology. She would then feel burdened and hurt by what she experienced as a lack of interest and unresponsiveness by the people around her. They, she believed, confirmed her own view about herself, namely that she should be able to get rid of her problems and be better.

Although there was evidence during this phase that Mrs T was becoming more concerned about her state, she still regarded the 'highs' that she was always trying to reach by being the provider to others as heroic and interesting, and certainly preferable to the alternative of an impossibly messy internal world. One vignette taken from her childhood well illustrates her fear of making contact with the underlying messiness. Mrs T was about 7 when an incident occurred at school, which had a profound impact on her. She had been carrying paint pots and someone had bumped into her. All the paint went down the front of her uniform and her mother was called to bring in a fresh one. The child Mrs T went to pieces, believing she had done something terribly wrong.

268

An example of this messiness came into the work over the issue of fees during Mrs T's second admission to hospital. The therapist received a number of calls from Mrs T's husband wanting to know if she would be charged for sessions while she was in hospital. The therapist herself experienced a variety of messy feelings about this, but she was helped in supervision to recover some perspective. Thought was given to the desperation of the husband, who must have concluded that since his wife was in hospital again, the therapy was failing. From his perspective, something should be done to make the patient well. If the therapy and the drugs failed to keep Mrs T out of hospital, it meant that therapist and doctors were failing. At this stage of the work neither the patient nor her family were at a point where they could accept that Mrs T had a problem that would have to be managed rather than eliminated.

Supervision helped to process some of the difficult feelings that the situation had stirred up in the therapist, mostly connected with feelings of guilt and responsibility that her patient was in hospital again. She was enabled to realise that the situation with Mrs T had been managed in a way that provided her with the containment she needed in hospital and that this represented an achievement, not a failure. The therapist came to recognise and reflect on how she had got caught up in 'thinking' very similar to that of Mrs T and her husband. A communication from the therapist that the fees were not an issue at this time allowed the focus to return to Mrs T and to the real nature of the problem.

The understanding gained in supervision of the kind of feelings Mrs T stirred up in the people caring for her had already become a helpful tool when it came to detecting signs of deterioration in Mrs T. They came to serve as a useful warning indicator of relapse. The following incident illustrates some of the dangerous confusions that can get stirred up in others by a patient like Mrs T.

Just before Mrs T's last hospital admission, material emerged in her session that Mrs T believed that the doctors and nurses treating her had had enough of her. It unfolded in this way. During the session, Mrs T reported suicidal thoughts, feelings and plans, which, although not unusual, had a quality that particularly concerned the therapist. The patient also expressed a belief that the medical professionals involved in her care, her GP and staff at the day hospital she attended were exasperated with her. With Mrs T's agreement, the therapist decided to speak to her GP about her state. When she made contact with the GP she was shaken by the irritation and exasperation towards the patient expressed by the usually sympathetic and supportive doctor – thoughts and feelings strikingly similar to those the therapist herself had experienced earlier in the work. She was alerted by these responses to contact the psychiatric service about Mrs T's relapse and possible need for admission. During that stay in hospital, Mrs T was able to attend regularly for her sessions.

This second phase of the work was marked by a growing recognition by both Mrs T and her therapist of the real nature of her problems. This put them both in a position to detect and explore what was going on beneath Mrs T's apparently attention-seeking histrionic behaviour and to appreciate the seriousness of her situation. The change in the therapist's countertransference during this second phase, resulting from the understanding gained in supervision, together with the growing recognition by the patient of the extent and nature of her illness, generated new life in the sessions.

During this second phase, Mrs T became more interested in the intricacies of her mental state and more able to reflect on the work done in sessions, in marked contrast to the earlier phase of the work. She experienced a great deal of relief when she became able to recognise that she was ill rather than 'attention-seeking' and 'bad'. This relief was associated with the gradual realisation that she would have to learn to manage the oscillations in her moods and feelings rather than get rid of them.

## The third phase

For the therapist, the changes that took place in the second phase of the work raised the key question of whether anything she could do in the session and any of the insights and understandings gained in the course of her work with Mrs T could have any impact on the autonomy of the self-destructive structures operating inside Mrs T.

Even though Mrs T appeared to respond well to the work in sessions, and cooperated in strengthening more thoughtful, reflective aspects of herself, there was an ever-present concern about whether there was a deadliness in Mrs T so powerful that it would kill off all links with the therapist and also with Mrs T's own capacity to think. The therapist's experience of Mrs T's acting out led her to remain concerned over an aspect of Mrs T that stood apart from what was going on in her therapy and carried on with business as usual, untouched by the work. However, through exploration of the question of whether any purchase could be gained on this deadly system a new third phase opened up in the work.

Gradually Mrs T was coming to be able to think about her object relationships both internally and externally and was growing concerned about what she might be handing on to her children. There was recognition of the possibility of an ego-destructive system, gathering pace through generations if nothing changed. There was some evidence that Mrs T wanted change. She now often talked about her efforts to bring her children up in a different, more free, way. Recently she had even talked about wanting to be more free herself. 'Things that have been coming up in my therapy are starting to make sense to me,' she said recently. 'I wonder why I am like this, why I seem to hate myself so much?'

She showed signs of being more able to stand up to destructive aspects of herself. Although the impulse to cut herself was often strong, she was no longer doing this at present. There was also evidence of something less cutting in her attitude towards herself and her limitations, linked to understandings of how sane, vulnerable aspects of her became lodged in her body and then attacked. She said:

'It's not easy, but I'm trying very hard every time I feel that I have to do things for other people to think about whether I can manage it or whether I'm sabotaging myself again. I know I like looking after other people, but I also realise it's often very bad for me.'

Mrs T showed increasing interest in evaluating the family version of Christianity, as well as thinking about the culture she experienced as a child and the parenting she received. She was even able to ponder with some humour her mother's extensive capacity to judge and criticise others, while at the same time seeing herself as an exemplary Christian. While Mrs T remained a committed Christian, she rejected the idea that if she prayed enough, or if the congregation of the church prayed enough, she would be cured of her depression: 'I think sometimes that I'd like to say it's all a lot of bloody bullshit and try and get on with my life and try to manage my illness.'

During one recent session she talked about her suicide longings in a different way: 'I was thinking earlier that I don't really want to kill myself, but I want the kind of attention that suicide brings me, that people are able to see how bad I feel sometimes.' Following an interpretation about using her body, and what she did to it in order to tell a story in such a way that the therapist and others would listen, Mrs T added:

'I'm also beginning to realise that it's not bad to want attention – that perhaps I need it now because for various reasons I didn't get it in the past. It doesn't make me bad because I want attention, but before I always thought it was selfish to want something for myself.'

271

After a pause, she added, 'It's interesting, too, that if I allow myself to have them, the longings, it doesn't seem so important whether I actually get them or not.'

However, even in this third phase of the work there were disconcerting echoes of earlier themes. For example, on the therapist's return from a break, she found Mrs T distressed and exhausted. Mrs T told the therapist that earlier that day a friend had congratulated her on her improved ability to think about and understand herself. This had left Mrs T feeling terribly alone and that she had no right to be feeling as exhausted and low as she was. Initially the therapist was very active with this material, making links to the break, to Mrs T's difficulty in communicating her state and so forth. However, when Mrs T said she wished her friend could see how bad she was really feeling, the therapist realised her mistake.

Mrs T showed relief when the therapist said that she had fallen into the mistaken belief that Mrs T was better than she was today, failing to take on board how exhausted she was. This had left her feeling that her therapist was as out of touch as her friend. In that session, and those following, it was then possible for both patient and therapist to see how a muddle occurred in Mrs T's mind, in which she made an equation between her advances in understanding and her being well. When she made this equation, it exposed her to a destructive aspect of herself that exploited these advances in order to make demands on her she could not meet. It came as a relief to Mrs T to realise that, although she now understood herself and her situation more than she had previously, which created a different state, that meant different, not well.

In this third phase the transference and countertransference shifted from the concrete into more of a relationship of interest and reflection. It became possible to explore with Mrs T her attempts to make the therapist into an ego ideal on whom she could depend. For example, the way that the environment must be perfect, with fresh flowers in the consulting room reflecting the perfect arrangements the therapist made for her. The therapist must also continue to wear a suit, in order that Mrs T could feel safe and depend on everything going on in a uniform way.

The object relationship that Mrs T was seeking was to a God-like figure, who would make everything all right for her. She felt that she had to be a 'good' patient, because if she did not fit in at all times, with the new religion of therapy, she would be cast out and rejected. If the uniform perfection of the therapist broke down, Mrs T feared she was with a frightening superego figure who was bored, critical and angry with her.

If she was severely depressed or had to go into hospital, she would feel a

272

conviction that someone had failed – that either the God-like therapist and doctors were false gods who promised salvation but failed to deliver, or that she had failed as a patient and wilfully squandered her opportunities. In this state of mind, her desire was for identification with an ideal object; there was no room for humanity, neither in her, nor in the therapist.

Over time Mrs T became more tolerant of a therapist who consistently frustrated her efforts to turn her into a god-like figure and psychotherapy into a new version of religion. She was the recipient of an experience with a therapist whose own superego has managed, sometimes with great difficulty, to survive the 'failures' involved in treating Mrs T, and to go on being interested and involved with her.

The clinical material illustrates how some of the therapist's early difficult countertransference experiences with Mrs T became modified and changed over time. However, it is also important to underline the fact that Mrs T's capacity to stimulate such strong emotions in the therapist and other professionals working with her, feelings of anger, exasperation and boredom that were often difficult to bear, also proved to be a vital factor informing the work, alerting those involved in her care to her dangerous underlying psychopathology.

## Discussion

The case material raises several technical issues that should be considered when confronted with a patient with an affective disorder.

### Attention-seeking

Often when patients are referred to as 'attention-seeking', this carries a pejorative connotation, implying that the presenting symptoms are being used for secondary gain, that the patient is opting for the 'sick role', and not making enough effort. However, this diagnosis can be made when we do not understand what is going on and such an attitude may cause a therapist to miss a hidden diagnosis, by dismissively categorising the patient as 'hysterical' (Slater 1965).

It is interesting that in this case the patient herself holds the belief that she should not need help, regarding herself as merely attention-seeking because of her need for a respite. In the countertransference,

Mrs T evoked a similar attitude of mind in both her therapist and GP, which carried the danger of underrating the severity of the underlying depressive psychopathology and attendant suicidal risk.

The lesson for us all as therapists is to be alert to the development of a dismissive attitude towards a patient with depression, as one may unwittingly have become the object of the patient's projections, which may lead one to underestimate the severity of the underlying disorder.

### *Differentiating the countertransference in depression and borderline states*

The patient showed no interest in doing any meaningful work in the sessions or in paying for them. She merely evacuated material, leaving the therapist dissatisfied that no meaningful intercourse was occurring and feeling like terminating the treatment. It was this sense of hopelessness in the therapy, together with a passing reference to the rope in the loft, that awoke the therapist to the underlying psychopathology and led her to seek more intensive supervision.

The patient had a history of acting out, including taking overdoses and cutting herself. Nowadays, such behaviour inevitably leads to a diagnosis of a borderline state. The clue to the fact that Mrs T's condition was depressive, not borderline, lay in the countertransference. With a borderline patient, the countertransference is directly to the therapist, who is held to be entirely responsible for all the patient's problems, a very uncomfortable situation for the therapist (Britton 1989).

Here, the countertransference experience was quite different with the patient unwilling to make any emotional or physical payment, engendering the feeling of an unrewarding situation for the therapist. The therapist's attitude changed, leading her interest in Mrs T to return, only once she realised that the patient's apparent lack of interest was being orchestrated by an underlying psychosis.

### *Depression, the forgotten psychosis*

Recognising an affective disorder as a psychotic state means that we can no longer rely on our ordinary empathic experience for understanding. We need to tune into the psychotic wavelength and identify the dominating phantasies to make sense of what is happening in the sessions.

The psychotic part here clearly has its own agenda. In the manic phase the patient feels identified with a role of God's servant, a universal provider for others. In this state of mind her children are seen as nothing but greedily demanding objects. Any respite from this role as God's provider, through attempts to gain admission, is felt to be fraudulent, leading to the projected countertransference feeling that she is exaggerating her needs. God's provider is not supposed to have needs of her own, as God attends to all, and no one else is felt to be giving thought to her predicament. When she becomes exhausted and depressed, this leads to thoughts of suicide as the only way out, and statistically speaking about one in seven patients with bipolar disorder do commit suicide (Angst and Sellaro 2000).

Once we are alerted to the underlying psychosis, we can then give further consideration to differing aspects that contribute to the patient's suicidal states of mind.

## Aspects of the suicidal state

Mrs T likened her striving to be at one with an ideal to trying to climb a sand dune, like the myth of Sisyphus. Death is seen as a welcome respite, like a peaceful return to the womb. The self-destructiveness is not addressed but superficially rationalised as 'God will probably forgive one sin'.

Awareness that a self-destructive attack is about to take place is kept at a distance through a dreamy, dissociated way of speaking. The projected anxiety from the non-psychotic part that was on the receiving end of the attack was manifest in the therapist's awakening to the dangerousness of the suicidal state.

Later the patient also became alarmed by her realisation of the dangerous dreamy dissociated state creeping up on her, as evidenced by the dream of being taken over by a stealth plane that dumps its deadly load, after which she woke in a fright.

The psychotic part of the personality may deny its murderous intent, but the non-psychotic part on the receiving end may convey frightened feelings, and awareness of the two distinct parts becomes crucial to understanding suicidal acts in such cases (Lucas 2003b).

Self-mutilation also occurs in this patient, in a different context, as an act of revenge towards the idealised object that is experienced as being totally unresponsive to needs through demanding perfect obedience. The dynamics behind this self-mutilation is different from that in a borderline state, where the patient attempts to make contact with feelings through cutting.

### *The autonomy of the bipolar state and the attempt to create a dialogue*

Behind the presenting facade of histrionic and attention-seeking behaviour is an attempt to underplay the dominion of manic depressive psychopathology that holds her in its grip.

In the manic phase, Mrs T is identified with God as his universal provider. She goes on until she needs a rest, but she has to justify this. It is an all or nothing state. In a collapsed state, hospital, however disturbed the ward, is seen as a respite. Her anger at the relentless demand by the ideal object is expressed in her bodily attack. Death is seen as a preferred option to going on as previously.

Having ventilated her anger in self-mutilation and had a respite in hospital, through manic reparation she forgives her God for having been over-demanding and goes back to serving him. In time, with therapy, a reflective part grows and sees this magical recovery for what it is, hence her criticism of the congregation's prayers for her recovery as 'bullshit'.

As the bipolar state seems to have an autonomy of its own, this left the therapist with the question of how she could make a lasting impact. She found that she could make salient interpretations that Mrs T seemed to respond to intellectually, but she felt unconvinced that these were having any lasting impact. Her concern remained that dangerous suicidal states could recur.

With no interjection from a sane part, the manic depressive cycle is expressed as an uninterrupted monologue. While the hidden psychotic part with its manic depressive agenda has been viewed as a cohabitee to be understood and talked to in its own right (Sinason 1993), the challenge clinically remains how to make an impact on its dominance. The way forward is to convert the monologue into a dialogue.

The dialogue must first arise in the therapist through challenging the assumption of the manic depressive transference by bringing in a different perspective. For example, the patient became disturbed when the therapist changed from wearing her usual formal suit and blouse. This black and white state was seen as a desired uniformity imposed in the sessions, with the patient not having to think but simply to follow the therapist's dictates, re-enacting her internal relationship with an idealised object.

For the patient to see this as a wish for an idealised uniformity in preference to breaking free and developing a mind of her own, the conflict had first to be experienced and realised within the therapist. Then the patient could be helped to consider another way of relating, a two-person intercourse rather than identification with the absolute. Insight does not remove the autonomy and forcefulness of the manic depressive cycle, and the need remains to support a reflective part of the patient who may recognise at times when she has become overwhelmed and exhausted and may need a further admission in her own best interests (see also Chapter 14).

Technically speaking, the central challenge for all analytic therapists in addressing patients with major depressive illness is furthering the move in the sessions from a monologue to a dialogue. Herbert Rosenfeld (1987) was fond of interpreting in a style that articulated different aspects of the patient's thoughts to them when addressing an impasse. Such an approach may help to stimulate dialogue, like an internal argument on how to respond to feelings, within the patient's mind, thereby moving them away from a total domination by a relationship with an ego-destructive superego.

### The concept of birth trauma in relation to depression

When we think in general terms about the purpose of a psychoanalysis, we may think of a central dynamic, in ego development, of reclaiming for the ego what has been taken by the superego. For example, in the special circumstances of training as analytic therapists there is tension between the need to learn from those who are more experienced, one's teachers, and the danger of overidentification with overvalued ideas at the expense of developing one's own mind (Britton 2003). We also talk of life beginning at 40. We all have a long gestation period before we can emerge with our own individual analytic identities and views.

In patients with major depression the presenting problem is very different. The difficulty is not only one of prolonged labour pains linked to the ego separating from a mature parental superego, but also that the patient did not come into the world as a separate being. It is as if the patient has been born into the world totally identified with an idealised ego-destructive superego, which remains tyrannically in control. In these terms, one might say that the patient has never been born as a separately formed individual.

There is a pull to remain in identification with the absolute in order to avoid all the confusing mixed feelings towards the ideal that result from starting to experience separateness, like Mrs T's wish to avoid 'messiness'. While Melanie Klein described the concept of the manic defence against depressive or persecutory guilt (Segal 1981d), here the defence is against the experience of an underlying mixture of inchoate feelings, from an ego never formed as a whole. The experience of separation from the ideal, with its attendant release of primitive emotions, accounts for the clinical presentation in puerperal psychosis (Lucas 1994; see also Chapter 14).

This accounts for the very disturbing countertransference feelings that the therapist was left with. She felt in the patient no sense of a whole person underneath with whom she could relate, only a series of reactions to events and interpretations. The therapist needs to be able to tolerate living with this state in the patient, since it might take a long period of time for a sense of a more integrated ego to develop. If this underlying chaotic state is not recognised in supervision, the supervisee may be left feeling uneasy because of being obliged to carry these feelings alone.

## Summary

This case illustrates that, for the therapist, relating to affective disorders presents many clinical problems, with an overriding need to develop a framework of understanding that can enable one to keep one's bearings. The psychosis underlying a hysterical facade that invites one to underrate the patient's psychopathology needs to be appreciated. It is important to be aware of the autonomous manic depressive part with its own agenda with the attendant risk of suicide. Working with a patient such as Mrs T faces us with the technical challenge of how to convert a psychotic monologue into a dialogue, and how to strengthen the presence of the non-psychotic part of the patient.

If progress is made, evidence of an underlying separate self may not present as a coherent ego but more in terms of a series of unconnected emotional reactions. In supervision it is important to realise that the supervisee is experiencing no coherent ego in the patient and that this is a very disturbing experience to stay with in therapy. Depression is the forgotten psychosis and, as in all psychotic disorders, projective mechanisms predominate. As illustrated in the clinical material, it is therefore only through close attention to the countertransference experience that understanding can arise.

# 20

## Education in psychosis

### Introduction

This chapter considers the need to provide educational settings where clinicians can learn about the applications of psychoanalytic thinking to understanding and relating to psychotic disorders. There is no substitute for direct clinical experience through contact with patients, followed by a setting for supervised discussion. This can take several forms. For individuals registered for an analytic psychotherapy training course, a six-month psychiatric placement attending ward reviews, ideally with a chance to clerk patients and discuss their formulation, is advocated for those without previous psychiatric experience.

For nurses and related professionals, the provision of courses to examine their reactions and responses to the demands made on them in their work is important for deepening their understanding, and capacities for containment and self-reflection. If ward managers can attend such courses, then what they gain can be filtered down to staff under them, enhancing an interest in a therapeutic attitude on the wards. Unfortunately such courses are in scarce supply, though there is an increasing awareness of the need for them (Evans 2006).

In this chapter, I am going to concentrate on three contrasting supervisory settings linked to the experience of the participants. First, for junior doctors starting in psychiatry, weekly informal psychosis workshops provide a setting for shared learning, and an example is provided (Garelick and Lucas 1996). Second, at specialist registrar level, a lot can be gained from the experience of seeing a patient with schizophrenia individually.

Third, material is provided from a highly experienced analytic psychotherapist, where the issues arising are different, namely how should psychotherapy departments respond when community mental health centres refer patients in psychotic states to them for individual psychotherapy.

## The role of the psychosis workshop

### *Case 1: Deciphering a somersault!*

At an informal weekly psychosis workshop, a problem was presented of a young man whose behaviour was very hard to manage. The young man, in his early twenties, had first presented two years previously with a psychotic episode and had predominantly been in hospital since then. His father had committed suicide, through hanging, five months before his first breakdown. He had been living with his mother and younger sister. When he first became unwell he had taken cannabis but not since then.

Prior to admission he had stood outside the house with a knife and declared his intention to kill his mother. There was observed 'high expressed emotion' between them and the family had been referred for psychotherapy but had never engaged.

His mother was angry, scared and very critical of the patient and it was noticed that she avoided looking at him when attending a tribunal hearing. His sister's reaction was very different. She had herself received psychotherapy, in relation to a past paranoid episode. She wrote a very polite letter to the doctors expressing the hope that her brother might receive psychotherapy but only when the doctors felt it was the right time.

Some months ago he had been moved from an admission ward to the acute rehabilitation ward. The nurses were worried because he kept turning somersaults. He would get down on his knees as if praying, move forwards, turn over in a somersault, and then get up again. At times he would also throw his food on the floor and walk into the shower with his clothes on, but these acting-out behaviours did not have such a disturbing effect on the nursing staff.

He was completely inaccessible to attempts to discuss his behaviour. When he went to occupational therapy he was sent back prematurely as his somersaults were disruptive to the group activity. When he returned to the ward, the senior house officer (SHO) asked him if he had wanted to go to OT and he tersely said 'No', but when he was asked if he had wanted to return to the ward early, he also said 'No'.

His only sign of activity on the ward was that he was reading a book called *The Watcher*, but as soon as anyone started to speak to him to try to engage him in conversation, he conveyed that he was bored with them.

The problem presented to the workshop was how to understand his behaviour and the other members in the workshop then started to ask questions in order to try to make sense of it all.

The question was raised of whether this was attention-seeking behaviour as he did the somersaults in the nursing office as well as elsewhere. The nursing staff were worried that if he was left unobserved he might do it on the stairs and injure himself. They also worried that if they did not intervene, he might go up to his bedroom and do it there on his own.

His behaviour was also considered in moral terms. While one view was concern over his behaviour, others wondered what was wrong with him doing it. The doctors and nurses were split in their reactions to his behaviour. The nurses felt concerned and wanted the doctors to do something about it, while the doctors were left wondering why the excessive fuss and concern. Some of the nursing staff also wanted to ignore the somersaults.

Attempts to involve the patient himself in discussing his activities received only a terse response. He had sat through a manager's hearing without saying anything, even when the discussion related to very sensitive matters about his state of mental health and diagnosis.

The nursing staff were now suggesting that he be sent back to the acute admission ward because of his disturbed behaviour, yet he was not smashing the place up or being aggressive.

The presenting junior doctor then recalled that before developing his illness, the patient had been going around with a Chinese gang, like the Triad, who carried machetes with them, and had the thought that he could have had his head cut off!

The junior doctor was also reminded of another a patient who he felt was like the patient but not psychotic. This patient was an adolescent who was not going to school but was not bad enough to be admitted and his parents were at their wits' end. The link in the doctor's mind was that, in both cases, they were very stuck. So the problem being presented was of the nurses' anxieties and the doctor feeling very stuck.

Other members of the workshop now started to associate to the somersault. One member thought of the somersault as an acrobatic act linked to an identification with a Chinese circus. This led onto the theme of aggressiveness linked to the Triad. The presenting doctor then recalled that he had talked about the case with a fellow colleague who had taken apart the word somersault into 'some assault'. This led to a consideration of the possibility that the assault in question was an assault on people's thinking; no one could make sense of it or find a way of talking with the patient about his disruptive behaviour.

The group then began to consider the question of why the somersaults were more disturbing than other behaviour, such as his repeatedly throwing his food on the floor. One idea was that this was because the somersault was not as readily understandable as throwing food on the floor. Mother's reaction to what she found unbearable was to cut herself off and demand it went away.

The question was then how to link the history and the group's associations in order to arrive at a meaningful psychodynamic formulation that would be helpful to the doctors and nursing staff. Within this context the following issues needed to be considered.

### The diagnosis

In the given history there were no diagnostic first rank symptoms, but the length of stay in hospital in a disturbed paranoid and socially withdrawn state, in the absence of an affective disorder, suggested the diagnosis of a schizophrenic illness. Indeed the length of time without remission suggested that we were dealing with a severe condition that would require long term professional involvement.

### The role of medication

While medication had an important role to play in this patient's treatment, medication alone was only part of the wider picture in his management. He was already on clozapine, the drug of choice in resistant cases of schizophrenia, augmented by fish oil and amisulpride, and still remained in a disturbed state.

### Recognising the onset of a severe and enduring illness

The onset of a severe and enduring schizophrenic illness is a frightening and bewildering situation for the patient, his relatives and the involved staff. The patient desperately tried to cope by identifying with the Chinese gang and distancing himself from his feelings by taking cannabis. The loss of his father around the time of the eruption of his illness exacerbated the situation. In her anxiety for him to become well again, his mother came to represent a non-understanding figure demanding that he conformed to standards he could not meet, resulting in his hostility towards her. She needed help in coming to terms with his condition so that she was not left to feel guilty and consequently blame herself, the patient or professional staff.

Nowadays, due to the shortage of beds, there is pressure to move patients to community care as soon as possible. However, every now and then, one may come up against a patient where in the early stages of the illness only a hospital setting can provide for his needs.

## Negative symptoms

If we are dealing with the emergence of an enduring psychotic disorder, we can expect to face much resistance to treatment, the negative symptoms of schizophrenia linked with strong anti-life forces. We can readily appreciate this in the patient's negative reaction to occupational therapy, his obliviousness to the tribunal proceedings and his terse bored reaction to any attempts to engage him in conversation.

## Countertransference experiences

The workshop was able to reflect on their own associations from a slightly distanced position, making it easier for them to think than the professionals at the coalface. They could appreciate the staff feeling stuck and the mother feeling frightened and angry. Some nursing staff wanted to return the patient to the acute ward, for a variety of reasons. His behaviour with the repeated somersaults was not understandable and they had no way to influence it. There was a fear that he might come to real harm if he happened to do the somersaults on the stairs out of sight. If they ignored the somersaults leaving him to do them in his bedroom they became concerned that he might withdraw into a totally inaccessible state. Through their associations the members of the workshop were able to understand that the somersaults had an aggressive component that disrupted any attempt to involve the patient in communication and that they represented an attack on thinking, i.e. really 'some assault'.

*Deciphering the meaning to the somersaults*

The somersault can be seen as an ideo-motor activity, an attempt to both relieve and communicate feelings. The patient's hostility to examination of his non-verbal communication led to his abrupt termination of any conversation on the grounds that it was boring. As a projected activity, we had to do the thinking for the patient. Through the countertransference experience we could start to understand aspects of his communication – his failure to solve his problems by acrobatic identification with the Chinese gang, his feeling of being stuck and going round in circles, his attempts to sort things out by himself by living in a world of his own making, and his fear that he might stay forever in an inaccessible state. All these were thoughts of the staff in contact with him and they had difficulty containing them. The challenge now was to find a way to enable the staff to feel more confident in relating to the problem and addressing the patient.

*The psychotic and non-psychotic parts*

The non-psychotic part of the patient is capable of thoughts and concerns over his breakdown and his inability to influence the situation. However, this part is under the domination of the psychotic part, which aims to eliminate all insight gained by the work of the non-psychotic part. The non-psychotic part is not allowed to speak and its content is evacuated by the psychotic part through projection. Bion (1957a) referred to this as the evacuation of the accretions of mental stimuli in ideo-motor activity. To make any sense of the patient's actions the workshop had to provide all the associations in order to bring out the different components making up the activity.

Having done this work, it might begin to be possible to talk with the patient about the plight that he finds himself in: how he feels unable to cope alone with the demands of life and how we need to provide a continuing support for him in hospital until he is ready to try the alternative of an outside supportive placement. His somersaults can be understood both as a means by which the psychotic part tries to relieve itself of feelings and an attempt by the non-psychotic part to communicate his needs to the staff.

The staff need to feel confident that they know what is going on and can safely contain and manage the situation of the early years of a severe psychosis in their own ward setting. Once they are orientated to what it means to have to contain the early stages of a marked schizophrenic illness, the staff may feel freer to help the patient's mother and daughter to begin to understand their relative's illness and to enable his mother gradually to feel less persecuted by it. If the staff convey their willingness to make a long-term commitment to the patient, then gradually a relationship can be built up between patient and staff.

## Case 2: An anorexic patient

### Background history

At a weekly psychosis workshop, in an informal setting, an SHO who was working on the eating disorder unit presented the case of a 19-year-old girl with a history of severe anorexia since the age of 15. She had spent eighteen months in a non-specialist hospital and had then been transferred for a year to an inpatient adolescent unit. After discharge, she started primary school teaching, but required readmission within a year. She had been on the eating disorder unit for two months at the time of the presentation.

We were told that although she was prepared to talk, she would neither eat nor drink. Under the Mental Health Act 1983 she was having to be forcibly fed twice a day through a naso-gastric tube. She kept pulling out the tube and it took six nurses to hold her down, while she screamed and resisted the tube being reinserted.

This young woman came from a Catholic background. She was the fifth of seven children. There was no family history of mental illness. She had always been shy, which was regarded as indicative of her being very determined or very stubborn, depending on how one looked at it.

She had been diagnosed as having a psychotic depression as well as anorexia nervosa, because she experienced visual hallucinations and kept saying that she wanted to die. The visual hallucinations involved seeing people who were dead. In the past, these visions of dead people had frightened her, but now she had started to say that she didn't mind if she joined them. Other people could stab her or give her an overdose, she said, but she would not do this; she could only try do die by starvation. As part of her treatment on the eating disorder unit she was seeing a psycho-therapist for individual sessions, but this person was not present at the workshop.

*Discussion*

In the ensuing discussion, the following issues emerged. First, in his countertransference experience, the presenting SHO felt her illness was like a bulldozer. He also complained of a monologue, mainly in the form of a controlling silence by the patient. There was no dialogue and only rarely did the patient seem near to tears.

Second, the SHO also wondered if her religious background played a part as she had initially asked to see the visiting Catholic priest. He was described as a warm and homely person. However, she now no longer wished to see him.

Third, another SHO at the workshop recalled a time when he had been on duty and had to be involved in her naso-gastric feeding. At first he had felt sad for her, then frustrated and angry with her resistance to intubation, which was extremely difficult for him to do. When at last he succeeded with the intubation, he felt as though he was raping her.

Fourth, another doctor felt that we were stuck at the physical level of intubating her in response to her actions, and that we had no other way of relating to her.

Fifth, apart from my SHO, all the other SHOs thought of the hallucinations solely in phenomenological terms as part of the picture of a psychotic depression. My SHO had been with me for several months and, unlike the other SHOs, was a GP in training, rather than a psychiatrist in training. He was not weighed down by phenomenology training for exam purposes. He expressed a different view, saying that he thought the hallucinations indicated a worrying shift in the balance of forces within her, since at first she had been frightened of an identification with dead people, but now she was not.

*Teaching points*

1   The psychotic wavelength
    If anorexia nervosa and depression can be thought of as psychotic disorders, this means that we cannot rely solely on our ordinary sensitivities to make sense of what is happening. We have to tune into and relate to the specific psychopathology.

2   The psychotic and non-psychotic parts
    In our work with patients with psychotic disorders, as Bion said, we need to think in terms of two separate parts, not one

287

person, and we have to deal with the psychotic part first (Bion 1957a). In anorexia nervosa, the psychotic anorexic part has a fundamental hatred of appetite and is murderous towards any sign of its presence in the non-anorexic part (Sohn 1985a). This way of thinking can help the SHOs to understand why the patient would not stab herself or take an overdose. In her madness, this behaviour would imply an appetite for something and thus represent a need, however destructive this was. Thus others would have to do these things to her; she could only kill herself passively through starvation.

3   The limitations of the phenomenological approach
While the phenomenological approach is important for diagnostic purposes, a different approach is needed in a dynamic clinical situation. The differing thoughts in the group about how to approach the visual hallucinations illustrate the possibility of viewing the patient's hallucinations from different perspectives.

4   From monologue to dialogue
The psychotic part of the patient repeatedly evacuates the insight arrived at by the work of the non-psychotic part, in the never-ending conflict between the life and death instincts. Hence the non-psychotic part had a need for a warm priest as a supportive figure. The psychotic part disowned these feelings, through projection, into the priest and then did not want to see him anymore. If one thought of the patient's behaviour in a more conventional way, one might simply have concluded that she had just showed ambivalent feelings towards religion.

The SHOs' basic problem, which applies to all cases presented at psychosis workshops, is how to find a way of talking to the patient meaningfully: how can we convert the psychotic monologue into a dialogue?

Her mental conflict has been reduced, through projection, to a physical battle around feeding. The conflict has to be reinstated as a mental problem while, at the physical level, the anorexic part is being made to realise that the non-anorexic part is being given equally powerful support, when it is having to survive during a dominating anorexic episode.

Over many years, with the aid of psychotherapy, the non-anorexic part may be helped to grow in reflective strength. However, at this moment in time the SHO needs a meaningful framework to orientate him and enable him to find a way of talking to the patient about the battle of the two parts, and help the staff to support the dominated tearful part that wants to live and train as a teacher, but is currently being held in a suppressed state. Only once this has been spelled out to the patient can periods of non-naso-gastric feeding be tried out in the context of an attempted mental dialogue, even if for long spells all sanity remains projected into the staff and the anorexic behaviour remains predominant.

In all psychotic disorders, staff may have to endure stages of seemingly never-ending intransigence, such as those that occur with protracted episodes of depression in hospitalised cases, where it is necessary to wait for the episode to relent. During these periods, it is important to keep a live dialogue going, even if at times it feels as though this is confined solely to the staff and carers.

The clinical situations encountered in general psychiatry may sometimes feel as though they have little relevance to the world of an everyday analytic psychotherapy practice, although they can help one to feel for analysands who may have had to cope with living with a parent with a major psychotic disorder in their childhood. However, if the analytic concepts introduced are pertinent to the presenting problem, they can be extremely helpful for the SHOs.

For a time, the SHOs are freed from the restrictions of purely phenomenological thinking and enabled to take an interest in their own responsiveness to the material. Through the introduction of the analytic framework, they are provided with the means to begin to develop confidence in speaking to their patients, and to move the relationship from a monologue to a dialogue, even if at first this takes place only in their minds. It is hoped that those SHOs most receptive to these ideas, and I have found this already to be the case in practice, will form the basis for the next generation of medically trained psychoanalysts, fulfilling Freud's wish that a psychoanalytic presence remains in the field of general psychiatry.

## A specialist registrar's experience of being with a patient with schizophrenia

I am grateful to Dr Sally Davies for permission and encouragement to use the following material for educational purposes.

The patient was a young man aged 27 with a diagnosis of schizo-phrenia. He was seeing a consultant general psychiatrist in his out-patient clinic and was on conventional antipsychotic medication. He had taken illicit drugs in the past, but not recently. He had expressed a wish for individual help and was referred by the consultant to the psychotherapy department for this.

The following material includes a précis from three sessions illus-trating the experience of direct contact with the mind of someone functioning in a predominantly psychotic way. He was being seen weekly. The specialist registrar, understandably, had great difficulty in following and recording the gist of the sessions, but they are presented as experienced.

### First session

The patient came in full of paranoid thoughts. He said, 'They know what he is thinking'. 'They look at him'. He stares at someone, and it is someone to check out feelings by the way he reads their response. He cannot mastur-bate at home. Perhaps this is why he has a homosexual relationship – mindless – with a friend. Then he feels ashamed of this, and becomes con-cerned over his mother's attitude and her disapproval of this behaviour. The therapist says so she, the mother, becomes the concerned one. The patient says that he brightens up when he plays tennis.

### Second session (two weeks later)

He misses the next week's session. He had a charity gig last week and completely forgot about the session that he had missed. Mother was away in Devon. They (he and his sister) found that they had run out of money and had no food. So they decided to have a party (as if this would be a way to get food).

As well as having problems with girls (meaning coping with the way they looked at him), he related another problem. He was picked for jury service. He was the foreman in a rape case. He was told not to discuss the facts of the case outside. He found it very difficult not to do this. There was not enough evidence to convict the person. He was worried that he was influencing other members of the jury. What if he was guilty? He was worried that other members of the family of the rape victim would find him and beat him up.

He had written a song called 'Sex Offenders'. People liked his song. A long time after playing it in gigs, a girl made a comment, which he took to indicate that she knew that he had written the song and he wondered how she knew this. He was worried over sexual feelings. A man had given him a massage. He said to the receptionist, 'Maybe you are a paedophile?' The receptionist said that it was him who was the paedophile (he had recounted this story before).

### Third session (a week later)

He had not slept very well. He worries that if he doesn't sleep and it continues, it means that he is becoming very unwell. It preceded breakdowns. Then he slept OK so it was all right. He said that the session last week had been very useful as he had spoken about the jury service.

He is working with a friend in the recording studio. He didn't sleep, then the friend didn't sleep (as if it was then the friend's turn not to sleep). He gets very emotional over music and can reach people (with it).

He says that there is a small room in the house where he sits with his mother and they don't use it very much. It is worse since the abortion of a girlfriend, also with cocaine. He gave up everything to be a musician, gave up normal jobs.

He feels responsible as a musician and has to keep doing it. He doesn't stop this when ill; there is a feeling with it that he can do anything.

There was some sadness around and the therapist said that the patient was sad that he still couldn't do everything.

He then talked of the effect of cutting his hair. He feels more free if it is longer and then creative. With medication, his hair is thinner, so he cuts it and feels like a schoolboy.

The specialist registrar noted in her mind that father was very distant compared to mother, and linked this with the patient's thought about mother's anger about the sex with the boyfriend, but she did not say this to the patient.

### The specialist registrar's countertransference reactions

The doctor felt that she had to act as the patient's ego function, without frightening him by doing this, but she felt that she should be realistic in her advice and response. She also had a fear of becoming an ideal object for him, with him becoming dependent on her for answers, as if she would be responsible for creating this unhelpful dependent problem for him. She felt that with borderline patients there was a theoretical framework for diagnosis and approach, but not with psychosis. She felt it was a different experience, but one which all senior doctors should have as part of their training.

### Discussion points

The doctor raises the question of whether there is a theoretical framework of approach to psychosis that differs from the approach with borderline states. Bion would say that there are two separate parts of the personality, the psychotic and non-psychotic and, in schizophrenia, one always has to deal with the problem presented by the psychotic part first.

A basic problem and one that led the patient to seek therapy is that the psychotic part needs someone to think for him, as he is incapable of doing this. However, since he attacks any separate person because they represent a threat to an omnipotent state, he gets into dreadfully confused states with his objects.

We can follow this theme in the material presented above. If he projects out into people, they immediately know his feelings and this is a disturbing experience. He has no container for his masturbatory phantasies, i.e. no container breast/mother. This contributes to the countertransference feeling that, unlike the situation with borderline patients, where the primary complaint by the patient is lack of under-standing containment from mother and a premature ejection into the real world, here there is felt to be no containing framework whatsoever.

The patient is aware that his view of mother's reaction to the homosexual relationship is linked to his attack on the mother or maternal breast. He doesn't really feel that he has an established adult homosexual orientation, and sees the homosexual relationship as mindless, the aim being to obliterate difference. He feels that the mother linked to an adult mind and sanity would not approve of this behaviour.

The need for some firm intervention, which is not occurring, may account for the therapist's thought about the patient's distant father. The patient brightens up by physically distancing himself from his conflicting feelings about the nature of his homosexual behaviour, by playing tennis. He then misses a session.

He then gets caught up in the excited mood of the charity gig, his own idealisation of his music (idealised masturbatory triumph over his conflicts) and he completely forgets the next session. The therapist is felt to have gone away, like his mother who is on holiday in Devon. He has turned the situation around so that it is the therapist that has left him rather than the other way round, with him missing the session.

He then runs into trouble, with no food being provided by the therapist mother, so resorts to manic states with idealisation and attacks on awareness. This is manifest in the material about influencing others' minds, the rape case and his idea of persuading the jury that the accused is not guilty, idealising his song on 'sex offenders', and worry that others will see through his behaviour and see his sexualised excited destructiveness, in the reference to the paedophile.

In the final session there seems to be an attempt to put his critical thoughts to sleep by becoming more manically excited over the power of his music, which gives him power over all others and enables him to become the universal provider, triumphing over the mother therapist. By projection of disturbing insight into others he distances himself from awareness and reduces the risk of a more extreme manic breakdown leading to hospitalisation.

The attack on the container is returned to in the reference to the abortion, use of cocaine, and his renunciation of life to be the omnipotent musician, leading to his comment on the very little used small shared room for him and the mother/therapist.

The therapist is subjected to the experience of a non-stop monologue, with very little room for the development of any shared reflection on the functioning of the patient's mind.

The patient's wish to actualise a state of total omnipotence where he could help everyone through his music was linked to his masturbatory phantasy that he could renounce the real world in which he needed a relationship in order to develop his thinking. The therapist articulated his sadness over his failure to achieve this. Perhaps taking on his feelings and becoming like a friend sharing his musical recording made him feel better because he had found someone to take his projections. This is suggested by his comment that he felt better after he recounted the jury service story to the therapist.

However, the wish to achieve some magical ideal state either by being the ideal provider, or alternatively by the therapist assuming this role, leads to the therapist's countertransference concern that she has allowed herself to be treated as an ideal and that this was not helpful for the patient.

Rey (1994a) described what he termed the claustrophobic-agoraphobic dilemma as a dominating feature in schizophrenia. The patient wants to distance himself in order to be free from awareness. He does this by projecting into the therapist and then missing the next session. However, he then finds himself without a needed mother/therapist so he returns to his sessions and the cycle of distancing through projection repeats itself.

The therapist, who has allowed herself to be open to receiving the patient's powerful projections, is left trying to process her feelings. The non-psychotic part of the patient's mind feels frightened of being taken over by the manic state of mind, while the manic state of mind does not take kindly to being scrutinised. So the feeling that the therapist is left with is that she needs to act as an ego function, to do the thinking for the patient, but without frightening him by exposing him to the full awareness of his state of mind.

One can appreciate that the issues to be considered here are very different from those in the case of a non-psychotic patient. For a specialist registrar an experience like this may help them to develop a deeper feel for the way that the mind works in psychosis. They will then be able to use the experience gained in other encounters within general psychiatry.

A common feeling that results from involvement with a patient in a psychotic state is of being left with a headache if one doesn't impose some rationality on the material. This is a reaction to the wish of the psychotic part of the patient to attack thinking and the therapist's mind. The case material illustrates this.

It is always easier to be in the role of the supervisor. The therapist brings the couple, the patient and themselves, to supervision. In supervision one has the opportunity to make slow action replays, as I have done here, to try to make sense of material that is produced with bewildering speed in the sessions. The trainee needs the opportunity to work with an experienced supervisor in order to enable them gradually to develop a framework of approach to the patient and begin to gain the confidence to make potent interpretations.

In an ideal world all specialist registrars would have the opportunity to gain one-to-one clinical experience with a psychotic patient. A period of personal therapy also helps enormously in gaining confidence in relating to the inner world, and is to be encouraged in all trainees who seek to learn to do this, not merely in those who wish to pursue formal analytic psychotherapy training.

## Referral of patients with schizophrenia: identifying the role for the psychotherapist

*Introduction*

I am grateful to Marcus Evans for his permission to use this clinical material, shared in a supervisory setting. He presents from the position of an experienced analytic psychotherapist, involved in relational work between an NHS psychotherapy clinic and local psychiatric services (Evans 2006). He often found that his view of the patient's needs differed significantly from that of the referring psychiatric team.

*Background history*

The patient was a 30-year-old man referred with a diagnosis of paranoid schizophrenia, although this was now disputed by his team. He had been seen in weekly psychotherapy for six months. Mr Evans took him on the condition that he continued to be seen by a psychiatric team for ongoing medication and psychiatric care.

The patient's parents separated when he was 3 years old. He was angry with his father because he did not take any interest in his upbringing, and angry with his mother because she remarried when he was 15 years old and no longer gave him her undivided attention. He successfully completed several O Level exams, but then started smoking 'skunk' (a strong form of marijuana) with a group of school friends and dropped out of the sixth form. The patient became obsessed with stalking his mother, and this resulted in her taking out a restraining order, for him not to visit.

When he was first admitted to hospital, the patient said that he was gathering evidence that he was the son of God. He expressed a belief that he would die when he reached 33, the age that Christ died. When the patient was put on antipsychotic medication, his mental state improved quite quickly. He then asked for someone to talk with and was referred for psychotherapy.

A week prior to the first of the sessions described below, the patient had stopped taking his medication and his therapist had told his CPN of his concern about this.

## First session

The patient began by expressing regret about the way he had treated his parents, saying that he should have had more control over his feelings and that he had been 'drugging' himself with the notion that his parents were to blame for his problems.

However, he agreed with the therapist that while he was expressing his wish to control his own thoughts, he also felt at times that he was being mocked like Christ, the son of God. He said that he was bored with those thoughts, but then added that he did not like to be seen on the way to his sessions. The therapist linked this to his humiliated feelings about his dependency needs, similar to his saying that he couldn't blame everything on his parents.

The patient then described powerful feelings of despair, 'I feel lost'. Towards the end of the session he reported paranoid delusions of being watched in his flat in the evening, which resulted in him going round to his mother in the middle of the night and repeatedly banging on her door until she called the police.

In the intervening week the therapist phoned the CPN and said that he was worried about the patient, and that he understood that he had stopped taking his medication. The CPN was again alerted to the therapist's concern over his mental state and said that he would phone the patient, but he was then not in his flat at the time of the arranged visit. The CPN told the therapist that he would try again, although the tone in his voice indicated that he thought the therapist was being rather anxious and overly protective of the patient.

## Second session

The patient admitted that he had received notification from the CPN of his visit but said that he had to leave the flat as people were following him. At the same time, he denied that he was in a paranoid state or that he was Jesus, but said that he was conducting his own studies on hieroglyphics and the meaning of numbers.

His therapist pointed out that while his feelings of need were indicated by his attempt to see his mother again, at the same time he was denying that there was anything wrong and claiming that he did not need help from the CPN. He recalled how the patient had on one recent occasion gone round to his father and tried to jump off the balcony. The patient said that it was a drug-related problem that had made him paranoid. In this way the psychotic part continually tried to minimise the extent of his illness.

A week later his CPN reported that he had seen the patient, could find no evidence of psychosis, and was planning to discharge him. This was despite contradictory feedback from his therapist, who then contacted the consultant psychiatrist, who felt that the patient had improved with therapy. The psychiatrist agreed that the patient was a vulnerable man and needed medication, but he did not have direct authority over the community health team's caseload. The consultant was not sure about the patient's diagnosis and thought that he might be suffering from a drug induced psychosis rather than schizophrenia, despite the psychotherapist's statement that the delusional system appeared pretty fixed and that the patient had not taken illicit drugs for several years.

## Third session

The patient came to this session in a very different mood – oscillating between feelings of pain, humiliation and mania. He had seen his consultant who had put him on some new antipsychotic medication. He had also been to court as a result of breaking his restriction order, and the judge had warned him that he would be sent to prison if he broke it again. He said that he felt very humiliated and was worried that he would be put in prison. At this point he felt in touch with the seriousness of his situation, but then he started to talk about a situation in which he was with someone who smashed up a snooker hall. He described putting numbers together in a way which revealed hidden meanings and elaborated on his understanding of hieroglyphics.

He did not turn up for his next appointment as he had been remanded in custody after another attempt to break into his mother's house. He subsequently received a lengthy prison sentence. His probation officer, who had interviewed him the day before the incident, felt guilty as she had asked him a lot of probing questions. He had become more and more bizarre as the interview went on and she worried that he could not cope with insight.

His therapist was left asking himself similar questions. He wondered whether the psychotherapy was making the patient worse as insight seemed to provoke a vicious counter-reaction and wish to 'smash up' his mind. Also when the patient talked in an insightful way, there was a question about the function of this talk: to what extent was the patient sharing a problem he wanted help with and to what extent was he was getting rid of the insight into his therapist?

## Discussion

Psychotherapy departments in the UK exist in a changing world where they will be expected to become more involved with psychotic disorders within the Community Mental Health Centres. Psychotherapists will need a different theoretical framework to the one they are accustomed to work with when approaching problems presented by non–psychotic disorders.

The first issue is to establish agreement with the general psychiatric team as to what the patient's needs are. In this case, the team disagreed on this patient's diagnosis as, for short periods, he was able to rationalise his paranoid states as the result of his previous drug related psychosis.

Evans observed that what appeared to be insight was in fact an evacuation by the psychotic part of awareness arrived at by the work of the non–psychotic part of the patient (Meltzer 1966), similar to the function served by dreams in psychotic disorders (see Chapter 12). The experience within the sessions indicated the patient's very limited ability to stay with psychic pain rather than evacuate and return to delusional solutions. The primary issue was not that insight made him worse, but rather that contact through the sessions and interview allowed him to begin to appreciate the fragile state of his mind.

From his work with the patient, it quickly became evident to Evans that the appropriate diagnosis was of a longstanding paranoid schizophrenic illness, with all the management implications attendant on such a diagnosis.

A diagnosis of longstanding severe paranoid schizophrenia means that a dedicated psychiatric team needs to be in place on an open-ended basis, with a designated key worker monitoring the patient's medication, and working gradually to establish an effective exoskeleton (see Chapter 17), consisting of supervised residence and day placement activity. The team working with the patient had not accepted his diagnosis and they were unable to respond appropriately to his relapsing state. In fact he should have been admitted to hospital on a formal basis and should not have ended up with a prison sentence, as it was clear that he was in a psychotic state when he broke the restriction order to visit his mother.

It was due to his background clinical experience that Evans was able to identify the lack of clarity and firmness within the team's approach and he did his utmost to try to ensure that it was addressed. This became his central role as the involved psychotherapist.

Psychotherapists are now being asked to provide a meaningful presence within general psychiatry, while still wishing to retain space and time for their own work with less disturbed patients. Becoming aware of how the issues presented in psychotic disorders differ from those in neurotic and borderline states can help psychotherapists to prioritise a review of the state of the support being provided by the responsible psychiatric team, rather than feeling that their role is confined to providing individual therapy for all patients on request.

## Overall summary

In this chapter I have considered the importance of education for those involved in the area of psychosis, highlighting the fact that the worker's needs will differ depending on their stage of training. Non-medical psychotherapy trainees need six months of psychiatric experience at minimum. For senior nurses, postgraduate analytically based clinical courses can deepen their individual capacities for self-containment. For junior doctors new to psychiatry, a psychosis workshop can serve as an important space for reflection. For those who are more advanced in training, seeing an individual case with supervision can be an enlightening experience. Finally, for experienced psychotherapists the challenge will be to find a way of relating effectively to the increasing demands from the local psychiatric services.

# 21

## Conclusion
## Psychoanalytic attitudes to general psychiatry and psychosis

Freud did not share the oft-expressed view that general psychiatry and psychosis are an arid area for analytic exploration.

In 1916, writing on the subject of 'Psycho-analysis and psychiatry' as part of his *Introductory Lectures on Psychoanalysis*, Freud commented, 'There is nothing in the nature of psychiatric work which could be opposed to psycho-analytic research. What is opposed to psycho-analysis is not psychiatry but psychiatrists' (Freud 1916–1917b, p. 254). This would make for a lively debate at the AGM of the Royal College of Psychiatrists!

In a later paper in the Introductory Lecture Series on 'The libido theory and narcissism', Freud goes further in support of the need for an analytic presence in general psychiatry. He writes:

> There are difficulties that hold up our advance. The narcissistic disorders and the psychoses related to them can only be deciphered by observers who have been trained through the analytic study of the transference neuroses. But our psychiatrists are not students of psycho-analysis and we psycho-analysts see too few psychiatric cases. A race of psychiatrists must first grow who have passed through the school of psycho-analysis as a preparatory science.
>
> (Freud 1916–1917a, p. 423)

Ernest Jones, the founder of the British Psychoanalytical Society, added his view in a paper entitled 'Psycho-analysis and psychiatry' (Jones 1930). He observed that the so-called normal individual, the

300

neurotic, and the psychotic have reacted differently to the same fundamental difficulties of human development, and commented:

> Parenthetically, I wish to express here my conviction that the strategic point in the relationship between the three fields is occupied by the psychoneuroses. So-called normality represents a much more devious and obscure way of dealing with the fundamentals of life than the neuroses do, and it is correspondingly a much more difficult route to trace. The psychoses, on the other hand, present solutions so recondite and remote that it is very hard for the observer to develop a truly empathic attitude towards them, and unless this can be done, any knowledge remains intellectualistic, external, and unfruitful.
>
> (Jones 1930, pp. 487–488)

This book has argued that in order to develop what Jones (1930) described as 'a truly empathic attitude', we need to tune into the psychotic wavelength; ordinary empathy, applied to non-psychotic disorders, is insufficient.

Over the years psychoanalysts have sometimes attempted to impose their own views to explain the behaviour of psychotic patients. Reacting to the inhumanity of the early physical interventions, leucotomy and insulin coma, Laing and the anti-psychiatry movement blamed schizophrenia on society's intolerance of eccentricity (Lucas 1998). The exponents of this approach later became disenchanted when the psychosis did not go away with their laissez-faire attitude. In the United States, at Chestnut Lodge, the roots of psychosis were attributed to infantile trauma, following Fromm-Reichmann's (1950) concept of the 'schizophrenogenic' mother. In the UK during the 1960s, emerging Kleinian theory was applied to the mind in psychosis and led to an enthusiasm for treating individual cases of schizophrenia through psychoanalysis. Many seminal insights resulted from this work (H. A. Rosenfeld 1965; Segal 1950; Sohn 1985b). The prevailing climate of optimism also led to the creation of specialist analytic units in the NHS at the Shenley and Maudsley Hospitals (Jackson 2001a). However, the enthusiasm faded and the specialist centres eventually closed, perhaps partly in consequence of the dawning realisation of the intransigent nature of chronic psychoses.

Following on from the work of Klein, and based on his individual analytic case studies, Bion introduced a completely new perspective to psychosis, with his consideration of a psychotic part of the personality which develops and functions completely differently from the non-psychotic part (Bion 1957a). Bion urges us to keep these two separate parts in mind and, in all major psychotic disorders, always to address the needs of the psychotic part first and foremost. It has been left to those few analysts still working in the field to add Bion's insights to preceding theories, in order to assemble a framework that is both relevant to the task of relating to patients with psychosis and can aid junior doctors in their work.

In modern-day psychiatry, with its emphasis on evidence-based approaches, everything that is undertaken is expected to be open to objective measurement. At present, this does not include evidence arising from a consideration of the individual clinician's countertransference experience. Such evidence would be regarded as too subjective and unscientific, and yet it is vital in enabling us to decipher the meaning of experiences with psychotic states. I have found it essential to provide space in psychosis workshops to support the SHOs in the exploration and valuing of their individual emotional experiences, helping them to learn not to dismiss these as idiosyncratic.

In the introduction to his book, *Sex, Death and the Superego*, Ron Britton (2003) compares the current emphasis on an 'evidence-based' approach in medical research to what he terms an 'experience-based' one. He points out that, in contrast to learning new medical skills, it takes decades to gain experience in psychoanalysis. In the mean time the young doctor has to rely on information gleaned from papers and from the supervision of others who have already gained such experience. He warns, however, that we all carry 'overvalued ideas' that we tend to treat as if they were 'selected facts' (Britton 2003). This means that we must always retain our own critical faculties when listening to others, no matter how experienced they may be in the field. This idea is very relevant for the SHOs starting in psychiatry who, when presenting at workshops, need to be encouraged to retain their own critical faculties and individual sensitivities. Using Winnicott's terminology, we need to foster a 'facilitating environment' for the development of the next generation of psychoanalytically orientated psychiatrists (Winnicott 1965).

Despite a psychoanalytic training and seven years at the Maudsley Hospital, including the privilege of working under Henri Rey in the psychotherapy department seeing borderline patients, and on the specialist psychosis inpatient unit run initially by John Steiner and then Murray Jackson, nothing prepared me for arriving at Claybury Hospital in 1978. The setting was a busy asylum, with responsibility for 28 acute beds, 125 long-stay beds, a day hospital, outpatient clinics and forensic visits. This was very different from the small caseload and academic atmosphere I had encountered at the Maudsley.

I found that I had to act as a scavenger, gleaning any useful analytic contributions on psychosis from wherever I could find them, while at the same time being wary of any overvalued ideas, in myself or others. In this way I began building up a framework with which to relate to patients and their psychopathology. This has been a difficult and demanding experience, but in the end it was a gratifying one through which I have been able to offer help to new psychiatrists starting on their own voyages of discovery.

## Developing a model of the mind applicable to psychosis

As a psychoanalyst who works in general psychiatry, and carries clinical responsibility for patients who are very ill and require protracted admissions, my perspective is very different from that adopted by the analytic psychotherapist in other areas of clinical work. The theory I work with is one which must take into account the following issues.

### *The usefulness and limitations of the medical model*

The medical model, as applied within psychiatry, is very limited in flexibility. While it helps to clarify that we are dealing with a major psychotic disorder, it provides only a snapshot, and cannot take into account dynamic movement, since this requires introduction of an analytic model. Without a psychoanalytically based teaching, SHOs will not be introduced to this perspective.

### *The role of medication*

Antipsychotic medication may help to act as a container and ease the pathway in relating to the patient. Antidepressant medication can sometimes be a helpful adjunct to facilitate the continuation of analysis in severe cases of depression where, for example, the patient is finding it difficult to get up for morning sessions. The fundamental point is that when we are dealing with psychosis, we have to relinquish the omnipotent views (whether analytic or organic) that only one pathway should prevail. In other words, we need to be prepared to introduce flexibility into our thinking.

## The notion of cure

Over the years many optimistic attempts have been made to cure schizophrenia, from both the organic and analytic perspectives. This illness does not fit into our familiar preconceptions. When the asylums closed in the mid 1990s, it was believed that chronic schizophrenia was the result of institutionalisation. In theory effective community care should have obviated the need for inpatient beds. In fact the closure of the asylums led to an acute shortage of beds in the district hospitals. During the alarming early years of schizophrenia, with potential for suicidal acts, the danger is that we may focus too much on an attitude of trying to achieve a cure. The consequence of this therapeutic zeal may be that we lose sight of the importance of providing support for the patient to come to terms with the condition, by working to assemble a containing environment or exoskeleton.

## Theories of infantile trauma

Most analytic models of the mind place a central emphasis on infantile trauma to explain development of psychopathology. However, over-reliance on this approach may lead us into difficulties when relating to patients with schizophrenia. What is needed is an open mind in each individual case.

## The need to differentiate psychotic processes from major psychiatric disorders

It is important to differentiate severe borderline states from schizophrenia, since each has different implications for modes of management and prognosis. Borderline patients can teach us a lot about psychotic processes (Rey 1994a), and they can be treated using an analytic approach. The transference has a particular intensity directed to the therapist, while the patient may well be very committed to the therapy.

## A view on the death instinct

Nothing in Freud's theorising has generated more controversy among his followers than his introduction of the notion of an inherent destructive force, the death instinct or death drive. Freud introduced the concept to his metapsychology belatedly in order to complement his notion of the life instinct. As Laplanche and Pontalis (1973) pointed out in a detailed review of the death instinct, a dualistic tendency is fundamental to Freudian thought. At first Freud was tentative about the notion, but ended up strongly endorsing it. He wrote:

> To begin with, it was only tentatively that I put forward the views that I have developed here, but in the course of time they have gained such a hold on me that I can no longer think in any other way.
>
> (Freud 1930, p. 119)

Klein viewed envy as the external manifestation of the death instinct.

The question often arises, why not just view aggressiveness as a positive reaction to frustration, without the need to invoke such a draconian measure as the death instinct? When this point arose some time ago in a discussion at a scientific meeting of the British Psychoanalytical Society, I recall Hanna Segal saying that the best way she could describe its manifestation in everyday life was 'human bloody mindedness' – something that we can all recognise. This certainly resonates with my own clinical experience when relating to patients with major psychotic disorders.

## Tuning into the 'psychotic wavelength'

Identifying the dominating psychopathology, while still retaining an overall empathy for patients in their struggles to cope with crises with

305

their limited mental capacities, is a central issue in teaching SHOs to regard their patients as human beings rather than objectifying them as 'the psychotic'.

A patient who came into hospital because he was unable to cope with a financial crisis had changed his name by deed poll to Jesus Christ, but he complained that he was angry with God. He was unable to cope in his present state, so in his psychotic way he had hoped that, if he changed his name, God would help him out. Unfortunately for him, changing his name had not resolved his financial troubles. We can feel sympathy for his attempts to cope within his limited mental resources, rather than just considering the presenting material in phenomenological terms.

## The importance of the countertransference experience

Since patients in psychotic states make extensive use of projective mechanisms, our countertransference experiences are of crucial importance when striving towards an overall understanding. For example, since there are two separate parts operating simultaneously in psychosis, we frequently find that we ask ourselves whether we are being fair in doubting the veracity of a patient's account. Is what the patient is saying evidence of psychosis or is it the truth? If we experience this doubting countertransference, it usually indicates that we are in the realm of psychosis.

For the leader and participants of a psychosis workshop, it is a common experience to feel that one will have nothing to contribute when one hears florid psychotic material that makes no sense. It is only with time that we come to recognise that we have been on the receiving end of powerful projections from the psychotic part of the patient. This part is engaged in evacuating and negating thoughts that have been arrived at through the work of the non-psychotic part. It is as if the psychotic part has a contemptuous murderous reaction, a 'so what!' response to any thinking that might take place. As the workshop proceeds, it begins to come to life as we hear everyone's associations to the projected material. This enables the initial aridity to turn into a workshop that becomes creative and fruitful.

*The deciphering of ideographs and the relationship between hallucinations and delusions*

Bion (1958) described how the psychotic part of the mind is incapable of thinking; it can only act as a muscular organ. It stores memories, termed ideographs, formed through the work of the non-psychotic part, in which it projects feelings, for the purpose of evacuation or communication. Our task in everyday psychiatry is to decipher the meaning of these ideographs. This is comparable to solving crossword puzzle clues and is helped by the simultaneous use of our countertransference experiences (Bion 1958). Such work, importantly, introduces humour and interest into the team's involvement in work which might otherwise threaten to become arid, demanding and soul-destroying.

> A patient in a manic state complained that he had contracted avian flu. If we think of this delusion as an attempt by the psychotic part to evacuate his sanity, the symptom becomes alive and interesting, rather than just a dry phenomenological description of a delusion requiring medication. I described the avian flu that the patient had caught from chickens as his attempt to fly away from his need to cooperate with our treatment for him. I said that he was chickening out of attending the day hospital and receiving full community support, rather than facing up to his problems with our help. Interpreting in this way made the patient smile and helped the care team feel less disabled by the patient's mania.

*The psychotic and non-psychotic parts of the mind*

Most importantly of all, I have learned to think always in terms of two separately functioning parts of the mind, rather than one person, when relating to individuals with such major psychotic disorders as schizophrenia, bipolar affective disorders, and major depressive episodes. I would also include anorexia nervosa, as in the case briefly described in Chapter 20.

As a general psychiatrist, whenever I am asked to consider sectioning a patient under the Mental Health Act 1983, I have to determine whether I am relating to a sane part of the patient, or to a mad part masquerading as normal. Denial and rationalisation, rather than hallucinations and delusions, are the commonest presenting symptoms in psychosis. The patient's denial and rationalisations can frequently fool us into underestimating the severity of the disturbance in their underlying state of mind. A common occurrence of this dynamic in everyday analytic practice is in severe depression, where we might think we are relating to a non-psychotic part which is seeking insight, whereas the dominating psychotic part is not in the least interested in understanding, since all it wants is fusion with an idealised object.

Psychoanalysts who are not familiar with working in general psychiatry may still feel uncomfortable with the notion of the two separate parts, rather than thinking in terms of split-off parts of the personality requiring reintegration. Reintegration of split-off parts, though a fundamental way of thinking in relation to the analytic process, properly belongs to the workings of the non-psychotic part of the personality. For myself, I find the concept of two separate parts of the personality enormously helpful when I am trying to orientate myself to the presenting psychosis. For example, if a patient says that he or she is feeling fine, yet the nearest relative has alerted the professionals to an alarming relapse, who are we to believe? It is crucial, in my view, that approved social workers carry this model of the two parts in mind when they are conducting assessments under the Mental Health Act 1983, otherwise they can be left with the view that asserts that the patient is fine and the problem lies solely with the nearest relative.

# Notes

1   Recently, on the initiative of the President of the British Psychoanalytical Society, Roger Kennedy, an NHS Liaison Committee was formed to rectify this.

2   Bion's complex interpretation of the ideograph, based on his knowledge of the patient, was as follows:

> The glasses contained a hint of the baby's bottle. They were two glasses, or bottles, thus resembling the breast. They were dark because frowning and angry. They were of glass to pay him out for trying to see through them when they were breasts. They were dark because he needs darkness to spy on his parents in intercourse. They were dark because he had taken the bottle not to get milk but to see what the parents did. They were dark because he had swallowed them, and not simply the milk they had contained. And they were dark because the clear good objects had been made black and smelly inside them. All these attributes must have been achieved through the operation of the non–psychotic part of the personality. Added to these characteristics were those I have described as appertaining to them as part of the ego that has been expelled by projective identification, namely their hatred of him as part of himself he had rejected.

However, in what Bion actually said to the patient in the session he describes, he concentrated on the psychotic problem, that is, the need to repair the ego. He said: 'Your sight has come back into you but splits your head; you feel it is very bad sight because of what you have done to it' (Bion 1957a, p. 58).

3   For a full appreciation of the breadth of his contributions, see Clifford Yorke's obituary of Tom Freeman in *The Times* (31 May 2002).

4   A version of this chapter was originally published as Lucas, R. (1998).

309

Why the cycle in a cyclical psychosis? An analytic contribution to the understanding of recurrent manic depressive psychosis. *Psychoanalytic Psychotherapy*, *12*, 193–212.

5   A version of this chapter was originally published as Taylor-Thomas, C. and Lucas, R. (2006). Consideration of the role of psychotherapy in reducing the risk of suicide in affective disorders: A case study. *Psychoanalytic Psychotherapy*, *20*, 218–234.

# References

Abraham, K. (1911). Notes on the psychoanalytical investigation and treatment of manic depressive insanity and allied conditions. In *Selected Papers on Psychoanalysis* (pp. 137–156). London: Hogarth Press (1973).

Abraham, K. (1924). A short study on the libido, viewed in the light of mental disorders. Part 1. Manic depressive states and the pre-genital levels of libido. In *Selected Papers on Psychoanalysis* (pp. 418–507). London: Hogarth Press (1973).

Alanen, Y. O. (1997). *Schizophrenia: Its Origins and Need-Adapted Treatment.* London: Karnac.

American Psychiatric Association (APA) (1994). *Diagnostic and Statistical Manual of Mental Disorder*, 4th edn (DSM-IV). Washington, DC: APA.

Angst, J., and Sellaro, R. (2000). Historical perspectives and natural history of bipolar disorder. *Society of Biological Psychiatry, 48*, 445–457.

Appleby, L. (1997). *Progress Report: National Confidential Inquiry into Suicide and Homicide by People with Mental Illness.* London: Department of Health.

Barnes, M., and Berke, J. (1991). *Two Accounts of a Journey through Madness.* London: Free Association Books.

Bateson, G. (1972). *Steps to an Ecology of Mind.* New York: Chandler.

Bell, D. (2001). Who is killing what or whom? Some notes on the internal phenomenology of suicide. *Psychoanalytic Psychotherapy, 15*, 21–37.

Bentall, R. P. (2003). *Madness Explained: Psychosis and Human Nature.* London: Allen Lane.

Bentall, R. P. (2004). Abandoning the concept of schizophrenia: the cognitive psychology of hallucinations and delusions. In J. Read, L. R. Mosher and R. D. Bentall (eds) *Models of Madness* (pp. 195–208). London: Routledge.

Beveridge, A., and Turnbull, R. (1989). *The Eclipse of Scottish Culture.* Edinburgh: Polygon.

Bion, W. R. (1957a). Differentiation of the psychotic from the non-psychotic personalities. In *Second Thoughts* (pp. 43–64). New York: Jason Aronson (1967).

Bion, W. R. (1957b). On arrogance. In *Second Thoughts* (pp. 86–92). New York: Jason Aronson (1967).

Bion, W. R. (1958). On hallucination. In *Second Thoughts* (pp. 65–85). New York: Jason Aronson (1967).

Bion, W. R. (1962). A theory of thinking. In *Second Thoughts* (pp. 110–119). New York: Jason Aronson (1967).

Bion, W. R. (1967). *Second Thoughts*. New York: Jason Aronson.

Bion, W. R. (1977). *The Grid*. Rio de Janeiro: Imago Editors.

Black, D. M. (2001). Mapping a detour: Why did Freud speak of a death drive? *British Journal of Psychotherapy, 18*, 185–197.

Bleuler, E. (1911). *Dementia Praecox or the Group of Schizophrenias*. New York: International University Press (1955).

Blom-Cooper, L. (1995). *The Falling Shadow: One Patient's Mental Health Care, 1978–1993*. London: Duckworth.

Blom-Cooper, L., Grounds, A., Guinan, P., Parker, A., and Taylor, M. (1996). *The Case of Jason Mitchell: Report of the Independent Panel of Enquiry*. London: Duckworth.

Bourne, S., Lewis, E., and Kraemer, S. (1993). Mothering skills of women with mental illness (letter). *British Medical Journal, 306*, 859.

Britton, R. (1989). The missing link: Parental sexuality in the Oedipus complex. In R. Britton, M. Feldman and E. O'Shaughnessy (eds) *The Oedipus Complex Today: Clinical Implications* (pp. 83–101). London: Karnac.

Britton, R. (1995). Publication anxiety: Conflict between communication and affiliation. Unpublished presentation to the British PsychoAnalytical Society.

Britton, R. (1998). *Belief and Imagination: Explorations in Psychoanalysis*. London: Routledge.

Britton, R. (2003). *Sex, Death and the Superego*. London: Karnac.

Britton, R. (2009). Mind and matter: A psychoanalytic perspective. In R. Doctor and R. Lucas (eds) *The Organic and the Inner World*. London: Karnac.

Cameron, J. L., Laing, R. D., and McGhie, A. (1955). Patient and nurse: Effects of environmental changes in the care of chronic schizophrenics. *Lancet, 269*(6905), 1384–1386.

Carson, J., Shaw, L., and Wills, W. (1989). Which patients first? A study from the closure of a large psychiatric hospital. *Health Trends, 4*, 117–120.

Clay, J. (1997). *R. D. Laing: A Divided Self*. London: Sceptre.

Cohen, M. B., Baker, G., Cohen, R. A., Fromm-Reichmann, F., and Weigart, E. V. (1954). An intensive study of twelve cases of manic-depressive psychosis.

In J. C. Coyne (ed.) *Essential Papers on Depression* (pp. 81–139). New York: New York University Press (1985).

Coltart, N. (1995). Attention. In J. H. Berke, C. Masoliver and T. J. Ryan (eds) *Sanctuary: The Arbours Experience of Alternative Community Care* (pp. 157–172). London: Process Press.

Cooper, J. E., Kendell, R. E., Gurland, B. J., Sharpe, L., Copeland, J. R. M., and Simon, R. (1972). *Psychiatric Diagnosis in New York and London. Maudsley Monograph no. 20.* London: Oxford University Press.

Cox, J., Murray, D., and Chapman, G. (1993). A controlled study of the onset, duration and prevalence of postnatal depression. *British Journal of Psychiatry, 163*, 27–31.

Cullberg, J. (2001). 'The parachute project': First episode psychosis – background and treatment. In P. Williams (ed.) *A Language for Psychosis* (pp. 115–125). London: Whurr.

Davies, E., and Burdett, J. (2004). Preventing 'schizophrenia': Creating the conditions for saner societies. In J. Read, L. Mosher and R. D. Bentall (eds) *Models of Madness* (pp. 271–282). London: Routledge.

De Masi, F. (2001). The unconscious and psychosis: Some considerations of the psychoanalytic theory of psychosis. In P. Williams (ed.) *A Language for Psychosis* (pp. 69–97). London: Whurr.

Evans, M. (2006). Making room for madness in mental health. *Psychoanalytic Psychotherapy, 20*, 16–29.

Fagin, L. (2001). Therapeutic and counter-therapeutic factors in acute ward settings. *Psychoanalytic Psychotherapy, 15*, 99–120.

Fagin, L. (2007). A brief narrative of in-patient care in the United Kingdom. In M. Hardcastle, D. S. Kennard, S. Grandison and L. Fagin (eds) *Experiences of Mental Health Inpatient Care* (pp. 8–16). London: Routledge.

Feldman, M. (2007). Addressing parts of the self. *International Journal of Psychoanalysis, 88*, 371–386.

Fenichel, O. (1946). *The Psychoanalytic Theory of Neurosis.* London: Routledge (1996).

Firth, W. (2004). Acute psychiatric wards: An overview. In P. Campling, S. Davies and G. Farquharson (eds) *From Toxic Institutions to Therapeutic Environments: Residential Settings in Mental Health Services* (pp. 174–187). London: Gaskell.

Flanders, S. (1993). *The Dream Discourse Today.* London: Routledge.

Fonagy, P., and Bateman, A. W. (2006). Mechanisms of change in mentalization-based treatment of BPD. *Journal of Clinical Psychology, 26*, 411–430.

Freeman, T. (1988). *The Psychoanalyst in Psychiatry.* London: Free Association Books.

Freeman, T. (1998). *But Facts Exist: An Enquiry into Psychoanalytic Theorising.* London: Karnac.

Freud, A. (1936). *The Ego and the Mechanisms of Defence*. London: Hogarth Press (1987).

Freud, S. (1900). *The Interpretation of Dreams*. In *S.E. 4–5*.

Freud, S. (1910). The future prospects of psycho-analytic therapy. In *S.E. 9* (pp. 144–145).

Freud, S. (1911a). Psychoanalytic notes on an autobiographical account of a case of paranoia (Dementia paranoides). In *S.E. 12* (pp. 3–79).

Freud, S. (1911b). Formulations on the two principles of mental functioning. In *S.E. 12* (pp. 213–226).

Freud, S. (1914). On narcissism: An introduction. In *S.E. 14* (pp. 67–107).

Freud, S. (1915). The unconscious. In *S.E. 14* (pp. 159–215).

Freud, S. (1916–1917a). Psychoanalysis and psychiatry. Lecture XVI, *Introductory Lectures on Psycho-analysis*. In *S.E. 16* (pp. 243–256).

Freud, S. (1916–1917b). The libido theory and narcissism. Lecture XXVI, *Introductory Lectures on Psycho-analysis*. In *S.E. 16* (pp. 412–430).

Freud, S. (1917). Mourning and melancholia. In *S.E. 14* (pp. 237–259).

Freud, S. (1920). Beyond the pleasure principle. In *S.E. 18* (pp. 3–64).

Freud, S. (1921). Group psychology and the analysis of the ego. In *S.E. 18* (pp. 67–143).

Freud, S. (1923). The ego and the id. In *S.E. 19* (pp. 12–66).

Freud, S. (1924). Neurosis and psychosis. In *S.E. 19* (pp. 149–153).

Freud, S. (1925). An autobiographical study. In *S.E. 20* (pp. 7–74).

Freud, S. (1930). Civilisation and its discontents. In *S.E. 21* (pp. 64–148).

Freud, S. (1937). Constructions in analysis. In *S.E. 23* (pp. 225–270).

Freud, S. (1940). *An Outline of Psycho-Analysis*. In *S.E. 23* (pp. 141–207).

Fromm-Reichmann, F. (1950). *Principles of Intensive Psychotherapy*. Chicago, IL: University of Chicago Press.

Garelick, A., and Lucas, R. (1996). The role of a psychosis workshop in general psychiatric training. *Psychiatric Bulletin of the Royal College of Psychiatrists, 20*, 425–429.

Gelder, M., Gath, D., and Mayou, R. (1990). *Oxford Textbook of Psychiatry*, 2nd edn. Oxford: Oxford University Press.

Gelder, M., Gath, D., Mayou, R., and Cowen, P. (1998). *Oxford Textbook of Psychiatry*, 3rd edn. Oxford: Oxford University Press.

Gelder, M., Mayou, R., and Cowen, P. (2001). *Shorter Oxford Textbook of Psychiatry*, 4th edn. Oxford: Oxford University Press.

Gelder, M., Harrison, P., and Cowen, P. (2006). *Shorter Oxford Textbook of Psychiatry*, 5th edn. Oxford: Oxford University Press.

Giovacchini, P. L. (1979). *The Treatment of Primitive Mental States*. New York: Jason Aronson.

Goldberg, P. (1997). *The Maudsley Handbook of Practical Psychiatry*. Oxford: Oxford University Press.

Greenberg, J. (1964). *I Never Promised You a Rose Garden*. New York: Holt.

Grotstein, J. S. (2001). A rationale for the psychoanalytically informed psychotherapy of schizophrenia and other psychoses: Towards the concept of 'rehabilitative psychoanalysis'. In P. Williams (ed.) *A Language for Psychosis* (pp. 9–26). London: Whurr.

Hargreaves, E., and Varchevker, A. (eds) (2004). *In Pursuit of Psychic Change: The Betty Joseph Workshop*. Hove: Brunner-Routledge.

Heimann, P. (1950). On countertransference. *International Journal of Psycho-Analysis, 31*, 81–84.

Hinshelwood, R. D. (1989). *A Dictionary of Kleinian Thought*. London: Free Association Books.

Hinshelwood, R. D. (2004). *Suffering Insanity: Psychoanalytic Essays on Psychosis*. Hove: Brunner-Routledge.

Holmes, J. (2004). What can psychotherapy contribute to improving the culture on acute psychiatric wards? In P. Campling, S. Davies and G. Farquharson (eds) *From Toxic Institutions to Therapeutic Environments: Residential Settings in Mental Health Services* (pp. 208–216). London: Gaskell.

Isaacs, S. (1952). The nature and function of phantasy. In M. Klein, P. Heimann, S. Isaacs and J. Riviere (eds) *Developments in Psychoanalysis* (pp. 68–121). London: Hogarth Press.

Jackson, M. (1989). Manic-depressive psychosis: Psychopathology and psychotherapy in a psychodynamic milieu. In S. Gilbert, S. Haugsgjerd and H. Hjort (eds) *Lines of Life: Psychiatry and Humanism*. Oslo: Tano.

Jackson, M. (2001a). Psychoanalysis and the treatment of psychosis. In P. Williams (ed.) *A Language for Psychosis* (pp. 37–53). London: Whurr.

Jackson, M. (2001b). *Weathering Storms: Psychotherapy for Psychosis*. London: Karnac.

Jackson, M., and Williams, P. (1994). *Unimaginable Storms: A Search for Meaning in Psychosis*. London: Karnac.

Jacobson, E. (1978). *Depression: Comparative Studies of Normal, Neurotic and Psychotic Conditions*. New York: International Universities Press.

James, W. (1902). *The Varieties of Religious Experience*. New York: Longmans, Green.

Jaspers, K. (1967). *General Psychopathology*, 7th edn (1959), trans. J. Hoenig and M.W. Hamilton. Manchester: Manchester University Press.

Johannessen, J. O., Martindale, B. V., and Cullberg, J. (2006). *Evolving Psychosis: Different Stages, Different Treatments*. London: Routedge.

Jones, E. (1930). Psycho-analysis and psychiatry. In *Papers on Psychoanalysis*. London: Maresfield Reprints.

Jones, E. (1972). *The Interpretation of Dreams* (1895–1899). In *Sigmund Freud: Life and Work (Volume 1)* (pp. 384–399). London: Hogarth Press.

Joseph, B. (1982). Addiction to near death. In M. Feldman and E. Bott Spillius (eds) *Psychic Equilibrium and Psychic Change: Selected Papers of Betty Joseph* (pp. 127–138). London: Routledge (1989).

Joseph, B. (1985). Transference: The total situation. In M. Feldman and E. Bott Spillius (eds) *Psychic Equilibrium and Psychic Change: Selected Papers of Betty Joseph* (pp. 156–167). London: Routledge (1989).

Joseph, B. (1989). In M. Feldman and E. Bott Spillius (eds) *Psychic Equilibrium and Psychic Change: Selected Papers of Betty Joseph*. London: Routledge.

Katan, M. (1979). Further exploration of the schizophrenic regression to the undifferentiated state: A study of the 'Assessment of the Unconscious'. *International Journal of Psychoanalysis*, *60*, 145–174.

Kendell, R. E., Chalmers, J. C., and Platz, C. (1987). Epidemiology of puerperal psychosis. *British Journal of Psychiatry*, *50*, 662–673.

Kennard, D., Fagin, L., Hardcastle, M., and Grandison, S. (2007). Things you can do to make in-patient care a better experience. In *Experiences of Mental Health Inpatient Care* (pp. 205–207). London: Routledge.

Kernberg, O. F. (1984). *Severe Personality Disorders: Psychotherapeutic Strategies*. New Haven, CT: Yale University Press.

Kerr, I. B., Crowley, V., and Beard, H. (2006). A cognitive analytic therapy-based approach to psychotic disorder. In J. V. Johannessen, B. V. Martindale and J. Cullberg (eds) *Evolving Psychosis: Different Stages, Different Treatment* (pp. 172–184). London: Routledge.

Kierkegaard, S. (1849). *The Sickness unto Death*. London: Penguin (1989).

Kingdon, D. G., and Turkington, D. (1994). *Cognitive-Behaviour Therapy of Schizophrenia*. Hove: Lawrence Erlbaum.

Klein, H. S. (1974). Transference and defence in manic states. *International Journal of Psychoanalysis*, *55*, 261–268.

Klein, M. (1935). A contribution to the psychogenesis of manic-depressive states. In *Love, Guilt and Reparation and Other Works 1921–1945* (pp. 262–289). London: Hogarth Press.

Klein, M. (1940). Mourning and its relation to manic-depressive states. In *Love, Guilt and Reparation and Other Works 1921–1945* (pp. 344–369). London: Hogarth Press.

Klein, M. (1945). The Oedipus complex in the light of early anxieties. In *Love, Guilt and Reparation and Other Works 1921–1945* (pp. 370–419). London: Hogarth Press (1975).

Klein, M. (1957). Envy and gratitude. In *Envy and Gratitude and Other Works 1946–1963*. London: Hogarth Press (1975).

Klein, M. (1958). On the development of mental functioning. In *Envy and*

*Gratitude and Other Works 1946–1963* (pp. 370–419). London: Hogarth Press (1975).

Klein, M. (1959). Our adult world and its roots in infancy. In *Envy and Gratitude and Other Works 1946–1967* (pp. 247–263). London: Hogarth Press (1975).

Klerman, G. L. (1990). The psychiatric patient's right to effective treatment: Implications of Osheroff v. Chestnut Lodge. *American Journal of Psychiatry*, *147*, 409–418.

Kotowicz, Z. (1997). *R. D. Laing and the Paths of Anti-Psychiatry*. London: Routledge.

Kraepelin, E. (1896). *Psychiatrie: Ein Lehrbuch für Studierende und Aerzte. Fünfte, vollständig umgearbeitete Auflage*. New York: Arno Press (1976).

Kraepelin, E. (1905). *Lectures on Clinical Psychiatry*. London: Baillière, Tindall and Cox.

Kraepelin, E. (1921). *Manic-depressive illness and paranoia*. Edinburgh: Livingstone.

Kumar, R., and Robson, K. M. (1984). A prospective study of emotional disorders in childbearing women. *British Journal of Psychiatry*, *144*, 35–47.

Laing, A. (1977). *R. D. Laing: A Life*. London: HarperCollins.

Laing, R. D. (1960). *The Divided Self*. London: Tavistock.

Laing, R. D. (1961). *Self and Others*. London: Tavistock.

Laing, R. D. (1985). *Wisdom, Madness, and Folly: The Making of a Psychiatrist*. London: Macmillan.

Laing, R. D., and Esterson, A. (1964). *Sanity, Madness, and the Family*. London: Tavistock.

Laplanche, J., and Pontalis, J.-B. (1973). *The Language of Psychoanalysis*. London: Hogarth Press.

Leff, J. (1994). Working with the families of schizophrenic patients. *British Journal of Psychiatry*, *164* (supplement 23), 71–76.

Lewin, B. D. (1951). *The Psychoanalysis of Elation*. London: Hogarth Press.

Lieberman, J. A., and First, M. B. (2007). Renaming schizophrenia. *British Medical Journal*, *334*, 108.

Lucas, R. (1992). The psychotic personality: A psychoanalytic theory and its application in clinical practice. *Psychoanalytic Psychotherapy*, 7, 3–17.

Lucas, R. (1993). The psychotic wavelength. *Psychoanalytic Psychotherapy*, 7, 89–101.

Lucas, R. (1994). Puerperal psychosis: Vulnerability and aftermath. *Psychoanalytic Psychotherapy*, *8*, 257–272.

Lucas, R. (1998). R.D. Laing: His life and legacy. *International Journal of Psycho-analysis*, *79*, 1229–1239.

Lucas, R. (2003a). The relationship between psychoanalysis and schizophrenia. *International Journal of Psychoanalysis*, *84*, 3–15.

Lucas, R. (2003b). Risk assessment in general psychiatry: A psychoanalytic perspective. In R. Doctor (ed.) *Dangerous Patients: A Psychodynamic Approach to Risk Assessment and Management* (pp. 33–48). London: Karnac.

Lucas, R. (2004). Managing depression – analytic, antidepressants or both? *Psychoanalytic Psychotherapy, 18*, 268–284.

McGlashan, T. (1984a). The Chestnut Lodge follow-up study: I. Follow-up methodology and study sample. *Archives of General Psychiatry, 41*, 573–585.

McGlashan, T. (1984b). The Chestnut Lodge follow-up study: II. Long term outcome of schizophrenia and the affective disorders. *Archives of General Psychiatry, 41*, 586–601.

McGlashan, T. (1986a). The Chestnut Lodge follow-up study: III. Long term outcome of borderline personalities. *Archives of General Psychiatry, 43*, 20–30.

McGlashan, T. (1986b). The Chestnut Lodge follow-up study: IV. The prediction of outcome in chronic schizophrenia. *Archives of General Psychiatry, 43*, 167–176.

Mahler, M. S. (1952). On child psychosis and schizophrenia: Autistic and symbiotic infantile psychoses. *Psychoanalytic Study of the Child, 7*, 286–305.

Martin, D. V. (1968). *Adventure in Psychiatry*, 2nd edn. Oxford: Bruno Cassirer.

Martindale, B. V. (1998). Cognitive therapy for delusions: Commentary *Advances in Psychiatric Treatment, 4*, 241–242.

Martindale, B. V. (2001). New discoveries concerning psychoses and their organisational fate. In P. Williams (ed.) *A Language for Psychosis* (pp. 27–36). London: Whurr.

Martindale, B. V. (2007). Psychodynamic contributions to early intervention in psychosis. *Advances in Psychiatric Treatment, 13*, 34–42.

Meltzer, D. (1966). The relation of anal masturbation to projective identification. *International Journal of Psychoanalysis, 47*, 335–342.

Meltzer, D. (1978). Part III: The clinical significance of the work of Bion. In *The Kleinian Development* (pp. 20–36). Perthshire: Clunie Press.

Michels, R. (2003). The relationship between psychoanalysis and schizophrenia by Richard Lucas – A commentary. *International Journal of Psychoanalysis, 84*, 9–12.

Milton, J., Polmear, C., and Fabricius, J. (2005). *A Short Introduction to Psychoanalysis*. London: Sage.

Mind (2000). *Environmentally Friendly? Patients' Views on Conditions in Psychiatric Wards*. London: Mind.

Mitchell, J. (1974). *Psychoanalysis and Feminism*. London: Penguin.

Morrison, A. P. (2004). Cognitive therapy for people with psychosis. In J. Read, L. Mosher and R. P. Bentall (eds) *Models of Madness: Psychological, Social and Biological Approaches to Schizophrenia* (pp. 291–306). London: Routledge.

Murray, L., Cooper, P., and Stern, A. (1991). Postnatal depression and infant development. *British Medical Journal, 302*, 978–979.

Niederland, W. G. (1974). *The Schreber Case.* New York: Quadrangle.

O'Shaughnessy, E. (1992). Psychosis: Not thinking in a bizarre world. In R. Anderson (ed.) *Clinical Lectures on Klein and Bion* (pp. 89–101). London: Routledge.

O'Shaughnessy, E. (1999). Relating to the superego. *International Journal of Psychoanalysis, 80,* 861–870.

Pao, P.-N. (1979). *Schizophrenic Disorders: Theory and Treatment from a Psycho-dynamic Point of View.* New York: International Universities Press.

Paykel, E. S., Emms, E. M., Fletcher, J., and Rassaly, E. S. (1980). Life events and social support in puerperal depression. *British Journal of Psychiatry, 136,* 339–346.

Proulx, F., Lesage, A. D., and Grunberg, F. (1997). One hundred in-patient suicides. *British Journal of Psychiatry, 171,* 247–250.

Quinodoz, J.-M. (2002). *Dreams that Turn Over a Page.* London: Routledge.

Rado, S. (1928). The problem of melancholia. *International Journal of Psycho-analysis, 9,* 420–438.

Raphael-Leff, J. (1983). Facilitators and regulators: Two approaches to mothering. *British Journal of Medical Psychology, 56,* 379–390.

Read, J. (2004). The invention of 'schizophrenia'. In J. Read, L. R. Mosher and R. P. Bentall (eds) *Models of Madness* (pp. 21–34). London: Routledge.

Read, J., Mosher, L. R., and Bentall, R. P. (2004). 'Schizophrenia' is not an illness. In J. Read, L. R. Mosher and R. P. Bentall (eds) *Models of Madness* (pp. 3–8). London: Routledge.

Resnick, P. J. (1969). Child murder by parents: A psychiatric review of filicide. *American Journal of Psychiatry, 126,* 325–334.

Rey, J. H. (1994a). *Universals of Psychoanalysis in the Treatment of Psychotic and Borderline States.* London: Free Association Books.

Rey, J. H. (1994b). The schizoid mode of being and the space–time continuum (beyond metaphor). In *Universals of Psychoanalysis in the Treatment of Psychotic and Borderline States* (pp. 9–30). London: Free Association Books.

Richards, J. (1993). Cohabitation and the negative therapeutic reaction. *Psycho-analytic Psychotherapy, 7,* 223–239.

Roazen, P. (1973). *Brother Animal: The Story of Freud and Tausk.* London: Penguin.

Robbins, M. (1993). *Experiences in Schizophrenia: An Integration of the Personal, Scientific and Therapeutic.* London: Guilford Press.

Rosenfeld, D. (1992). *The Psychotic: Aspects of the Personality.* London: Karnac.

Rosenfeld, H. A. (1950). Notes on the psychopathology of confusional states in chronic schizophrenias. In *Psychotic States: A Psycho-Analytical Approach* (pp. 52–62). London: Hogarth Press (1965).

Rosenfeld, H. A. (1952). Notes on the psychoanalysis of the superego conflict in an acute schizophrenic patient. *International Journal of Psychoanalysis, 33,* 111–131.

Rosenfeld, H. A. (1954). Considerations regarding the psycho-analytic approach to acute and chronic schizophrenia. In *Psychotic States: A Psychoanalytic Approach* (pp. 117–127). London: Hogarth Press (1965).

Rosenfeld, H. A. (1963) Notes on the psychopathology and psycho-analytic treatment of schizophrenia. In *Psychotic States: A Psychoanalytic Approach* (pp. 155–168). New York: International Universities Press (1965).

Rosenfeld, H. A. (1965). *Psychotic States: A Psychoanalytic Approach.* London: Hogarth Press.

Rosenfeld, H. A. (1969). On the treatment of psychotic states by psychoanalysis: An historical approach. *International Journal of Psychoanalysis, 50,* 615–631.

Rosenfeld, H. A. (1971). A clinical approach to the psychoanalytic theory of the life and death instincts: An investigation into the aggressive aspects of narcissism. *International Journal of Psycho-Analysis, 52,* 169–178.

Rosenfeld, H. A. (1987). *Impasse and Interpretation.* London: Routledge.

Ryle, A., and Kerr, I. B. (2002). *Introducing Cognitive Analytic Therapy: Principles and Practice.* Chichester: Wiley.

Scadding, J. G. (1967). Diagnosis: The clinician and the computer. *Lancet* 2(7521), 877–882.

Schneider, K. (1959). *Clinical Psychopathology.* New York: Grune and Stratton.

Schwartz, J. (2001). Commentary on David Black: Beyond the death drive detour – How can we deepen our understanding of cruelty, malice, hatred, envy and violence? *British Journal of Psychotherapy, 18,* 199–204.

Searles, H. F. (1961). Phases of patient–therapist interaction in the psychotherapy of chronic schizophrenia. In *Collected Papers on Schizophrenia and Related Subjects* (pp. 521–559). London: Maresfield Library (1965).

Searles, H. F. (1963a). *Collected Papers on Schizophrenia and Related Subjects.* London: Maresfield Library (1965).

Searles, H. F. (1963b). Transference psychosis in the psychotherapy of chronic schizophrenia. In *Collected Papers on Schizophrenia and Related Subjects* (pp. 654–716). London: Maresfield Library (1965).

Segal, H. (1950). Some aspects of the analysis of a schizophrenic. *International Journal of Psychoanalysis, 31,* 268–278.

Segal, H. (1973a). *Introduction to the Work of Melanie Klein.* London: Hogarth Press.

Segal, H. (1973b). Manic defences. In *Introduction to the Work of Melanie Klein* (pp. 82–89). London: Hogarth Press.

Segal, H. (1979). Bion's clinical contributions 1950–1965. In N. Abel-Hirsch (ed.) *Yesterday, Today and Tomorrow* (pp. 203–210). London: Routledge (2007).

Segal, H. (1981a). Notes on symbol formation. In *The Work of Hanna Segal: A Kleinian Approach to Clinical Practice* (pp. 49–65). New York: Jason Aronson.

Segal, H. (1981b). Countertransference. In *The Work of Hanna Segal*. (pp. 81–88). New York: Jason Aronson.

Segal, H. (1981c). The function of dreams. In *The Work of Hanna Segal* (pp. 89–97). New York: Jason Aronson.

Segal, H. (1981d). Manic reparation. In *The Work of Hanna Segal* (pp. 147–158). New York: Jason Aronson.

Segal, H., and Bell, D. (1991). The theory of narcissism in the work of Freud and Klein. In J. Sandler, E. S. Person and P. Fonagy (eds) *Freud's On Narcissism: An Introduction – Contemporary Freud, Turning Points and Critical Issues* (pp. 149–174). New Haven, CT: Yale University Press.

Sharpe, E. F. (1937). *Dream Analysis*. London: Hogarth Press.

Silver, A.-L. (1997). Chestnut Lodge, then and now. *Contemporary Psychoanalysis*, *33*, 227–249.

Sinason, M. (1993). Who is the mad voice inside? *Psychoanalytic Psychotherapy*, 7, 207–221.

Slater, E. (1965). The diagnosis of hysteria. *British Medical Journal*, *1*, 1395–1397.

Slater, E., and Roth, P. (1969). *Mayer-Gross, Slater and Roth's Clinical Psychiatry*, 3rd edn. London: Baillère, Tindall and Cassell.

Sodre, I. (2004). Who's who? Notes on pathological identifications. In E. Hargreaves and A. Varchevker (eds) *In Pursuit of Psychic Change* (pp. 53–65). London: Routledge.

Sohn, L. (1985a). Anorexic and bulimic states of mind in the psycho-analytic treatment of anorexic/bulimic patients and psychotic patients. *Psychoanalytic Psychotherapy*, *1*, 49–56.

Sohn, L. (1985b). Narcissistic organisation, projective identification and the formation of the identificate. *International Journal of Psychoanalysis*, *66*, 201–214.

Sohn, L. (1997). Unprovoked assaults: Making sense of apparently random violence. In D. Bell (ed.) *Reason and Passion: A Celebration of the Work of Hanna Segal* (pp. 57–74). London: Duckworth.

Steiner, J. (1979). The border between the paranoid-schizoid and depressive positions in the borderline patient. *British Journal of Medical Psychology*, *52*, 385–391.

Steiner, J. (1987). The interplay between pathological organisations and the paranoid-schizoid position and depressive positions. *International Journal of Psychoanalysis*, *68*, 69–80.

Steiner, J. (1993a). The retreat to a delusional world: psychotic organisations of the personality. In *Psychic Retreats: Pathological Organisations in Psychotic, Neurotic and Borderline Patients* (pp. 64–73). London: Routledge.

Steiner, J. (1993b). Problems of psychoanalytic technique: Patient-centred and analyst-centred interpretations. In *Psychic Retreats: Pathological*

*Organisations in Psychotic, Neurotic and Borderline Patients* (pp. 134–146). London: Routledge.

Steiner, J. (1994). Foreword. In M. Jackson and P. Williams (eds) *Unimaginable Storms: A Search for Meaning in Psychosis*. London: Karnac.

Steiner, J. (2005). Gaze, dominance and humiliation in the Schreber case. In R. J. Perelberg (ed.) *Freud: A Modern Reader* (pp. 198–205). London: Whurr.

Steiner, J. (2008). Transference to the analyst as an excluded observer. *International Journal of Psychoanalysis, 89*, 39–54.

Stengel, E. (1964). *Suicide and Attempted Suicide*. London: Penguin.

Sullivan, H. S. (1962). *Schizophrenia as a Human Process*. New York: Norton.

Taylor-Thomas, C. and Lucas, R. (2006). Consideration of the role of psychotherapy in reducing the risk of suicide in affective disorders: A case study. *Psychoanalytic Psychotherapy, 20*, 218–234.

Thompson, C. (1999). The confidential inquiry comes of age. *British Journal of Psychiatry, 175*, 301–302.

Thorgaard, L., and Rosenbaum, B. (2006). Schizophrenia: Pathogenesis and therapy. In J. O. Johannessen, B. V. Martindale and J. Cullberg (eds) *Evolving Psychosis: Different Stages, Different Treatments* (pp. 64–78). London: Routledge.

Trilling, L. (1955). *The Opposing Self: Nine Essays in Criticism*. New York: Viking.

Turkington, D., and Siddle, R. (1998). Cognitive therapy for the treatment of delusions. *Advances in Psychiatric Treatment, 4*, 235–242.

Turkington, D., John, C. H., Siddle, R., Ward, D., and Birmingham, L. (1996). Cognitive therapy in the treatment of drug-resistant delusional disorder. *Clinical Psychology and Psychotherapy, 3*, 118–128.

Welldon, E. V. (1991). Psychology and psychopathology in women: A psychoanalytic perspective. *British Journal of Psychiatry, 158* (supplement 10), 85–92.

Wernicke, C. (1906). *Grundrisse der Psychiatrie*. Leipzig: Thieme.

West, R. (1992). *Depression*. London: Office of Health Economics.

Willick, M. S. (2001). Psychoanalysis and schizophrenia: A cautionary tale. *Journal of American Psychoanalytic Association, 9*, 27–56.

Wing, J. K., and Brown, G. W. (1961). Social treatment of chronic schizophrenia: A comparative study of three mental hospitals. *Journal of Mental Science, 107*, 338–340.

Wing, J. K., Cooper, J. E., and Sartorius, N. (1974). *Measurement and Classification of Psychiatric Symptoms, and Instruction Manual for the PSE and the CATEGO Programme*. Cambridge: Cambridge University Press.

Winnicott, D. W. (1960). The theory of the parent–child relationship. In *The Maturational Process and the Facilitating Environment*. London: Hogarth Press (1990).

Winnicott, D. W. (1965). *The Maturational Process and the Facilitating Environment*. London: Hogarth Press.

World Health Organisation (WHO) (1994) *International Classification of Diseases* (ICD-10). Geneva: WHO.

Yung, A. R., and McGorry, P. D. (2007). Prediction of psychosis: setting the stage. *British Journal of Psychiatry*, *191* (supplement 51), s1–s8.

Zachary, A. (1985). A new look at the vulnerability of puerperal mothers: A clinical study of two inpatient families at the Cassel Hospital. *Psychoanalytic Psychotherapy*, *1*, 71–89.

# Index